Scottish Writers Talking 4

Scottish Writers Talking 4

Jackie Kay
Allan Massie
Ian Rankin
James Robertson
William (Bill) Watson

interviewed by
Isobel Murray

Kennedy & Boyd

Kennedy & Boyd
an imprint of
Zeticula
57 St Vincent Crescent
Glasgow
G3 8NQ
Scotland.

http://www.kennedyandboyd.co.uk
admin@kennedyandboyd.co.uk

First published 2008
Copyright © Isobel Murray 2008.

Author's Photographs:
Jackie Kay © courtesy of The Herald & Evening Times
picture archive
Allan Massie © courtesy of The Herald & Evening Times
picture archive
Ian Rankin © courtesy Ian Rankin
James Robertson © courtesy Marianne Mitchelson
William [Bill] Watson © courtesy of The Herald & Evening
Times picture archive

ISBN-13 978-1-904999-88 1 Paperback
ISBN-10   1-904999-88 3 Paperback

Acknowledgements

Grateful thanks, first and foremost, to my five victims, for all their patience and cooperation. And to Bob Tait, as ever.

Special thanks to C Duncan Rice, Principal of Aberdeen University, for supplying fees for the interviewees.

Special thanks too, to the Strathmartine Trust, for a generous contribution to publishing costs.

Thanks for help of all kinds from Flora Alexander, Mig and Frank Brangwin, Professor Ian Campbell, Dr Barbara Fennell, Professor David Hewitt, Dr Jeannette King, Dr Alison Lumsden, Professor Alan Spence, Alan Taylor, and Maureen Wilkie.

Contents

Introduction: The Tables Turned

Here a self appointed representative of the literate reading public, 'Q', questions Isobel Murray about her interviewing project, of which the current volume is the fourth and final product.

Q: So, what exactly is an in depth interview?

IM: For me, it's an interview which involves a lot of work for the interviewer. I try to read as much as possible of the writer's whole oeuvre before I stick a microphone in their faces. I'm primarily there to listen, but I must learn as much as possible, so as to ask the right questions, and sense the direction the interviewee wants to go.

Q: So, what does it involve for the writer?

IM: That's much less formal. The writers know they have made a date to talk about themselves and their work for a minimum of two two-hour sessions, and often more, so inevitably they think it over, considering what they most want to say, whether over breakfast, or standing at a bus stop, or waiting in a queue. I've never had to deal with a subject who hasn't devoted some time to this.

Q: What do you want or expect them to say?

IM: You never know until you get going, and then it's a delight. I usually start by asking about a writer's background, youth and education, and we go on from there, with the writer often indicating the direction he or she wants to go, and with a gentle barrage of roughly chronological questions ready if they want prompting.

Q: But really, what's it worth? Surely any writer worth his or her salt says what they want to say in their published work, and anything else is beside the point?

IM: That's certainly a point of view. No one puts a higher value on the details of a published text than I do: much of my academic research has been specifically directed to producing dependable texts. And my teaching has been devoted to studying them. And I'd never suggest reading interview material instead of the published work, but I believe strongly that anything that helps a reader to read a work with more understanding, or context, or explanation, is worth considering. That was really the basic motivation for starting the series of interviews, many years ago. Of course an interview cannot change the published work, but it may change the reader's capacity to understand and respond to it. We might learn for example, that the order of publication was not the order of composition: Iain Banks was very interesting on his early works, and how he went back and rewrote early, unpublished novels after his initial dramatic success with *The Wasp Factory*. Or the passage of time may have obscured resemblances: Mitchison let drop that a character in *To the Chapel Perilous* was based at least in part on journalist James Cameron: a future scholar may thank us for that. We may get a hint of motive to tease out for ourselves: asked why he went into detective fiction after *Docherty*, Willie McIlvanney immediately replied that he wanted to disappoint people who were wanting a sequel to that fine historical novel. Giving himself time to reflect as he spoke, he went on to give other reasons; which may seem more credible; that he wanted to return to the contemporary world; that he wanted the freedom of the detective genre to chap any Glasgow door, that he was already conscious of a voice, Laidlaw's voice: the reader can consider all of these at leisure. Or we can get an insight into the little tricks some writers indulge in just to please themselves: both Bernard MacLaverty and Janice Galloway admitted to things they didn't expect readers to pick up, but that helped them through the solitary writing process. It is fascinating to go back to the texts and see how it's done. And Iain Crichton Smith acknowledged how important a particular early review of his poetry by Lawrence Graham had been throughout his poetic career: unusually, I was able to include both this fascinating early review and Graham's contemporary reaction to Smith's remarks in my text.

But these are just small happenings that spring to mind. To me, it is the impression one gets of a new wee window on the writer, from reading the whole interview, that matters, and indeed will go on mattering more as time goes on.

Q: You say 'the whole interview', but you edit it: how much of it ends up in the wastepaper basket by your editorial fiat?

IM: Good question. Rarely much, actually. Transcribing takes a lot of time, and I excise very little. But a writer under pressure of microphone has not got the time to polish his or her prose as they would for publication, so I may tidy it a wee bit, taking out 'sort of's and 'kind of's and the like. And it's important to put in '(L)', because the text does not necessarily indicate the tone, or the irony. Or they may over-use the same adjective. And few people obey the 'rules' of English grammar as they talk: it isn't really human to talk in measured sentences all the time. Listen in for a moment to other people's talk in the garden centre or the coffee shop, and you'll see what I mean. Jackie Kay talks with different rhythms than other people, and I had big problems with her: I didn't want to 'normalise' her too much, because her delivery is both unique and delightful.

Q: Why do you always start by saying how well you know your victim?

IM: I think that's important. You are going to overhear a conversation between two people you probably don't know, and it should help to know if they've just met, as was my experience, for example, with Jessie Kesson and Naomi Mitchison, or if they are old friends, as was the case for both myself and Bob, with George Mackay Brown and Iain Crichton Smith. Or indeed former students, as with a great sparring match with Ali Smith.

Q: While we're on that, what part does Bob Tait play in all this anyway?

IM: You probably know Bob was Editor of the magazine *Scottish International* from 1967-73. He lived in Edinburgh, and saw it as his job to be aware of the literary scene as well as others. So he was a great help with Norman MacCaig, for example: they were very old friends. But the poor man had his own job, in the field of education, let alone his regular broadcasting and his work with a housing association. He did not have the time I had for all the reading and/or rereading. So he read what he could, but his main job at first was working the fiendishly difficult tape-recorder as sound engineer, and just intervening in the conversation as he chose. This could complicate matters, of course, as when he and Mitchison started on a heated discussion of Scottish history programmes on contemporary television! I had to drag her back to her books.

As time wore on he had less time for the reading: in-depth interviewing is never an economical use of time! And I got a simple wee modern tape recorder. So he sits in sometimes, as was very useful, for example, in the case of Bill Watson, whose journalistic career at *The Scotsman* he put in context for us.

Q: Why the long gap from the mid-eighties to the late nineties?

IM: Partly, finance became very difficult, and I've had great difficulty finding fees for authors, on which I insist. And it was partly that my research time, such as it was, was occupied with Oscar Wilde, who demanded a share of it until 1998. And partly I was the victim of our success. I was often asked to write about authors I'd interviewed, an instant expert, as it were. No one much else was writing about Robin Jenkins and Naomi Mitchison then. I wrote chapters on writers, and pressed for new editions, and was pressed in turn for introductions... And for several years I was an Assistant Editor of the *Oxford Dictionary of National Biography*, commissioning articles on writers from 1840 to 2000. Then I was asked to write the biography of Jessie Kesson, an all-consuming task for a while.

Q: So how did you choose your subjects, then? Are these the twenty Scottish writers of the century you think are most important?

IM: Oh dear no, it wasn't that ordered. I got money at first from the new University of Aberdeen Development Trust, for interviews, they said at first, on Northern Scottish writers. So we started with George Mackay Brown in Orkney! Then it seemed no one cared too much whom I chose, so I went for older folk – Mitchison was 87, and how was I to know she'd live to be 101?! Then MacCaig. I first interviewed Kesson when I was introducing her at a Book Festival session, and she obliged in the middle of a horrendous day. I tended to avoid writers who were well-covered already, such as Alasdair Gray or Irvine Welsh. Money was always tight, so I victimised our University Writers in Residence, taping Willie McIlvanney, Bernard MacLaverty and Iain Crichton Smith. Iain Banks was here in Aberdeen to speak to students...

Then I began to realise I wasn't as young as I used to be, and had better start stopping, so I went for obvious glaring omissions, like Allan Massie. And it seemed important to include Ian Rankin, continuing the detective genre McIlvanney had adopted. There are so many interesting writers out there, it is hard to stop. But with any luck I may have set a precedent, and someone else will take up a microphone...

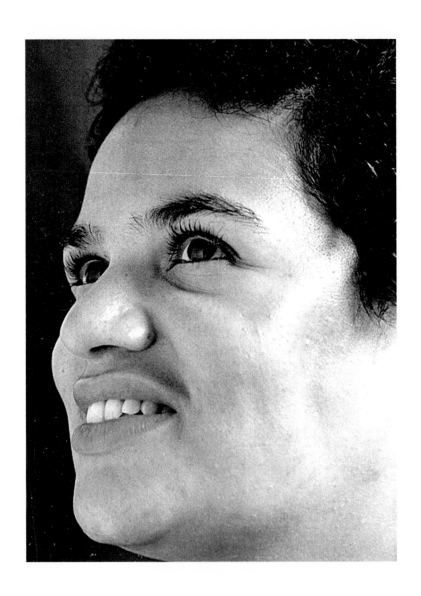

Jackie Kay

Before the interviews, I had met Jackie Kay briefly once or twice, after readings. She was open, friendly and easy to talk to, with a bubbly sense of humour. I found it difficult to pin her down to dates for the interviews; she was very busy: but once she had agreed to it, she was very positive and helpful. One problem made itself evident only later. Kay's conversational delivery is a problem for the transcriber, because she talks very fluently, but without pause or punctuation! Her voice flows, without natural full stops, and she often builds up her meaning by repetition and amplification, a kind of incremental repetition. I have 'normalized' it a bit, but only slightly, as her delivery is part of her impact, which is unique, and it is not hard to follow, unless you get breathless between full stops! When she repeats 'very very' or 'really really', her voice does not allow a comma. She naturally uses 'I' and 'you' almost interchangeably, and I have kept this. The keynote of the interviews became her infectious giggle.

As readers will know, her work often inhabits an area close to but not necessarily identical with her own experience: thus, meeting her for the first time, but soaked in her work, I had to keep asking questions like, do you have a brother? A fear of mice? Experience of farming? A religious granny? Jackie's little dog, Dinkie, voiced mutters of jealousy at my usurpation, from time to time, and had to be placated with biscuits. It was occasionally hard to start Jackie talking, if she felt a question was too general, or not specific enough. There was a great deal of laughter on the tapes: at first this may have been rather nervous, as it was our first real conversation, but it developed naturally as part of an enjoyable conversation. (The taxi driver who took me to the airport, said, a propos of nothing in particular, that her smile made him cheerful all day.)

IM: I am in Manchester, and it is the 23rd of March 2006, and those present are Jackie Kay and Isobel Murray. As usual, I'd like to start by asking Jackie to tell us what she'd like us to know about her youth, her background, her education.

JK: Well, I went to Balmuilday Primary School in Bishopbriggs, and I really liked that school. I liked a lot of my teachers: you have teachers for a whole year when you're in primary school, and you're in the same class between five and twelve, and you get to know those children in your class really really well, and you don't appreciate that at the time. It's only looking back that you think how well you got to know people, because you were with them in the same class for seven years. It's still astonishing to me now, when I look back and think of any single girl in that class, and remember all their names. I did OK at primary school. I wasn't like the dux of the school, I wasn't the brightest. I had trouble with long division I remember (L), although I really loved long multiplication, and I loved being able to work certain things out. I remember once making a model of a mine, and I had to find out a lot about mines for that in Primary Seven, and that was my favourite school project. It had all the different layers of the coal face, and I took it really seriously, and later I wrote a play about the mines –

IM: Which was called?

JK: Which was called *Twilight Shift* [1992]. But it's fascinating that these wee interests that you develop quite early can hold on! I probably liked my very last teacher in Primary Seven best, and I probably felt myself coming into myself in Primary Seven. Before that I used to think of myself as a very slow child, below average or just average. And then I went to secondary school, and I really seemed to get an awful lot brighter quickly! I think it was maybe due to the fact that you could study what you wanted, and I was only good at certain subjects, and absolutely rubbish at others (L), and that's still the case. I'm completely ignorant of certain subjects: there are whole areas which are just completely dim to me: the lights are turned out! (L)

IM: Like what? Science?

JK: A lot of science. My son explains basic science things to me. He's really quite an all-rounder in that way. Like common sense (L), sense of direction, practicality!

IM: That was an all girls primary, was it?

JK: No, no: it was a mixed primary.

IM: And you went on from there to a secondary. Where was the secondary school?

JK: That was Bishopbriggs High School.

IM : Tell me about that. No, hold on, before that: you've got a brother: is that true, or one of the stories?

JK: Yes, I've got a brother. He's older than me.

IM: So he'd been through all these various things   before you.

JK: Yes. He's two years older than me.

IM: So, was that an advantage, did you feel? Was he at the same school?

JK: Yes, he was. It wasn't an advantage or a disadvantage, really. It was just that you had a brother there. Most of the people in the school had a brother or a sister in the school, so it wasn't unusual.

IM: So, what subjects particularly excited or interested you?

JK: When I went to secondary school, the subjects that really excited me were English, and Spanish, and History. These are the subjects that actually excited me, and I did very well in those. I did French as well, and I did Maths too, and I was good at Maths. And I liked Maths; I really liked Algebra, and I liked working out all these problems, liked that area. And then there were subjects that didn't excite me. I don't know if that was to do with the way they were taught, because I'd like to have a chance at doing some of those subjects again, and pay more attention! Like Science, or Latin. I think if it had been taught in a more exciting way Latin

3

might have been good. Or even Geography. It didn't excite me at school at all.

IM: But you've been making practical discoveries about it since!

JK: Yes. But it's quite interesting, because primary and secondary school gives children a chance to see what their interests are, and what they might pursue, and often they will identify something that they're good at quite quickly. But they'll miss some things too, along the way.

IM: You were interested in music right from the start? Dancing the Black Bottom and all the rest of it, and having a teacher being rude to you about that! She said, it's supposed to be in your blood. [*See AD,1991, 'Chapter 7: Black Bottom', and* Bessie Smith *1997, p 70*]
      You were interested in dancing and performance generally? You're quite a performer now.

JK: I've always been a performer. I used to perform for my Gran and my Mum and Dad. When we went to a croft on Mull, my brother would sit up on the roof, a sort of corrugated iron roof of the croft, and my Mum would sit at the bottom, so I had somebody in the Gods, and somebody in the stalls (L), and then I'd just do these shows, for as long as anybody would listen. Dancing up and down, clapping, making up my own songs, singing... I really loved that as a kid. That's when I felt happiest, was just completely making things up. Even though I couldn't really sing; I don't have a good singing voice, one of life's great sadnesses.

IM: Did you have any other major out-of-school interests?

JK: Yes; sport. I really liked running. I went in for the Scottish Schoolgirls Championships, long-distance running, and was very good at hockey, and I used to train five days a week; I was incredibly athletic and fit. I had a school trainer, Mrs Fife, me and Fiona MacKay went to Mrs Fife out of school hours, and did our hill starts up this incredibly steep street. Running and doing a whole workout really regularly was good for the brain and the mind, and I really got into all of that. Also I went to the Royal Scottish Academy of Music and Drama, between the ages of ten and sixteen, every Wednesday and every Saturday, Wednesday afternoons and Saturday mornings, and that became a bit of a conflict with sport, because Mrs Fife didn't really want you to have any other interests: she was jealous, really, of you going to drama, so that became quite tricky.

IM: And was it basically drama you were doing there?

JK: It was speech and drama, improvisations. A lot of things that have actually helped me to this day, because you learned how to project your voice, make things up. We didn't actually get to do any parts, I kept thinking it would be about going for auditions, but actually what we did was probably a lot more useful, because it was very imaginative and creative. It was a lot of fun, and we made different friends. I made friends whose parents had things like Lapsang Souchong tea (L): I discovered Lapsang for the first time. A lot of these friends were quite middle class, quite well off, and lived in completely different parts of Glasgow. So that was interesting; you got to go to their houses; it was just another world. I'm still friends with some of them.

IM: Great. That finished at sixteen, so when you were coming up to Highers, you did English and History and Spanish.

JK: And French. I was going to do Maths as well, but I dropped the Maths about halfway through; I just decided that five was too many. I didn't really need the five, so I thought, why bother? But my Dad was very disappointed: he's very good at Maths, and thought Maths would be good for life, but I fail to see how Maths is good for life! (L)

IM: You went to Stirling to University. What made you choose Stirling?

JK: I chose it because of the kind of courses it had. They had very different courses in literature: they had a course on the Indian novel, and I thought that would be great, to be able to go beyond the narrow reading that you got at school. There I didn't come across any black writers at all hardly, except for Wole Soyinke's 'Telephone Conversation' [*a 35 line poem in which a black man enquires warily about lodgings*]. I also chose it because it was a campus university, and I thought that would be safer, because I was only seventeen! (L) I was worried about going away from home. But mainly I chose it because they were flexible about what you wanted to major in. I hadn't decided if I wanted to do English, or History, or even if I might want to do Sociology. Or even I might want to do Spanish: I couldn't decide what I wanted to do a degree in.

IM: And had it occurred to you at this time that you would like to be a writer?

JK: No, not really. I did write! But I didn't dare think that.

IM: What kind of thing were you writing?

JK: I wrote a novel when I was twelve, about a hundred and odd pages of the jotter – I've still got that jotter! 'One Person, Two Names ' it was called. It was about this girl who was black. And then I wrote lots of poems, a mixture of stories and poems.

IM: But you weren't doing anything about trying to get them published?

JK: I sent some of them off to newspapers: I had some published in newspapers, like *The Morning Star*, when I was twelve (L).

IM: Having mentioned *The Morning Star*, we'll recap for anyone who doesn't happen to know that your adoptive parents are Communists. And you've written very entertainingly and sympathetically about that, about your mother hiding books and things all round the house before she let the adoption lady in. [AP, *'Chapter 3: The Waiting Lists'*] Did you always more or less go along with the gist of their ideas? Or did you at school or at university even, think, I don't know if I am naturally left wing?

JK: No, it never occurred to me to think that I wasn't naturally left wing. It did occur to me to think about the specifics, whether or not I would define myself as a Communist, or as a Socialist, or anti-racist, or a feminist. And it occurred to me to think about those things, and the differences between those things, when I was seventeen/eighteen. But I always thought of myself as being on the side of Socialism, and I still do.

IM: Yes, I think that's fairly clear from what you've written.

JK: I think the Communist Party round the world made lots of mistakes, definitely, but for me, being brought up in a Communist family was a very very positive experience, and it's taught me a huge amount, a way of thinking, and a way of looking at the world, which I've obviously adapted and readjusted to fit my own eyes (L), and my own vision. So I never think of myself as being an indoctrinated child, or somebody who couldn't think for themselves at all, because my parents encouraged us both to think for ourselves. In fact my brother once said he was going to be voting Tory, I think just to wind up my parents (L). And at the age of eight, I decided I'd gone religious, and made my Mum come to the church, and joined this choir, and made her come to church three weeks in a row. I used to say the Lord's Prayer out loud in the house! (L). So it was quite possible to have different opinions to them, and for them to respect that. They were never doctrinaire, and I really resent the idea that people who have strong beliefs have to force them down other people's throats. In fact religious people do that far more often, because they've actually got a calling to do that. The job of extreme religious people is to go about finding converts. They don't discuss an idea without wanting to convert. With Communists, at least with the ones I met, they enjoyed discussing an idea for the idea's sake. They didn't necessarily go on to say, now will you take out a Party card. Some of them might have done, but a lot of people actually enjoy discussion for discussion's sake. My favourite people in the world are people like Ali Smith, people who enjoy discussing things for discussing's sake. Doing good things as well, but enjoying discussing.

IM: If the questions I ask sound cheeky, it's only because I often don't know when you're writing about yourself or not. Was there a religious granny?

JK: Yes, there was a religious granny.

IM: So you did get a taste of that?

JK: I did get a taste from her, yes, because she took me to church, and I quite liked going to church with her. I suppose I was always writing: I think perhaps we talk about being a writer in possibly the wrong terms. We should really re-evaluate what being a writer means. Being a writer doesn't necessarily mean writing a book; or writing a book right away. It means observing people and observing things from really early on, and looking at the world in a certain way. Later on you discover that you can actually write about that way, but that way of looking at people and finding people interesting you've had really probably from very very early on, from when you were a kid, and I can remember those people from my Gran's church, and those particular characters and their hats, and their ways of putting the threepenny bits into the collection box, and their slightly patronizing manner with me, and their warmth (L), and their clothes, and I took it all in, and it was very different from hanging out with my Mum and Dad's friends.

IM: Was it Catholic or Protestant?

JK: Protestant.

IM: It's just interesting, what you've been as it were exposed to.

JK: If I'd had a chance, I'd have rather been exposed to Catholicism. More colourful and rich, and there's all that guilt thrown in, and you get a wee wafer (L). You get something to eat and then you get all these ceremonies; exciting things when you're seven; exciting things happen later on, and you have godparents, I think all of that would be quite nice. But obviously it does a lot of people's heads in as well.

IM: Now, you went up to Stirling, and you wanted to read English or History or Sociology. How did you make your mind up?

JK: All the different teachers kept trying to persuade me to take their degree, which was very flattering at the time. I remember we had two very famous Sociologists, Becky and Russell Dobash, and I remember Russell Dobash coming up to me and going, let me get this right: you're black, you're gay, you're Scottish - are you working class?? (L) So he really desperately wanted me to do a Sociology degree, and Sociology I found really interesting at that time, because it was political, and because you were looking at the yeast of the media, and you were looking at bias, and you suddenly saw the world really differently. But everybody said a Sociology degree was worthless, that it was toilet paper: people were very rude about Sociology then; I don't know if they still are.

IM: I think it's got bigger since then.

JK: The English Department at Stirling was an absolutely fantastic English Department: it still is. It still has a lot of really exciting teachers there. And so I decided to stick with the English, because if I majored in English I could do a dissertation, and I liked the idea of doing a dissertation, rather than a final exam. That was the other reason that I chose Stirling above Edinburgh or Aberdeen or Glasgow, because I got offers at all of those places. Now I think maybe I should have gone to Edinburgh, because they have a more stream-lined education, . . . Who knows.

IM: A dissertation; what was it about?

JK: I did women and madness in nineteenth- and twentieth-century women's literature.

IM: Isn't that fascinating! I couldn't have guessed that at all. It's really funny. Having read all your books recently at least twice, the things in your life that I am expecting, and then you come out with the sports, and the women and madness! I don't know what I expected, because you don't quote much, you don't refer in the way some former English students do.

JK: I do that quite deliberately, not quoting all the time.

IM: Did you do any American literature?

JK: We did a course on the American novel, so we did Faulkner. I remember writing an essay about *Light in August*'s racism, because, you know, the black blood made him pick up the gun, the white blood made him put it down, the black blood, and so on (L). I did all this research and found out that Faulkner really did hold racist beliefs: he thought that black people's brains were smaller, and whatever, and I found a quote, actual documenting, but my tutor went, in what context? (L) In what context does thinking a black person's brain is smaller make it OK??!!

IM: There's a very big academic just been forced to resign the presidency of Harvard, because he's still suggesting women can't do science, and black people have smaller brains. [*Lawrence Summers*]

JK: Oh yes, I was reading about that – shocking. Thank God he's had to resign.

IM: So. You did English. And you did the Indian novel.

JK: I loved that course on the Indian novel. I discovered Anita Desai for the first time. I've read all of her ever since. I loved that writer from her very first book *Cry, the Peacock*, and then *Fire on the Mountain*: she's just fantastic. She's like Toni Morrison: you can completely see her development from her first book, which is rather rough and raw, to now, and I like being able to do that with writers, to trace how they've become who they've become.

IM : Talking about the Sociologist guy who was trying to poach you for his subject, you said that one of the things he knew about you was that you were gay, so you had, as it were, 'come out'. Before you went to Stirling, or when you were there?

JK: In my first year at university.

IM: Was that hard?

JK: I suppose it was, in some ways. Yes, I suppose it was. It was hard telling my family, and it was probably hard just trying to think what you are. And also because I had a boyfriend, a farmer boyfriend at the time whom I loved. I found that hard, letting him down. It makes you really reassess yourself. It's a big questioning time, and the whole question of sexuality: and you put quite a burden on yourself, when I think about it. We put quite a burden on ourselves, to have to say, we're gay or we're straight. That seems to be loosening up a bit now, but then, because there was so much prejudice, people felt that they had to really make a stand, and bisexuality was a bit of a cop out. People that were bisexual; there were rude names for them- 'bike' (L). Looking back on that, I wouldn't want it for my kid. I would like my child just to be able to be free about that, and not to feel that you have to define yourself. There's so much emphasis that we have on self-definition in our society, and so much obsession with it, what we call ourselves, the names we call ourselves, whether we call ourselves Scottish, or working-class, or lesbian. We're obsessed with it. As human beings we keep on trying to understand the story that we tell ourselves, but in doing that we don't realize that we could possibly make up another story that isn't necessarily true for ourselves, because we've had to.

IM: You say you were a bit anxious about what your parents would think.

JK: I was then, yes.

IM: Were they upset?

JK: No; they were great; they were wonderful.

IM: Was anybody particularly upset?

JK: No, nobody was particularly upset. Often these fears are just in people's heads. Although I do have friends who had the most awful experiences. One friend told his mum and she said, I'd rather you'd told me you'd murdered somebody! Which I then put in a poem (L). But that's really extreme. I remember my Dad saying to me, you don't know. You might have a relationship with a man at some point in your life again. I said, I do know; I do know that I won't! (L)

IM: We know so many things at seventeen and eighteen!

JK: I remember some of these arguments that I used to have with my Dad, about all sorts of things, from – I used to think that if somebody was really right wing then they couldn't be a good writer; but he'd say, unfortunately that's nonsense: look at Balzac! We'd have all these arguments back and forth. Some of them you look back now and feel embarrassed, but that's just part of being young.

IM: Absolutely. At the risk of asking you another question too big to get hold of, it says on the blurbs, 'has written widely for stage and television'. Would you like to say a bit about when that is central to what you're doing, and when it is more a nice way of earning money? Or if it's ever just one or the other?

JK: I haven't written that widely for stage and television in my own head. I've written six or seven plays now; I've written one song cycle that was made into a libretto; and another opera. And I've written a few poetry documentary things that have been on television.

IM: Can I ask here, because I can't find it anywhere, about Amelia Rossiter? I can't Google her.

JK: Yes. She was a real woman, who was imprisoned for life for killing her husband, and a whole cycle of poems was written about her, but keeping it open so that it wouldn't expose her. That was *Twice Through The Heart*. It was originally a poetry documentary done by Peter Symes for BBC [*1991*] Then later Mark-Anthony Turnage made it into a song cycle. And it was on at the Aldeburgh Music Festival, and at the Queen Elizabeth Hall. I met her quite a few times, and I read up all the case notes, and the judge's summing up. I tried to get to see her in prison, but they wouldn't let us in because we were from the BBC. She was involved in the whole process, and so was her family, and her lawyer and her daughters.

IM: So: she was guilty, or she wasn't?

JK: She was found guilty, yes.

IM: But she wasn't?

JK: No: she wasn't guilty in my eyes, because of the law of provocation. I was really writing about the law of provocation. We did do that documentary and she did get released. I don't know if one thing affected the other. And then I went to see her. Years later, when Mark-Anthony Turnage did it as a thing for English National Opera, her daughter came, and it was at the Queen Elizabeth Hall

IM: Were these poems published in your poetry books?

JK: Some of them. [OL]. I often do that. I've just written a whole lot of poems for the launch of National Theatre Scotland, that recently took place on the Shetland ferry. Some of these poems I probably will publish in a poetry book, and some of them I won't. Sometimes poems are good for the thing itself, but they don't really deserve to have another life, or they wouldn't translate out of that world they were in into the ordinary world. The reader isn't on the boat, basically! (L)

IM: Having mentioned Amelia Rossiter, this is probably a stupid place to ask it, but I might forget. The story of Billy Tipton was an inspiration for *Trumpet*. How important was that story? [*Tipton was a musician who lived as a man, but was discovered to be a woman on his death.*]

JK: It was important. I read about it, and it sparked me off. I read a little piece in the *Guardian* initially, just saying that this jazz musician had died. In the bit that I read, his son was quoted as saying, he'll always be Daddy to me, which I thought was really lovely, and it made me think about how you understand people, and what makes somebody who they are. It made me think about love. If you love somebody enough, you'll believe them. Love and belief, really, and to me *Trumpet's* a novel about belief. I didn't then try and research Billy Tipton, or get too bogged down in his actual story, or the fact that he'd three different wives and three different adopted sons.

IM: I didn't realise that!

JK: Or the fact that none of his wives knew, and he told them all that he'd had an abdominal injury, and they'd all believed him. And that is true. And sometimes truth is, as the old cliché goes, stranger than fiction. The funny thing about writing a novel is that in a funny way it's got to be more believable than real life, and also in a funny way less. It's got to be imaginatively true, but also true true. It's quite interesting as a novelist when you try to find that, what that is, what it's about. It's not necessarily about writing about things as they happen. If I'd written that in a novel nobody would have believed it, even though it was true. I decided that in my novel I had to have a son who wasn't as accepting as that, because otherwise where would the story be, and I'd have to have a wife who knew, and I'd have to have a tension between the knowing and the not knowing, and what that meant. And I wanted to set it in Scotland, and I wanted to make him black, so it's kind of a million miles away from Billy Tipton, because he was a white piano player, an American. But there are certain little details that I discovered: somebody had said that Billy Tipton had a high voice and a baby face. There a few little details in *Trumpet* that do relate to Billy Tipton – even the bandages.

IM: We started talking about what you write for stage and television. When you've done things for television, do you think about it differently? Is it more just for the money, as a job?

JK: Well, the things I've done for television I haven't got much money for; they've still been artistic things, so I could never say I've done anything just for the money. I've never been in a position where somebody's offered me a lot of money and I've just written, and it's been for the money. I've done it because I'm interested in trying to experiment with a new form: I'm trying to see whether I can do it or not. Even recently, I've just finished writing a screenplay for *Trumpet*, and even that I didn't do for the money, and it wasn't really all that well paid as yet – it might be eventually, if it gets made. I did that for the experience of trying to write a screenplay, and also because the person who wanted to make it into a film [Gurinder Chadha] wouldn't have anyone else do it: she said, I want to do this, but only if you do it yourself. So I had to learn how to do a screenplay. But I must say that trying to do different forms really excites me. I tried with plays; I've written six plays now, and I've rather given up now with plays, I don't think I'll write another one. I don't really think I can write them; I think that certain people can write them well, and are wonderful at them; and certain people are very bad at them, including me. I think with plays it's all the architecture and the structure and the dramatic concept, and getting it to really work: you can't just have reported action or monologues or a thing that's interesting that's happening having already happened. It's quite difficult in contemporary drama to get something up and running and unfold before your eyes in the now of that moment – very very difficult to do. I keep striving to try to find a way to do this. The closest that I came to it was in a little play that I had on most recently, which was at Oran Mor last year. It was called *Two*. As far as little plays go that was the one I've been most happy with. But that wasn't a lot of money! (L)

IM: I wasn't even going to ask about that! You're not keen to do more plays; do you want to go on doing things for television?

JK: I think I'd like to write another screenplay. I'm not really interested in television.

IM: Radio is where I've come across you more.

JK: Yes, radio I'm interested in. I think that radio's wonderful. When I lived in America for six months [*as Holloway Poet, University of Berkeley, California, 1996*] the things I missed most were the newspapers and the radio – and the curry (L). They've got national public radio there, but it's nothing like the radio here, and we really take our radio stations for granted here. We have such a wide variety. Is it a Radio Four day? Is it a Radio Three day? Is it a Jazz FM day? Is it – heaven forbid, but I'm getting to be the age – a Radio Two day? (L) Shocking, really.

IM: Have you given up on Bessie Smith?:

JK: No. I'd never give up on Bessie Smith.

IM: You wrote a play about her, as well as the book and the poems.

JK: Yes. [*See* Outline: Bessie Smith,*1997, and poems in OL1993*]

IM: So she was obviously very important for you. Do you still play her music?

JK: Yes, I do.

IM: You admired her enormously, as your book makes clear, but it fascinated me because she seemed to be such a different person from you. What is it that connects these two? I think she's marvellous too, but she's so blatant and dramatic.

JK: I know, it's funny: my Mum read the Bessie book, and she didn't like it. It's the only one of my books that she's actually said to me she didn't like, and she said, why couldn't you have picked a nice negro?! (L) Paul Robeson, or Nelson Mandela, somebody kind and good.

IM: Poetry. *The Adoption Papers* made an enormous impact. I read somewhere that it was done dramatically on the radio before the book. Did you do it?

JK: No, I didn't do it. They got three actors. My Mum didn't like the one who played the adoptive mum; she said, that woman's terrible; I've been miscast! (L) It was interesting, though, because the book wouldn't have been published in the way that it was if I hadn't done the radio thing, because I wrote a whole lot of poems. 'The Adoption Papers' were originally a bunch of poems that were all separate voices: they weren't counterpointed. And then when this person [*Frances Anne Solomon*] approached me and said she'd like to make it into a radio play, she said she'd like the voices to interact more, so then I went and rewrote them, and then having rewritten them I suddenly decided that that was the best way to publish them, not all separate but in this counterpointed, interactive way. And so it was quite lucky, really; it was one of those chance things, because I probably wouldn't have thought to do that.

IM: And you've done it since, not as elaborately, but poems not standing on their own, but building up together. Is structure something you think about a lot when you're writing?

JK: Yes, I think that structure's everything, really. I think some people are wonderful at structure, naturally gifted, and some are not. I don't think I'm naturally gifted at structuring things, but I have to have a sense that I am creating something – it's almost like a physical thing, a house, the house of fiction. It's got to have a door, (L) and you've got to be able to get in. You've got to be able to see out of it: that's really important, that you've got to be able to see out of it. And sometimes there can be an extra wee room, a surprise room, that you didn't know was there. (L) *Trumpet's* structure, that bugged me the whole time I was writing *Trumpet*. The reason it took me so long to write that novel was trying to find the structure. I knew the story I wanted to tell, I knew roughly what might happen in the story, but trying to find a structure that would get all these things to work together was quite difficult, and I found that quite late on.

IM: Roughly how long did it take you?

JK: Five years. A ridiculous length of time really. But I stopped writing *Trumpet* altogether, and wrote that Bessie book. Because somebody asked me to write the Bessie book, a nice man called Nick Drake, and he said, we need the book in a very short period of time, nine months or something. And I thought well, maybe it won't do me too much harm to completely immerse myself in blues for nine months and then go back to *Trumpet*, because I was stuck with *Trumpet* anyway. That was really lucky too, because then I read lots of jazz biographies, and immersed myself in music, and thought about Bessie, and the way in which music tells a story. And then I went back to *Trumpet*, and somehow it gave me a jazz structure, and then I thought about the structure of *Trumpet*, and it's kind of staring you in the face (L) that the structure should be musical in some way, and I could have solo pieces and it could be like a piece of music.

IM: Had you read that life of Billy Tipton? [*Diane Middlebrook*, Suits Me: The Double Life of Billy Tipton, *1998*]

JK: No, I hadn't. I was aware that it was going to come out, but it hadn't yet come out: *Trumpet* was published before that. Somebody did say that the Billy Tipton book was coming out. I could have got hold of the proofs of that book, and read it whilst I was still writing *Trumpet*, but I just didn't want to. I felt really strongly that I didn't want to, I didn't want *Trumpet* to be about that, and it irritated me when people kept going on too much about Billy Tipton, because that really wasn't the point.

IM: No! I only discovered Billy Tipton in a footnote, preparing for this. The first couple of times I read *Trumpet* I didn't know squat about Billy Tipton, nor did it matter!

JK: Oh, that's nice.

IM: Going back to *Trumpet* again, I liked the way you fought against labelling what Millie and Joss had as lesbian or anything else: even they don't think about it. It said so much about the individuality of an individual relationship, and you were saying a wee while ago how we all want an identity. Sometimes all we want is a heap of labels. This is a book that absolutely refuses to turn into labels, doesn't it?

JK: I think so, and I think that was really important to me. I thought some lesbians might read it and think it was a bit of a cop out, wishy-washy book (L), I did worry about that when I was writing it, but it seemed important to me that they didn't define themselves. As characters, the characters I made up just didn't, and they wouldn't have done, and I felt really certain about that, so I couldn't put that on to them. Also it allows more people to come in, when you don't rigidly define in that way: otherwise you begin to say them and us, and us and you. Their story is a love story. It's quite interesting to me the amount of people who identify with Millie as a widow. My old neighbour, Isabel Aird, whom I've known all my life, has read *Trumpet* five times! (L) She was made a widow twenty years ago, and she finds it very comforting. She always asks me, Jackie, how did you understand a widow like that? Somebody wrote to me recently from the University of Las Vegas saying that they'd done *Trumpet* in a reading group with this older group of women and men, a lot of them Bush supporters! The woman running the course had worried what they were going to think of *Trumpet,* and this sort of Bush-supporter woman began the whole discussion by saying, I am Millie! (L) That kind of thing really tickles me; it means it's transcended specifics. These are two women having a relationship: at the end of the day the reader knows that, but people still identify. I think the thing about reading is you have to find a way to get the reader to think that's them, to identify with your characters, because it's when we identify with characters in books that we don't read the book, the book reads us, like Auden said.

IM : Very often, whether in poems or stories or novel, you have a story, a story that grips. Often I've wondered, how did you know to stop a story here or there? Christian Sanderson, for example.[OC] That's a fine poem, and a fascinating one, but every time I read it I want to know more about it! Is she real?

JK: Yes, she is real. I wrote quite a few poems for this programme about black characters in British History, a whole hour programme that was on the radio. I only published a few of them, because it was one of those things that I was talking about earlier. Christian Sanderson we came across, me and the researchers. There she was; she was sent to Australia for the stealing of sixteen shillings, for seven years, there she was. And if it hadn't been in the records that were kept in Edinburgh, 'mulatto' in brackets, nobody would have known that she was black. That's what really fascinates me, that the only way of finding out about black people in British history, because they haven't been documented in any way, is if somebody does something wrong! (L)It makes you wonder about all the people that are lost. I think we all find the idea of lost people, lost history, fascinating, because it's the untold stories that move us in some ways. I'm always really drawn to telling them: and stories about adoption! Everybody talked about adoption, shows from Dallas to Dynasty, from Coronation Street to East Enders in a very negative way, or *Wuthering Heights* even (L): it's a great adoption story, come to think of it. I've always wanted to write something about *Wuthering Heights* as the great adoption novel. If I was an academic, I'd look at that theme, adoption in literature, in all sorts of different ways, and write something about that, because I found that really fascinating, the idea of the outsiders coming in, and ruining the family! (L) It's all the way through literature: it goes right, right back.

IM: Did you like James Robertson's *Joseph Knight*?

JK: I haven't read that. I must read that. I keep meaning to read that: is it good?

IM: I think it's very very fine. But James is very careful: he doesn't actually bring Joseph Knight on stage for any length of time. He relies on court records and things. I think he was afraid, as a white man of now, to voice a black man of the time, a slave reared in the West Indies, for fear that it wouldn't work. I think what he did worked extraordinarily well: but it also leads me to that whole area of things, like: most of your characters most of the time, are women: it that conscious, or deliberate? Do you feel, in a Jane Austenish way that you don't know what men talk about when they're alone together, so you don't write about it?

JK: I find women very interesting.

IM: (L) That's not the same!

JK: I find women very interesting to create, and I think that's the case, with a lot of women writers. Alice Munro does that, most of her very interesting characters are women. Margaret Atwood, Carol Shields. I think woman writers often do get drawn to creating women characters. I have created quite a few men, and I find that every time I do create a man, I feel quite excited! (L) Just by seeing if I can get that voice to be authentic. In my new book of short stories I've got quite a few male voices in it. I've got the character Malcolm Henry Jobson, in 'How to Get Away with Suicide', and I've got either off-stage men that are talked about through their women, or centre stage –

IM: The two that go climbing together

JK: Yes, that's right, I've got them too, Hamish and Don. So that book feels quite new to me, in the sense that there's more men there for their own sake. In *Trumpet* though, there was a few men. There was the drummer –

IM: I thought Colman worked brilliantly!

JK: Yes, *Trumpet* has quite a few men. So it's not quite true to think that I only have women, or mainly women, because there's still quite a few men kicking about – there's the Registrar, and the funeral director -

IM: All carefully chosen of different racial and national types! (L) This lady is politically correct! But given that the 'I' voice dominates the poetry on the whole, and the I voice is usually female – have you written many poems from the male point of view?

JK: Yes, I wrote quite a few. There's 'Close Shave', about a gay man down the mines. 'Dance of the Cherry Blossoms' – that's from the point of view of a man dying of AIDS. I think that's it as far as the voice goes. Most of the poems are in female voices. Oh no, 'Dressing Up' is in the voice of a male transvestite. [*All in AP, 1991*]

IM: Oh right; that's very interesting. But if you are about to attempt a male character, does it make any difference if he's gay or heterosexual?

JK: No. Because the world of maleness is the Other country. Sexuality I already know about in a sense, so it doesn't make any difference in trying to get an authentic voice. That's all I try and do when I write, is to try and find a way of creating a character-

IM: And a story!

JK: And a story, yes, that's right.

IM: The story is very important. Re-reading the poetry again, I kept thinking they were unwritten short stories, or unblown-up novels, that were all there *in posse*. Do you always know, when you start writing, what it's going to be?

JK: Yes, I do. Because to me an idea comes, and it's already got clothes on it. It's already dressed. It's arguable you could say such-and-such a poem could have been a short story, or *The Adoption*

Papers could have been a novel. These things are arbitrary decisions, but they're mine! And when I have the idea I know; I think, this is an idea for a short story. I never change half way through. It's something to do with the angle at which you are looking at something: the angle's different, depending on what you are going to write.

IM: So, why don't we impose a little order on my chronology by going back. You left Stirling; what do you do, what do you write, where do you go?

JK: After I left Stirling in 1983 I went to London. I first of all worked with a publisher, Sheba, a feminist publisher.

IM: Why did you go to London?

JK: I went to London because I had a lot of friends in London, a lot of black friends there, black, gay friends there, and that was very exciting. And also because I thought I would get more work there; that I'd have more of a chance: it's a bit like Dick Whittington! (L) The streets of London are paved with gold: we all think that, in a slightly fairy-tale-ish way. I already knew London well, because I'd spent every summer there: at the university, I'd spent four months every summer in London, working. Working at Westminster Hospital as a hospital porter. So I already knew my way about. I'd lived in Vauxhall, and Hampstead. John Le Carre's house: I was his cleaner for a while: that was one job I had! (L) So that was quite fun.

IM: That explains why you could write that bit in *Trumpet* –

JK: About the cleaner? Yes!

IM: So, you knew London quite well; you went to work for this publisher, Sheba. Did you know yet that you wanted to be a writer?

JK: I wrote all the way through university. But I didn't think that I would necessarily get published, and I didn't connect the publishing of things with a job, or an occupation. As far as I was concerned I was a writer, I wrote. But I wasn't a published writer, and that was the difference, really. But I did start getting things published in magazines. I had something published around that time in a magazine called ArchRage, a multi-cultural Arts Magazine, and that was very exciting. And also, bizarrely, I got a few readings, and the readings led to the publications, not the other way around. You go to these conferences, with all different people, so you think, I'll just chip in! (L) 'The Adoption Papers' was originally two poems that I wrote, 'The Mother Poem 1' and 'The Mother Poem 2', and I read them at the Commonwealth Literature Conference, where they had a free spot for people to just get up and read, people that were attending the conference. I read the two Mother Poems, and they got an *incredible* response: it was just amazing. I thought, it was such a response, maybe I should write more. So I went and wrote more.

IM: Were 'The Mother Poem 1' and 'The Mother Poem 2' about the two mothers?

JK: Yes. There wasn't a daughter in it at all, to begin with. And when I did come to do the daughter, I found her the hardest one to do.

IM: Did you? I suppose you have to select down to the daughter, whereas you're selecting up to the mothers. If I am allowed to ask this, did you ever actually meet your birth mother?

JK: Yes, I did.

IM: And was that successful?

JK: I don't know how you'd define success –

IM: Nor do I! (L)

JK: I was pleased to have met her. I was very pleased to have met her, and pleased to be able to put a face to her, so that was good.

IM: One of the results of your having touched a nerve in your audience with the adoption poems is that that was the first noise you made, nationally, as a writer. So people think of it as being almost your cause.

JK: Yes: that's an unfortunate thing, actually (L). That's very true; yes.

IM: And really it was almost accidental that you wrote more. It might have been something else. The other half of that book of poems is called, 'Severe Gale Eight'. Would you like to elaborate on that title?

JK: It's just the weather, a weather cycle.

IM: Is it tied to a time?

JK: No, it's just a weather title. When we had terrible winds and gales, I think I wrote them about the time of the Poll Tax demonstrations. I was really thinking about a vision of society. So that poem is really quite ambitious in what it's trying to do. I didn't quite pull it off, but I was trying to think about a world where nothing could be controlled for the good of people, but everything was controlled for the bad of people.

IM: So we're in London. Do we contact the BBC early on?

JK: No, I didn't! (L) It's a nice idea, Isobel!

IM: It was just when you said that somebody wanted to dramatise The Adoption Papers.

JK: She heard. She heard about them through these readings that I'd started to do. After that first one, I started to get readings. I remember that first one: I had terrible period pains, and I wasn't going to go. Thank God I did! (L) It's just the little things that change the course of your life. More importantly, it changed how I thought of myself, because it was just shocking. There were about three hundred people there for some reason, and one person had been on after the other, and I was the very last one. They hadn't really been responding much to anybody, or even seeming to be listening, and then suddenly they did, and it was just an extraordinary moment: it was very exciting. I think she got in touch with me because she'd heard of some of these readings, and she got in touch. Quite a few people did that, like Robin Robertson. He wrote from a publishers, and said he'd heard, and one time he came to one of my readings, and he said, really sarcastically, I've come to see what this phenomenon is that I've heard is called Jackie Kay. I could tell he wasn't very impressed! (L) It was very embarrassing. He wrote to me afterwards to send the manuscript to him, which was very nice: I'd a few people write asking me to send it to them, which was very unusual. But then they'd send it back, and they'd say, we like these; we think there's something going in them, but we can't be fully committed to them. I remember Robin Robertson saying that, can't be fully committed, and not knowing quite what that meant. Then it was ages before they were published; I had three or four years of just that manuscript sitting about. So by the time it did come out, it felt to me to be very out of date.

IM: Had you been trying to publish it all this time?

JK: Oh yes! When people asked me, I sent it to them. And then you'd wait, for months to get a response. So he kept to his promised three weeks.

IM: Did you do anything, at that time or later, about having an agent?

JK: No, not at that time. I remember that I wrote plays first. So the plays were on before I ever tried to get any books published. I suppose I became known for writing plays first, and that was in

1985. And they were on at the Drill Hall. I didn't have an agent when I wrote those, because I remember they said to me, the theatre company, that I would get some royalties, and I thought that was really too much, because I'd been paid for writing it, so I said that the company could have it, and they got me to sign something, (L) and all the money went back to them! I'd no idea that that money was due to you! Funny and naïve! I suppose I felt grateful for getting a chance. I got my current agent that I've been with really all the time after *The Adoption Papers* was published.

IM: And is it an important relationship in your life?

JK: Very. Hugely important.

IM: Name of the current one?

JK: Pat Kavanagh.

IM: What does she do? With you, for you? Does she suggest things? Does she criticise things?

JK: She's more like having somebody to consult and refer to. She doesn't particularly do anything for you, really. She'll organise a book deal; she'll try and get you a better advance, that kind of thing, or like after I wrote *Trumpet* she negotiated the contract for me to write the next novel before it was written. Actually, I've decided that's a bad idea: I'm not going to do that again, because it makes you feel then that you've got to write a tombstone (L). You do it because you've got no money, and you can't afford to not. Rich writers don't do it. But writers who are not rich try and get advances; but then the advances become a weight, a terrible weight and a terrible pressure. I've still not written a second novel, and I've only now managed to get my publisher to take this new book of short stories, and swap the contract for the second novel, which releases me, and now I feel a free woman! (L) It's all psychological, of course, but it's very important. You find these psychological things very important.

IM: That was partly why I was asking about the agent. So, now that you don't have to write the second novel, are you feeling like doing it?

JK: I might, it feels more possible. In a way I don't know the point of writing a novel, unless you feel that you've got a novel to write. I don't see that we should write novels just because we've written a novel. I might have only one novel in me.

IM: Perhaps we still need to establish how the young poet who was writing plays and publishing poems in London becomes the still young poet, author, dramatist, novelist – you name it - who is talking about it now. Emote!

JK: So what did you want me to talk about – relationships? Or -

IM: Don't bother about the relationships if they don't affect the writing career. Just in time: how did you get here from there? How have you developed?

JK: It's difficult to think of your own development.

IM: That's why it's easier just to tell a story.

JK: But it's difficult to tell the whole story of your life, because your life doesn't really happen like that. You'll need to ask me something more specific, because I can't just ramble: I need to have specific questions.

IM: OK. How long did you work for Sheba?

JK: I think three years. And I also worked at the Dalston Children's Centre, at the same time: I had two part-time jobs. I picked the children up in a minibus from their schools, and brought them back, and drove the minibus around London, and I liked that.

After those two, I had Matthew. Quite young, really; I was

twenty-six, which is youngish for then. And after I had Matthew I got a job as the Hammersmith and Fulham Writer in Residence, [*1989-91*] and then my writing career seemed to take off, after having a baby, which is quite funny. I also had my second play on at the Drill Hall, *Twice Over*, about a gay grandmother. [*1989*]

IM: I read that one.

JK: Goodness, you're well versed in it all!

IM: That book falls to bits: every page falls out.

JK: I know.

IM: But before we leave Matthew. You had Matthew out of the blue: did you mean to?

JK: Oh no, I didn't have him out of the blue: he was really planned. I think gay people, when they have children, plan them. I really wanted to have a child. And I wanted to have a child in the traditional way; I didn't want to have artificial insemination or anything like that. I was very good friends with the writer Fred D'Aguiar, and he caught me looking at a kid one day, and said, you seem to really like kids. I'll be the dad if you like. So that was really lucky. And he was smart, and handsome, and I thought he would be a good father for my child. So that was it, and we're still very close friends, and Matthew's very close to his Dad. He sees him; Fred lives in America now, but Matthew goes and spends four weeks there in the summer, and Fred comes over here quite frequently. I always wanted Matthew to know who his father was, and to have a relationship with him, because that seemed very important to me, given that I knew so little of my own birth parents. Not that it disturbed me, but I did know and have met an awful lot of people that it does really disturb; so I didn't want to hand a child a lot of unknowns. That has been very good, and I'll never ever regret that decision. Of course I'll never regret having Matthew!

IM: Did you always intend to stop at one?

JK: No; I would have like to have had more. But I think I read something by Alice Walker saying that a woman writer should only have one child: with one she can travel! (L) No; my life would have just been too difficult with more than one child. I couldn't really afford it, and I couldn't have travelled in the way that I did, and it would have been difficult for Fred, because then he of course got married, and had other children. I didn't want to get another dad, and have loads of men in my life.

IM: How old is Matthew now?

JK: Seventeen.

IM: Is he still at school?

JK: He's doing his A levels, at a sixth form college. He'll be home any minute.

IM: So Matthew happened, and you were getting on with publishing and so on.
A play went on, *Twice Over*, just after that, and then what?

JK: Well *The Adoption Papers* didn't come out until 1991, so it did feel like a long wait. I got published in different anthologies, and I did various different readings, and that side of things took off, and I did more radio work. But it did seem slow, getting started; and then I had a small book published; it's called *That Distance Apart*, which is very hard to get hold of, and is a rare little book, and has the Adoption Papers poems as they would have been if they hadn't been mixed up, so it's quite interesting to see. (L) [*It does not figure in JK's cv.*]

IM: (L) A PhD there sometime!

JK: And I met Carol Ann [Duffy] in 1991. I met her when I'd already heard that I was having *The Adoption Papers* published; that was quite nice timing. And my relationship with her began then and went on till a couple of years ago. We lived together. I think we started living together when Matthew was six, so the break up would have been in 2004. We were together for about fifteen years.

IM: And she has a child too?

JK: Ella – yes, she has Ella.

IM: So Matthew and Ella were company for each other, approximate ages; good.

JK: No, they weren't approximate ages, because Matthew's seven years older.

IM: Leaving the personal side of the Carol Ann thing as far aside as we can, do you think you influenced each other's writing?

JK: I think probably we did, because we shared a love of both being Scottish, and a love of language, so we did influence each other in that way, in that we'd have this thing, that we gave various different names to but it was almost like a private language. Yes, I think that was very rich, creatively very rich for both of us, and we were both very excited by each other's writing. That's something that we gave each other that can't really be taken away.

IM: When did you start writing for children?

JK: I started writing for children after I had Matthew, and I wouldn't have done if I hadn't had Matthew, but having a kid yourself takes you back through your own childhood. It's like a key opening the door back through there, and you start to think that childhood is actually a way of seeing; being a child is a way of seeing too. Children are writers all the time, if you like.

IM: Do you write poetry for children, stories for children, because someone asks you, or because you want to do this?

JK: Because I want to. And I never do it till I have an idea, or something that I actually want to do. I've got a contract for a book – I've got these contracts for books I haven't written, quite a few of them (L) – they start to plague you: the unwritten book is like the granny you haven't visited, you haven't even taken a scone or a hazelnut toffee to her (L): she just has to stand and look out the window! I've got a new book of children's poems that I'm writing at the moment, and a new children's novel that I'm about to start –

IM: Oh goody!

JK: I'm about to start the new children's novel, which I hope to set in Shetland, or at least by the sea; and it's going to have a lighthouse in it, I know that. And it's going to be inspired partly by Grace Darling, who was sixteen when she did the lighthouse rescue, not in Scotland at all, but I think I might take that story and readjust it (L) and reinvent it, relocate it to Scotland. [*Grace Darling and her father, a light-house keeper on one of the Farne islands, rescued nine people from a shipwreck in 1838*] I have the voice of that children's novel in my head already, so the thing I'm most excited about at the moment is getting a time to just get down to that: I really can't wait to start writing that. And that will be quite good, because I'll have written two children's novels then, and that might lead on: for some reason the idea of writing a children's novel is more appealing to me, exciting. The idea of writing another adults' novel is the absolute opposite.

IM: Wait till it comes up your back, as they say.

JK: That's good advice, Isobel.

IM: But I loved *Strawgirl*. [*2002*] Absolutely marvellous; so I'm delighted to hear you are doing another one. I loved it as me, adult, but I would also have loved it as a child. I think the using again of this idea of there being more than one of you, or having a secret friend with the same name was great: perhaps you could say a little about that. Why is it so important? I remember the lady who wrote the Introduction to *Two's Company* said that you were more or less obsessed (L) with this idea. [*Anne Harvey, 1992*]

JK: I think it's a Scottish obsession.

IM: *Justified Sinner*? (L)

JK: Yes, exactly. I think it's everywhere in Scottish Literature, isn't it; this theme of the double, the doppelganger. For some reason we Scottish get very attracted to that. It's Jekyll and Hyde; the doubleness. There's always more than one way of looking at a situation. It perhaps comes from being a smaller nation, and perhaps England and Scotland are the doubles, and perhaps the ghost-self is England. (L) Perhaps England is Jekyll, (L) - or Hyde! – at any given moment. Perhaps it comes from that, or perhaps it's just in the psyche. I do believe that nations actually hand their people, particularly their imaginative, creative people, their own obsessions. You can see that happening if you take a collection of writers, say from the American South, you'll see that they all come up with a similar kind of theme. Or if you take writers around the period of the Harlem Renaissance, you will see that quite bizarrely these writers all appear in the nineteen-twenties, and then all concern themselves with issues that are different but complementary. It always fascinates me why you have renaissances of writers or painters or whatever, and why they link in or tap into what must be a phenomenon that we don't understand, that makes us sound frankly barking to even speak about it! (L) A collective unconscious! I find it interesting when you go to Nigeria, for instance which I went to recently, you'll find that there are superstitions and myths that are deeply, deeply embedded into the culture itself, and the same goes for Scotland. The trouble with westerners is that they don't realise they are superstitious: we like to say that Africans are the only people that are superstitious, when actually our society is riddled, shot through with superstition like a terrible illness. Look at footballers! Look at sports men and women! So I think these things are collective unconscious.

I think myself, the reason personally that I'm interested in doubling, is because I could have had another life. Always to the other side of me is this other life that I could have had, and I think if you're adopted there's a very plausible reason for having this doubleness, because it's partly your imagination; it's partly your imaginary self; it's partly the imaginary mother, the imaginary father. You have literally two mothers, and two fathers. You have one real Mum: to me the real one was my adoptive Mum. And you have one imaginary one: and the imaginary one's the birth one. So to me it's completely the opposite from the way that people talk about it in our society, when they say, have you met your real mother? It's a question that always annoys me, because I've lived with my real mother all my life (L). She's the one that was there for everything.

IM: She/you has a good way of putting that in *The Adoption Papers*. [*See 'Chapter 6: The Telling Part'*]

JK: So the actuality is interesting between the imaginary and the real, and between fact and fiction in the ordinary and the extraordinary, and that border country that exists between the two places, the real and the strange. That is the country that I'm interested in exploring as a writer. I think the duality definitely comes from being adopted, but it gives me a richness, it's not something that I regret, and I'm really really pleased that I was brought up in Scotland. And that I was adopted. I don't think I would be the same writer, if these things hadn't happened to me, so I'm really lucky. I feel really lucky, but there still are things that you want to explore.

IM: One of the interesting things is that you live in England.

JK: Yes, that's right: very interesting. Scottish people will always say that to you with that wee smile, that self-pleased smile that you just put on your face! (L) Scottish people do it everywhere in the world – so do English people – but Scottish people are somehow childish about this: they're the only country that I know of anywhere in the world that kind of berates people who have left: why don't you still live in Scotland? (L) Do you know what I mean?

IM: I can see it entirely, but it's also an interesting question: I asked it because you were talking about Scottishness.

JK: I know. Well, Scottishness I think happens and is there whether you are living in Scotland or not, and in fact sometimes it can happen even more intensely because you're not living in Scotland. You look at the Scottish people in New Zealand, Australia, Canada and all over the world, and you'll see that they've actually developed a peculiar brand of Scottishness, kitsch Scottishness, because the homesickness and the nostalgia for being Scottish, and for Scotland itself is so intensified that it has become almost cartoon. You go to somewhere like Nigeria, and you meet expat Scottish people that have haggis flown in to Lagos to celebrate Burns' Supper ! (L)

IM: We were talking about dualism and all the rest of it, and I asked you what I thought was a harmless question (L) about not living in Scotland, fresh as I was from you talking about the Scottish unconscious, and fresh as I was from rereading, at Manchester Airport, the end of *Trumpet*, where Joss talks about his/her father, always saying that you always have this big nostalgia thing for your own country: do you?

JK: I do, yes. I think all Scottish people are soppy sentimentalists at heart (L). Nostalgia is a pining, literally: the word comes from that, doesn't it, the Swiss pining up in the Alps and pining for the little towns below. The reason that I've fallen in love with Shetland recently is because it answers that yearning. And you never know what the yearning is for: is it for the land; is it for the people; is it for some land that you have actually inside you? Do we keep land inside us as well as visually seeing it? I think we do, probably in some ways. My current little Walter Mitty dream-plan is to get a little croft in Yell! (L)

IM: Or perhaps Unst? There's a lot of empty houses in Unst, because the services have moved out. You'd probably get a very cheap croft there!

JK: Maybe I should go to Unst, and get a but-'n'-ben. I haven't been to Unst yet, you see, but I have been to Yell. Anyway I thought that I'd go there, and people would say, that mad woman jumping from peat-bog to peat-bog used to be a poet! (L)

IM: Nostalgia then is very complicated. When you went to Nigeria, did you have any sort of bizarre nostalgia for there?

JK: That's an interesting question.

IM: 'the hot dust on the red road?'

JK: In a way I did, because V S Naipaul says, all landscapes exist in the imagination. I think that's true too, that we have imaginary landscapes that we carry about with us that are really quite detailed in their imagining. And when I went to Nigeria the red dust and the red road were there! And that was very extraordinary. But it didn't affect me in the way that Scotland does. I think my imaginary landscape must be more Scottish.

IM: But given that you had a traumatic meeting with your – what do we call them? – Birth fathers? Conception father! [*See many poems in LM, and the prose account published in* Granta, *?? 2006*]

JK: Yes! (L) I never thought of that! That's quite good, Isobel; I like that!

IM: You can use it! Obviously that was an unpleasant experience: it must have been quite distressing, but did you feel an openness to the rest of the place? Did you feel any sense of, oh yes, I can see that parts of me belong here? Or not?

JK: I did in some ways. People said that to me, which was very nice. I did a lot of readings out there: I was also doing a tour there. In fact that was the reason I was in Nigeria, that I'd been invited there. Then I decided to try and find my father, because I was going to be there anyway. Lots of people at the readings would come up and say things like, how come your sense of humour is so African, when you weren't brought up in Africa? I thought, well, that's lovely, and that was something I hadn't realised. And actually, the longer I was there, the more I realised that there *were* some things that you could call African. Sense of humour, and rhythm and language, and even a way of speaking that is not altogether all-Scottish.

IM: And was there any factual truth at all in the poem about meeting the chap in the train? [*OC, 1998, 'Pride': the poet meets a black man on a train who proudly declared that she is an Ibo*]

JK: Yes, there was! Gosh, you've read your stuff well, haven't you? (L)

IM: Well, just the day we have this interview, I should know your work better than you do, in some ways! (L) But I'll forget most of the detail by next week.

[Tape change to 3]

IM: This is the twenty-fourth of March 2006, and I'm still in Manchester with Jackie Kay, and I am still Isobel Murray. Overnight I read a piece Jackie gave me about her meeting her conception father in Nigeria (N), and I listened to yesterday's tape .Well, one of the things that I fantasised about you, just reading your work; have you had real experience of living on a farm?

JK: No. I haven't had real experience of living on a farm.

IM: I thought the *Strawgirl* farm was very, very believable!

JK: Yes, well. Imagination is a wonderful thing. I did have a farmer boyfriend, and I did visit him in Auchencairn. His farm was called Torr, which is also the name I use in *Trumpet*. I did love it down there on the Solway Firth, on that coast. I spent quite a lot of time down there, and I used to watch the cows and so on, and he'd get up for the morning milking: I didn't. I did go to another farm on the Isle of Wight, when I was writing *Strawgirl*, and I stayed there for a week, and got up with them for the morning milking, and did some actual farm research. And the woman there on the Isle of Wight was lovely, and told me a lot about it, because she had a small herd of organic cows. Organic cows, we say: I don't know that the cows are organic! (L) She told me a lot about them, and I observed them, but I haven't actually lived properly for a long length of time on a farm.

IM: Well, I think it would be hard to work that out from the book, which is a nice thing to be able to say. A similar question: had you had any horrible times at the dentist? [*See OC, 1998*]

JK: Yeah. Haven't we all? (L)

IM: I find it painful, reading some of those poems!

JK: Yes, I've had terrible times at the dentist.

IM: Your teeth look so perfect.

JK: I know. They're not, unfortunately. My most recent horrific time at the dentist was actually in Italy last summer: it was just a nightmare from hell! I won't even go into that.

IM: Well, going back to pick up some things we started on yesterday, one thing I thought I should have asked you about was the writers that you most admire. Obviously you've mentioned some of them, like Margaret Atwood and Anita Desai.

JK: I really admire Jean Rhys; I like her voice, and I like the quality of her work, in *Wide Sargasso Sea* and *After Leaving Mr Mackenzie*; I think it's a nice body of work, unusual and distinctive. I like George Eliot a lot, if we stick to dead writers for the moment. I liked Pablo Neruda. I'm trying to think of people who have really really been important to me – Robert Burns, Hugh MacDiarmid, Norman

MacCaig. And then I really liked Audre Lordes, a black American poet. She made a huge impact on me when I first came across her work. Toni Morrison also made a massive impact. Quite a few of the Indian writers that I read I really liked, like Anita Desai. Wole Soyinka; Chinua Achebe. And then a lot of the Scottish writers who are around and about and alive and kicking, and well now. Like Ali Smith, and Tom Leonard, Liz Lochhead. They've all been really important to me in one way or another, James Kelman.

IM: Liz has been a foundation stone for Scottish women writers.

JK: That's right. I think without Liz Lochhead we wouldn't really have any of us: she's the kind of mother of us all.

IM: Well, you'd have had to wait for somebody else to –

JK: To come and do it. She really made it all possible, and she got up there and she kicked ass, and she was fantastic, really fantastic. I remember seeing her when I was sixteen! I got taken to see her at sixteen; I was really lucky. She just blew me away. And then I bought *Memo for Spring*, which was the only book she had out then, and I just read it over and over and over again, so I know a lot of those poems off by heart. Even daft lines like 'you left a/you-shaped/ depression in my pillow'. (L) I wondered about that for ages, because the word depression, I hadn't quite got its double meaning then! (L) So I just thought, oh the depression is a sad depression. [*See 'Inventory' in* Memo for Spring]

IM: And how important have the books been that you concentrated on for your dissertation? Which did you choose to concentrate on?

JK: I concentrated on *Jane Eyre* and *Wide Sargasso Sea*. I wrote a whole chapter on them. I wrote about Toni Morrison's *The Bluest Eye*. I wrote about Janet Frame, *Faces in the Water*, and Janet Frame is another author who is hugely important: I don't know how I managed to leave her out. I think she's just fantastic. A mixture of writers, really. I wrote about *Uncle Tom's Cabin*.

IM: There's nobody mad in *Uncle Tom's Cabin*! (L)

JK: I know! They were all perfectly sane, but they were depicted as mad, and it was also about how we are actually seen, and how we are depicted, and the monster; the Mad Woman in the Attic kind of figure. Who else did I write about? There was a Virginia Woolf one, but I didn't write too much about Virginia Woolf, because she'd been so written about at that time, and it was boring to me, the idea of writing more about Virginia Woolf – why? I tried to pick writers they didn't know too much about. Obviously they knew a huge amount about *Jane Eyre*, but they didn't know much about Toni Morrison then: she hadn't yet published *Beloved*, and she'd only published the first three then, *The Bluest Eye* and *Sula* and *The Song of Solomon*.

IM : It was *Sula* that I was teaching at that stage. (L)

JK: Yes. I'm trying to remember what else.

IM: That's a lovely conspectus.

JK: Oh, Joan Barfoot. There was a Joan Barfoot one, which was good, because it really had this idea of a woman returning to herself, as a kind of a wild woman – I'm trying to remember the name: it's gone out of my head. [Dancing in the Dark,*1982*]

IM: You suggested yesterday that you more or less deliberately don't quote or echo or refer to writers.

JK: Well I do, if it comes up, but some writers do it as a matter of course all the time, which is sometimes interesting, and sometimes not. And sometimes the reason people do that is because they somehow don't feel their work is enough on its own. It just can be slightly awkward, because I'd never want to be comparing myself all the time to people that I think are much better than me, (L) and so there's a slight awkwardness in saying, as Auden says, in the same breath as talking about your own work, so it seems to me to be slightly uncomfortable: so that's one problem with it, and then the other problem is that sometimes it's just a way of bolstering the self, and I think the self should just stand on her own. I read writers all the time, and I read what they've got to say about writing, and I find that endlessly fascinating – and comforting, actually. Because you find that the doubts that you have and the paranoia (L), the suspicion, is rife amongst writers, so I do read writers a lot, but I don't like to over-quote them. I find it irritating when other writers do that, over-quote. I think it's insecurity, actually.

IM: Well, if we were thinking about poetry, it started as we roughly covered it yesterday, writing things and reading things. How do you put a poetry book together? Obviously the case of *The Adoption Papers* is a special one, because it was made into a unit, but did you look at all the poems you had written, or all the poems you were pleased with that you'd written when you were publishing the book?

JK: I selected hugely. Part of *The Adoption Papers* was four times its length originally, and I decided that some of it was far, far too sentimental, and some of it too self-pitying; and I didn't want it to seem self-pitying, at all, at all at all! So most of The Adoption Papers ended up in the bin! And what was left got published. But I really wrote a lot then, because I hadn't yet learned how not to write things; I had to write screeds of rubbish in order to find something good, whereas now I don't disappoint myself too much, in that way of having to write rubbish. (L) I find that quite disheartening now. I don't work in that way any more. I think for much longer before I even put pen to paper, and don't just go off exploring with my notebook, writing screeds of rubbish. Sometimes I do, of course, and there's still a lot of things end up in the bin, but it's not quite the same working method (L), if you can call it that.

IM: But all four of the main poetry books that you've published do have something – I don't mean they all have one subject and one theme, that would be horrendous - but they do have a kind of thematic unity. Would you exclude poems because they didn't fit in that way?

JK: Yes, I would. I exclude poems that don't fit into the book, even if they're good poems. I don't think, you see, a book of poems has to be forty unrelated poems, like a lot of people do. Those books are OK, but they don't satisfy me properly in the terms of a book. I think the poems should talk to each other, and that there should be a reason for the order, the sequence of poems in any poetry book, and that they should be constantly revealing and hiding, if you like, from each other, so that the whole book should be an experience, like a novel is an experience, or a play. It's a whole, it's not a book of fragmented parts. Every poetry book I've written, I've written on that basis, and some are more obviously like that. Like *The Adoption Papers*, as you say, has a narrative that you follow, in the way that a novel might have a narrative. But in all of them, in *Other Lovers*, *Off Colour* and *Life Mask*, they all have a very definite order. Of course these orders that you put things in are up for grabs, but I found that if you change the order for instance of the poems in *Life Mask*, you get a very different book. You get a book that you can almost hardly bear to read. I had *Life Mask* in all sorts of different orders, and eventually I found an order that allowed me to read the bloody book! It also felt like you were going on a journey from darkness into the light, and that's the other thing that's really important for me in books of poems, that there should be some sort of journey that you go on. In each of the books I've written, whatever the book is, actually, whether it's short stories or whatever, there is still, through the order, something that's being told to the reader, covertly, if you like.

IM: But you don't necessarily write them in that order?

JK: No; never. Never write them in that order.

IM : You just write them when the spirit moves you, and then it's almost a craft in itself to select for the book.

JK: That's right. The writing of them is a bit like going and getting loads and loads of different ingredients for this big feast, and you've got no idea exactly yet what you're going to make, and then you find some way, some meal to make of them.

IM: I'm also interested in titles. Are you interested in titles? Do you take a lot of thinking about them?

JK: Yes, a massive amount of thinking about them. I love titles: I love the business of being able to have titles. It's a lot of fun. And angst, thinking of the title. And I do give a great deal of thought to titles: I think most writers do; I think everybody has to.

IM: The poetry books especially. *Other Lovers.* There are so many potential puns and layers, I don't know where to start. It's a brilliant title. Oh, and I was going to ask in brackets whether you've got a fear of mice. [*See OC, 1998, 'Love Nest', and the children's poetry book* Two's Company,*1992, 'Phobia – the year of the mouse!'*]

JK: Yes I do, actually: I'm terrified of them! (L)

IM: Leaving the mice aside, *Other Lovers* is if anything in one way a trendy title, because all the academic trendies talk about 'the other' these days. *Off Colour* I thought was a *brilliant* title, how many times a pun! I've given up writing about colour (maybe), and no' weel, all that disease and things! It is quite a sombre book.

JK: It is. I was going to call it Sickbag, and then I thought it would be off-putting. It's even gone on Bloodaxe's list on the Amazon site, the record of a book of mine called *Sickbag* that never was published, because that's the title that changed to *Off Colour*. (L) I didn't quite have the balls to call it *Sickbag*.

IM: I think *Off Colour* is a lot better, and it contains all the resonances. But it wasn't particularly an obsession at the time: it was just that you were picking out the poems that had to do with illness and with social ills?

JK: No, it was an obsession at the time. I was thinking what the links are between social illness and physical illness, and mental illness. Societal illnesses. Just the lot, really: the laws, the immigration laws, the institutions. I was just thinking around those. I was thinking that you could unify or link with the society through the ills, and the way it treats its ill people, and how racism itself is a kind of an illness. Any kind of deep, deep prejudice which is the real madness. Often when I'm writing a book, for some reason you end up sort of circling a subject. It's as if you had an aerial view of a patch of land, you would just keep flying round and round that particular patch of land: that's your territory for the course of these poems. I think of books of poems like that, as a series of wee fields (L), to go back to agricultural imagery, that you're seeding, and you're planting, and all of that. You have fallow periods with it: you have crops, but you have a whole period where you actually see the interrelations between your thoughts. It might take a while for that to emerge. The poems that I'm writing at the moment, for instance, are still unrelated. But something's starting to emerge that is linking them. I don't know yet what it is; I have to discover that myself. That's my job as a writer, particularly with poems, to discover. I think it's different really for fiction, and it's a different process. Obviously you're still finding things out, but it's different, because you might have already made some decisions beforehand.

IM: Decisions that you make beforehand: formal decisions? Do you know, I'm going to write in five-line stanzas, with a one-liner at the end, or whatever?

JK: I know sometimes. I'm not a great formal poet: I'd love to be, actually. Perhaps I'm too lazy. Perhaps I should learn more, but I like giving myself certain restrictions, like saying, I'm going to write four stanzas of four lines each, and I'm going to have this rhyme-scheme. I quite like working to those kind of restrictions. But I don't like it if I feel that the rhyme is leading the poem; or that you're boxing yourself into corners. Sometimes structure is a great freeing thing, because there's more freedom within a structure than there is within chaos. There's always more freedom within a structure than there is within chaos - that's what we have to tell our teenagers! (L) But I'm not really someone who with ease sits down to write a sonnet, nor do I write easily in iambic pentameters, nor do I scan and have a perfect ear. I think I have a musical ear, and I can hear what I want the language to do, and I can hear how I want it to sound, but I don't think I'm as skilled as someone like Don Paterson, or Glynn Maxwell or Simon Armitage, or any of these contemporary poets, or Carol Ann, at containing rhymes and forms.

IM: And you were saying that earlier on you discarded a lot of poems. Do you tend to write them and finish them, and that's them, or do you put them in a drawer and come back, and edit them, change them a bit?

JK: It depends, really. I tend to write and finish them, and that's it for now; then when I come to work on the whole book I go back to them, and there might be things that I take out or change, depending on how they fit in with the poem that they're going to be next to. I'll change them once they come to fit in the whole book.

IM: Right. We must mention The Broons. I think 'Maw Broon Visits a Therapist' is a wonderful poem.[OC 1998] It is obviously a wonderful performance poem, but it's got quite a lot to it, hasn't it? I was very upset when I found out that Paw Broon had been two-timing her. (L) [See 'There's Trouble for Ma Broon', LM 2005] Mind you, it did seem unlikely that they would have a wee but-'n'-ben. They don't, do they?

JK: Oh, they do! In the cartoon, they've got the but-'n'-ben.

IM: Well, I'm glad I asked that, because

JK: Yes, a lot of these details in the Broons poems are often completely faithful to The Broons.

IM: 'The Broons' Bairn's black?' (L)

JK: They're completely faithful to the notions, like if it mentions a pinny, you know that she has a pinny, usually, and if her hair's up in a bun -

IM: Oh God, that bun! And obviously you refer to them because they're such a wonderful Scottish archetype, but why them particularly?

JK: I've always loved the strip. I think he's one of the great cartoonists of all time, Dudley Watkins, absolutely fantastic cartoonist. He led the way, really, and my Mum lived next door to him in Fife, and when she was a wee girl he gave her drawing lessons. He stayed with this lodger; I keep meaning to write an article about that for *Granta*, because it's such a fascinating story, and I must try and do it, before it all kind of slips away. She's not got those drawings any more, which is a great shame. She gave them to Uncle Willie in Lochgelly, Uncle Willie lost them. They would be worth a bloody fortune now, and it would be really nice to see. But anyway, she was and still is good at drawing and cartoons. Actually, she wanted to be a political cartoonist. That was her ambition, and she never got to do it. I like cartoons, and how much they can say, and how much they can comment on our society. They give us a laugh; they're jokes in pictures, but they're wee films as well. They're like film screens of stories. They're poems, in the case of The Broons, because they always begin with a double line rhyming couplet, which is lovely. And I just think they're an archetypal Scottish family, so it's quintessentially Scottish that you can have fun with if you're black and Scottish. You can play around with it; 'The Broons' Bairn's Black', or whatever. Or you can keep on upsetting the cart of what it means to be a woman, what it means to be a man. I think in the next book of poems I write there'll be a Broons poem too. I've kind of decided that I'm going to publish at least one Broons poem in every book of poems that I write till I die! (L) That's my minor ambition! I could probably write a whole book, all at once, on them, but I think that'd be tedious. I like them just to come out in wee dribs and drabs like that.

IM: You might later on collect them, and publish them, with the odd wee cartoon.
That could be fun.

JK: That would be fun, if you got the rights to do it.

IM: I'm sure they would: *The Sunday Post* would be fair taken up with itself.

JK: Quite a good idea; it's a great idea, that! (L)

IM: When we come to *Life Mask*, the most recent book of poetry, the mask is really clear, from all sorts of angles, and your notes about it, about how they were casting you in bronze and all. I felt these poems were extraordinarily spare, honed down. Did you have that feeling? I don't mean that the earlier ones were ornate: far from it, but here you're almost coming down to ballads. We talked yesterday about how people empathised with Millie in *Trumpet*, although they weren't women in her situation. I think anybody could empathise with the voice in *Life Mask*, because they're so – they are particular, but they're just universal in the themes.

JK: That's nice of you: thank you. Yes, I think I really did want to write spare poems. I wanted the poems to be lyrical, and there should be a lot of space in them for the reader to come in, so that the poems wouldn't just reveal me, but hopefully reveal the reader to themselves. And that there would be a process of stripping away, because so much of the book is about stripping away, and about layers, and about masks and about the faces that we put on. And all the different kinds of masks that there are. I've read them quite a lot now, and I've also done workshops in schools around that theme of masks, it's quite astonishing when you start to talk about it, how many masks people perceive – even children perceive – that they have to wear, or don, in order to get through an ordinary day. And it's quite a good discussion to have; very simple, in a way. An interesting idea that's interested writers for years, but also a very complex idea. And one that still intrigues us, because we're really intrigued with faces, and these faces not being who they seem to be in our society, the doubleness of faces.

IM: 'Give a man a mask, and he will tell you the truth.'

JK: Exactly. The mask says more than the face. That's Oscar Wilde. But yes, exactly that.

IM: I was going to ask about illustrations. The children's books are illustrated. Do you choose the illustrators?

JK: No, usually the publisher chooses them. In fact I haven't really had an illustrator that I've been really excited about as yet, to be truthful. I quite liked the ones in *Three Has Gone*. Kind of odd woodcuts.

IM: But you don't as it were have a say in that.

JK: They'll send you examples of people's work, and then you get to say, yes I like that one; but you don't just go out and pick someone that you like, and get them to get that person, which would be really great if you could. I suppose some writers might get to do that.

IM: I think it depends on your clout with the publisher, which usually has to do with how much money you're making for them (L).

JK: Exactly.

IM: I want to talk in particular still about short stories, in fact I think we should do that right now, because otherwise the tapes are going to be a bit skewed towards the novel and the poems. Are titles important here too? *Why don't you stop talking?* (L).

JK: Yes, they are very important. *Why don't you stop talking* is really a note to myself! (L) Good to have a title that's a note to yourself!

IM: It's a savage book, in some ways.

JK: It is. It is a savage book, and it's all about change and metamorphosis, and the changes that are forced upon us if we don't create enough space in our lives to be ourselves. We're forced into sometimes quite horrific changes. Most of the stories are unified in some way or another through that particular theme, which again wasn't a theme I necessarily set out with, but it was something that came, the longer the stories went on for.

IM: I keep looking for bigger ideas behind, like the one about sharks. ['*Shark! Shark!*'] Is it just irrational fear, of anything, that can destroy you?

JK: I think in his case he's frightened of death, and the shark's a metaphor for death. He's absolutely terrified of death in a really really deep way, in the way that some people are, and he's put that fear of death onto sharks, but in the end the fear of death kills him. That's what the story is about, really; it's about how our fears kill us. And that is a very deep subject, and it's true; we know ourselves that when we really fear something, we can make it happen, because we've put so much energy into the fearing of it. That's not to say that we're responsible for really nasty things that happen to us, like people jumping out on us from behind bushes (L) or whatever! But it's just on some quite inexplicable psychological level, our fears define us. We are reduced by our fears. For instance, if you're in an unhappy relationship, and you're absolutely frightened of being on your own, then you'll not leave the unhappy relationship. But you might shrink; so as you get smaller and smaller within that, so your fear has defined you, literally, changed you. Whereas if you confront the fears that you have, then you've got a chance of surviving. That's really what *Why don't you stop talking?* is about. A lot of my stories are about that, because they're all quite edgy. For me, it's quite an edgy form, the short story. Quite dark and troubled.

IM: It is. Even the lovely one that ends with the woman becoming a tortoise. ['*Shell*'] I wondered if that was supposed to be a happy ending or not! (L) She seems so happy.

JK: She's delighted, yes. It is a happy ending for her, the tortoise gets peace.

IM: And she enjoys eating the earth, so why should one worry? And so, like the poetry books, *Why don't you stop talking?* is very much linked, very much a whole. The stories obviously stand separately, but –

JK: Yes, I like to think of it as a whole.

IM: And some of them are also very funny; that's the confusing thing. 'Physics and Chemistry' I thought was just wonderful – Plain and Purl. So the book that is forthcoming, *Wish I Was Here* – that's another brilliant title, and it's such a perverse title! (L) The whole of that story, of going on holiday to interlope with the old lover and her new one: and she's so determined to do it! Does she think it will make her happy?

JK: I know; it's bizarre, isn't it. She starts to sing and dance along (L). Actually that story had a different ending; and I took the last three lines out, because I thought it was better to end with her going 'look who's-a here!'. After that, those three lines where the lover, Jan, looked at her and said, 'What do you think you're doing, you spooky cow?' (LL) Which really made me laugh out loud when I wrote it! Then I decided it was better to just leave it out. The funny thing was, I started writing that story, as I do with quite a few stories, not particularly liking that character: I started off actually really disliking her, and then by the end of the story I felt really sympathetic towards her. And that was the course that I hoped the reader would go on, and that's quite an interesting thing, that little journey that you take with your own character, and you don't know that you're going to change towards them.

IM: 'How to Get Away with Suicide', for example. The things that go through that man's head, and the reasons he finally has *not* to commit suicide, yet. Is that a happy ending?

JK: I think so, yes. I think it's a happy ending for him. I think the stories in *Wish I Was Here* are on the whole slightly more positive. (L)

IM: Yes. I'm not sure about 'My Daughter the Fox'. Giving birth to a fox instead of a baby is bad enough, nobody else liking it. But then when the foxes call outside and –

JK: And she has to give her back: that's very sad, that one.

IM: A very folktale-ish ending. It seems to speak back to an older way of talking and writing: it's very interesting. I was appalled with 'The Silence'. Just because it does so well the meaningless conversations people have, and the way they stop listening to each other.

JK: That comes from even a wee place like one of those garden centres that also have a café. You look at the couples in them; particularly when I'm in Milngavie with my Mum; we're always going there. And I really like going to places like that. And you look at the couples that are having what they usually have, and the amount of them that are really not saying a single thing to each other! They're like paintings! Hopper paintings. But it just makes me think a lot about what it must be like. Just hell, 'The Silence'. To me it's the saddest story in the book. That would be my idea of hell, to be in a relationship where nobody really talked to me any more. Although I try to find a way to make that positive for these characters, because in a sense the silence gives them peace in the end.

IM: It's not terribly positive, though! Communication is so important. It doesn't have as much savagery as the stories in *Why Don't You Stop Talking?* But an awful lot of sadness. Tell me about the composition of 'Sonata'.

JK: Well, 'Sonata' is really a story sparked off and inspired by *The Kreutzer Sonata* by Tolstoy. [*Novella published 1889. An in-depth, first person description of jealous rage by a man who killed his wife, who had had an affair with the violinist with whom she played Beethoven's Kreutzer Sonata.*] I'd been rereading that story a while before, because I'd been picking some pieces of music for this radio programme, and the Kreutzer Sonata was one of the pieces that I picked. The one by Janacek, not the original one. I thought that interesting: there are three different Kreutzer Sonatas, and I couldn't call a story The Kreutzer Sonata because of that thing I was talking about earlier, about setting yourself up to fail! (L) Not being Tolstoy, and knowing that I'm not Tolstoy. So I thought I'd call it 'Sonata'. I set off to write a story, going across Russia in the snow, in the train, taking some of the same things that Tolstoy has in that story, jealousy. And that was it. But I wanted to write a lesbian story, because all of these stories are all so heterosexual. I wanted to write a story which is in a sense the same as the first story, 'You Go When You Can No Longer Stay'. I wanted to put the woman against the Martin Amis, so although it's a story about the break-up of a relationship, it's also a story asking, what is the main stream? It challenges what the main stream is. And that's what I like to try to do as a writer, is to constantly ask what the main stream is, and to challenge it. I didn't realise that 'Sonata' would become a dual narrative story; I didn't set out to do that; it was just that I wrote the first four pages, and then suddenly the other voice came through, and I thought, oh, I don't know if I can get away with that. That doesn't happen in Tolstoy's story. I quite like that feeling when you're writing, when you think, can I do this? It's really scary! (L) Am I allowed: I'm not sure! Then you think, yes, you can do it; you are allowed, and keep on with it. I kept on with it, and I didn't really decide when one voice would stop, but it became like a process of the music itself, and it became like passing the baton between one and the other, very musical. I needed to have the two voices, and I needed to have the two voices being foreign, it seemed to me, and to speak English in a very fluent way, not in a silly staccato way, but in a way that we could properly hear, especially people that do languages, I think. All my friends who have read that that speak fluently in Spanish or French or anything, completely think the voices are authentic. Whereas the friends who don't speak foreign languages don't! If you see what I mean. (L) 'Sonata' is a story that has divided people who have read it so far. Ali Smith didn't like it at all, for instance: she said she did it all for the green scarf! (L) Which is so beautifully Ali, I forgave her for it! (L) Her favourite is 'My Daughter the Fox'. Which was your favourite? Did you have a favourite?

IM: I find some of them really quite upsetting. I thought 'You Go When You Can No Longer Stay', although it's got comic elements in it, like that. I didn't terribly like 'Not the Queen'. I'm kind of bored with the Queen.

JK: Yeah; I don't like that one either.

IM: I saw the point of it, and the fact that she'd put up with it because it would upset her husband -

JK: I wanted to take that story out, because I think it's the weakest story in the book, but other people really liked it, and they thought it gave the book a different angle, because otherwise it would all be jealousy and such. I think they thought it opened it out a bit. Ali thought it was good, 'Not the Queen', but I absolutely hate that story; it's my least favourite. It's almost I hate it so much I almost didn't write it, if you know what I mean. I think, how did I write that shite? (L) But I did ask the people at Picador, and they all really liked it, and it's even been The One. It's been picked up by *The Bookseller*, this book, in advance of it being published, and the one that they talk about is 'Not the Queen'. But they liked 'Not the Queen'.

IM: I didn't hate it; but partly because as I say I find the Queen very boring.

JK: But what one did you like?

IM: You make me feel like I used to make my students feel! I would say, did you enjoy *King Lear*? What are you talking about, enjoying *King Lear*! I thought 'You Go When You Can No Longer Stay' is a favourite, and 'Wish I Was Here' is a favourite, and I didn't get on quite so well with 'What Is Left Behind'. I think 'Wish I Was Here' is probably it. And it's a marvellous title for the whole thing. I just think it's rather a waste of time to talk about 'Not the Queen' when there's so much else! I liked 'Sonata' very much: I haven't read the Tolstoy for yonks – you could say in living memory! And I don't know that much about sonata form, how closely the passing the baton worked musically. But I thought it came off very well; in a way perhaps it's the sort of thing that Ali might have done herself.

JK: She didn't like it anyway.

IM : And I liked 'The Mirrored Twins.' Apart from anything else, just the fact that they were so lovely and ordinary, a hospital porter and a refuse collector. And the detail, the opposite of what I was talking about, the spareness of the *Life Mask* poems. A wonderful accumulation of details: that works, I think.

JK: That's my favourite story, 'The Mirrored Twins'. It's my favourite because it's an adventure story; and I hadn't written an adventure story (L) before, and I didn't know if I could do that, and I could really really see them, exactly where they are. I could see the twin peaks; I could see the whole thing.

(tape turns over)

IM: Another thing that I've read, which doesn't belong to any obvious genre – one of the things you said yesterday was how interested you were in all sorts of different things – the piece you wrote for *Granta,* for example, doesn't act as a short story, doesn't act as a poem. Well, it does act as a short story, but the reader doesn't know whether it's a true story or not.

JK: Well, it is a true story: I think the reader will know that, that it's true when they read it, definitely. It's part of a memoir that I have written . I've written a whole book.

IM: Ah! How did I get into that? Just by accident.

JK: And that's one part of it, and I've written this whole book: I've finished it, but I just didn't know whether I wanted to publish the book or not. People want to publish the book, and I just couldn't make up my mind whether I wanted to publish it or not, so I thought, if I took a little bit of it, a tiny fraction of the words that the book makes up, and published it on its own, and saw how that felt, it would help me decide whether to publish the whole memoir, which is called *Tracing*.

IM: And you haven't decided yet, obviously.

JK: No, because I haven't yet had any response. I had a response from the people at *Granta* that have read it, and the other people who have read it, and everybody likes that particular piece a huge amount. I suppose it's more an emotional thing that I'm thinking about, of how exposed you feel, so I'm waiting for that. It's also going to be in the *Guardian* Review: the *Guardian* and the *Telegraph* both wanted it, and they kind of fought over it (L), which was quite funny. But I couldn't have something in the *Telegraph*, even though they'd have paid me more money. And once it's been in the *Guardian*, I'll be able to see how I feel about it. I might just decide not to.

IM: Or to wait a wee while.

JK: The book was finished two years ago. I wrote the book quite soon after I came back from Nigeria, while everything was still fresh in my head, and it didn't take me that long to write: it only took me about six months. But I probably would want to do other things, if I was going to publish it anyway, like go back to Nigeria again, go to Ibo country and see if I could find out brothers and sisters, and do all that kind of stuff. I don't know if I can quite get up the energy for that! (L)

IM: Obviously, not yet, if at all, is the answer. Just let it simmer away.

JK: Exactly, I think that's good.

IM: Unless you're starving at any point! But no, you should never publish: what is it Sammy says to Colman? Don't do anything that you might be sorry for in five years time.

JK: Yes.

IM: If you don't know, not yet. I'm very good at giving advice! Free! Is there any other genre that you haven't tried?

JK: No; I think I've tried different genres, and I quite like the way that writing in one genre, or trying to, helps with writing another. For instance, when I came to write the screenplay, having written poems and short stories really helped. Having written a novel doesn't help at all – in fact, it anti-helps! (L) So I quite like that thing of experimenting with form. There isn't another form that I'd like to try: I'd just like to try some of the ones that I've done again, and some of them I'd like to never try again. Like writing plays, I think. I never want to write another play, unless I suddenly woke up one day and had the whole thing in my head. The form that I'm most comfortable with is the short story form, and the reason that I like the memoir and the short story form is that you can play quite closely to the truth. I quite like to write quite close to the truth, or to give a semblance of the truth: I like the border country, that I was talking about yesterday, that exists between these two things. And I like the sense of danger that you get, and also the sense of authenticity that a reader gets from reading. That's why we live in the time of the memoir. We live in the time of recording and documenting ourselves ad infinitum. We don't live in a time where the imagination is properly valued, and it's extraordinary the capacity we have in this society to keep on recording real moments. That's why celebrities' TV has taken off in that way, and 'Big Brother', and all those kind of programmes that make some people recoil in horror and other people grin in glee. But we live in a society that is obsessed with documenting and recording ourselves, and obsessed with what the truth is. It seems that when you are trying to write a memoir or a short story you really are examining that quite seriously, what is the truth; what do you want to say; what don't you want to say. What do you want to leave out. And you always have to ask that question when you write a short story: what don't you want to say? Because what you don't say in a story is just as important as what you do.

IM: Were you suggesting that 'Sonata' kind of slipped out from under your control, got longer and so on: do short stories normally just write themselves in the right length?

JK: Well 'Sonata' I always intended to be a long story, because the Tolstoy one is about ninety pages, and I needed to have about forty at least; otherwise it would be silly. And I couldn't really have done a ten page 'Sonata'. And I wanted to see if I could do a long story, because most of my stories in *Why Don't You Stop Talking* are all about ten or twelve pages long. I wanted to see if a story would sustain itself over that kind of period of time.

IM: There wasn't any problem with that!

JK: What was your question? (L) Do I normally have a sense of the length of them before I start? I don't know what the length of them's going to be before I start . Except the little ones in 'What Ever': the little bird ones. I did have a sense of the length of them before I started, because one I counted the words, and it was two hundred and twenty, and so I thought I'd do another one at six hundred and sixty (L). And I gave myself sort of arbitrary maths to do that, just because I wanted to see if I could do it, and because it was a really short one that began that series of stories, it was the shortest, the one that's at the last, 'Gull': that was the first one I wrote. And so I had to have other little ones to go with it, because I wanted to publish that little story. And that's how that came about. But they all had to be very short. And then 'The Silence': I wanted that to be very short too. So I suppose I know if I want something to be very short, or I want it to be longer, but I don't know exactly the word count or the length at all.

IM: I don't think anybody does, except someone like me who's spent so many years reviewing new fiction: I can write six hundred words without counting! (L)

JK: That's a good facility to have! I want to do a save the short story campaign, and I think the time of the short story is NOW! And I think that it's a much much under-valued form. Poetry has its own prizes, but there isn't a proper short story prize. In this country for books. You can't just enter books of short stories for the Booker, for instance, or the Whitbread. There is a Whitbread poetry prize, and there is a Whitbread children's book prize, but the short story, of all the forms, is the least supported by other institutions and prizes, and the kind of things that support literature.

IM: We should mention the Macallan.

JK: The Macallan short story prize is an exception, and Orange sponsor a new big short story prize that just came out last year, funded also by the Book Trust. But these are all things that are happening now, that are recognising the short story. There are very few outlets for short stories, while poetry has lots of different magazines. And the few places that there are tend to publish writers that they already know. I'm lucky enough to be able to get my short stories published,
But lots of people don't. I really do think it's a great freedom form: it's a pioneering form, and you can keep on changing it, reinventing it. there's still lots of things to do with it.

IM: I just love getting into a novel. And I love being able to stay there for quite a while.

JK: I'll have to try to write a novel for you.

IM: Tell me also a little bit about your teaching at Newcastle.

JK: I teach a short story course there, and I teach a course in children's literature. I supervise four PhD students, and I really enjoy it. I really enjoy particularly these two courses that I teach, for six weeks in a row, and I really really like them. I like making up the course; deciding what goes on it for their reading, and also the courses are practical, because they are reading and writing. A lot of these students are doing an MA in Creative Writing, so they actually want to be writers themselves, but they are supported with the reading. I find it interesting, find teaching interesting.

IM: You enjoy it?

JK: I love it!

IM: And how much do you do of it?

JK: Not a lot. That's probably why I love it. (L)

IM: Two six week courses?

JK: Yes. I teach for six weeks of each term. That's perfect really. I think if it was half time, I couldn't do it, with all the things I have to do in my life, and I'd start to feel resentful of it, in the way that you do, or even feel it was affecting how I could be creative myself. I'm still much much too busy, and I'd like to have more time in my life just to write, and I really envy and admire people who can do very little else except write, and promote their book once they have it out: that must be great!

IM: Like Martin Amis?

JK: (L) Even he writes huge pieces for *The Guardian* on tennis and things, doesn't he? He wrote to *Granta*, because that's where it was printed, 'You Go When You Can No Longer Stay', saying, tell Jackie Kay I really liked her story! (L) So that was very sweet, wasn't it? And that story got picked for this award in America, a short story award called the O Henry, so that was nice.

IM: I think it works very well. But Martin Amis was the right person. It could I suppose have been Ian MacEwan.

JK: Well there's Ina MacEwan; there's my character Ina MacEwan: he's in there as well! (L)

IM: Oh, I am thick: I didn't notice that!

JK: There are all these wee things in that book that are planted for people to notice eventually, hopefully. Like these two scones with rhubarb-and-ginger jam in two different stories. (L) When Janet says to Ina, why don't you have a wee scone with homemade rhubarb-and-ginger jam. And in 'You Go When You Can No Longer Stay' she comes back to the kitchen and she picks the tracing paper off the jar. In that book, more than in *Why Don't You Stop Talking* there's little details from story to story that are chimeable, hopefully, that you can pick up and interlink things. There's even a sense that the one character that appears in one story could be another one in another, and things like that. I can imagine that if you made a film: when you say, what form would you like to try now, I'd like to make my own film. I'd like to write the screenplay, and direct it, and have a film that was a bit like short stories. A bit like 'Short Cuts', say, by Altmans - that kind of film, when you are getting glimpses of windows opening into different people's lives, and the people don't seem to be that related, but it's quite richly satisfying, the way that they all connect. I'd really love to do that. That's my next ambition, apart from learning to play the trumpet. (L) Carol Ann bought me a trumpet once. God knows, it must be under the stairs in the old house: I could get it back.

IM: Was it true, the piece in *Granta*, that your mother had become a Mormon?

JK: Yes, that's true; yes, yes.

IM: That was when I thought it was a story.

JK: No, no, it's really true. It's like a story! That's why there was no point for me in writing that as a story, because to me it was a true story that happened to me: that's what the whole thing felt like, a story that was happening to me, unfolding. It's all so wild, it has to be true. She's a Mormon, he's a born-again Christian, and both my parents are Communists! (L) One way or another, I'm surrounded by strong belief systems!

IM: You're having quite a good time with them, making good use of them all.

Books by JK mentioned in the interviews

For Adults

Gay Sweatshop: Four Plays and a Company (includes the play *Twice Over*) 1989
The Adoption Papers   1991
Other Lovers 1993
Outline: Bessie Smith 1997
Off Colour 1998
Trumpet 1998
Why Don't You Stop Talking 2002
Life Mask 2005
Wish I Was Here 2006

For Children

Two's Company 1992
Three Has Gone 1994
The Frog Who Dreamed She was an Opera Singer 1999
Strawgirl 2002

Allan Massie

I have had a friendly but tenuous relationship with Allan Massie since some time in the late seventies, when we both served on the Grants to Publishers subcommittee of the Scottish Arts Council. We were all strangers, and all became friendly, but Allan was the one fellow member with whom I found myself in critical agreement time after time. There followed a gentle acquaintance, mostly at a distance.

Massie is an extraordinarily prolific writer. At the time of the interview he had published maybe nineteen novels, and various biographies, critical works, appreciations of cities, histories. There are books on Rugby, Glasgow, Edinburgh, Colette, etc, besides the ones I raised here as of special interest for the novel-reader. On top of that he is a prolific journalist, producing by his own recent estimate an average of 200 newspaper articles per annum! There is, of course, a very big difference between a novelist and a columnist. The latter is sometimes paid to be opinionated, to take sides, to make political points. Such shades of Massie's 'opinions' as are also discernible in the novels will be very much more tentative; exploratory, analytic. Here I was clearly interviewing not the columnist but the novelist.

Massie is widely respected as a novelist, but often omitted in surveys of the 'Scottish scene': why is this? Maybe the very fact of his being a journalist and commentator marks him off unfairly for some people: maybe his public school background sets him apart from the current fashions. Certainly I think his cosmopolitanism has a part to play. He gained a unique new perspective on Scotland as well as Europe from his years in Italy. We might compare what Robertson learned about Scotland from America. Maybe the question is slightly generational, too: he has this in common with Bill Watson, as well as the public school and Oxbridge element. Both of them were profoundly touched by the war: Watson tells of his time as an evacuee, and Massie grew up fatherless, with his parent a prisoner of war in Singapore.

Again, Massie is clearly not 'just' a Scottish novelist. His interests embrace the whole of Europe in modern times, the whole Roman Empire and the 'Dark Ages' in historical terms. Indeed, some readers probably do not know how many of his novels are set in the part of

Scotland from which he hails: the posher farmfolk of the North East, the worlds of Drumtochty and Glenalmond. And like Watson, he has a firm traditional admiration for Dumas, Scott and Stevenson: his novel about Scott, The Ragged Lion, is one of his own favourites.

IM: December 9th 2004, at the Aberdeen home of Bob Tait and Isobel Murray. Allan Massie has been very kind, and come to see us, thus saving our venturing to Selkirk. I'd like to start by asking Allan a bit about his background. It says in all the books that he was born in Singapore, but we think of him as very Scottish. How long were you in Singapore?

AM: I think I was probably in Singapore only for a few days. My father was a rubber planter in Malaya, in Jahore, which was just across the causeway from Singapore, so my mother would have gone to the hospital in Singapore for the birth, and then would have gone back to Jahore, but I left Malaya when I was about six months old. In 1939 my father was on leave, which came every four years. We came home, - mother, father, elder brother and myself. My mother was pregnant, and my father went back in 1940. We stayed at home. My sister was born in May 1940. Then he was taken prisoner in Singapore, of course, and was in the Japanese camp up in Thailand, so like everyone there had a very rough time, and very nearly died, but did survive. The result was of course, that when he came home, which would have been probably early 1946, one didn't know him.

IM: Yes: it must have been strange for all parties.

AM: That was the case of course for so many people of our own generation, that fathers had been away – even if they'd been in the services on the home front, they were still away most of the time, and the children just didn't know them.

IM: Have you ever been back?

AM: I've never been back: my brother's been back; I haven't. I'm not likely to now.

IM: The next thing I know about you is that you went to Glenalmond. At five, or…?

AM: No: Glenalmond didn't take us till we were thirteen. We were in Aberdeenshire, farming on both sides of the family. Father went back to Malaya to continue as a rubber planter, and so we went to boarding school, first of all at Prep School, at Drumtochty Castle. [*Drumtochty Castle, Kincardineshire: "a neo-Gothic early nineteenth-century pile which was a hospital during the war, then a boys' school, followed by a restaurant, before reverting to a private home again"* . *See a wonderful fictional account of the school in Elspeth Barker's* O Caledonia *1991*] Then I went on to Glenalmond when I was thirteen. I suppose if my father had not gone back to Malaya, in that event he would have farmed here. My mother had inherited a fairly small farm from her father, and we'd probably have gone to Aberdeen Grammar – or Gordon's – and Aberdeen University, and I've often thought if I had done that I'd probably have become a lawyer in Aberdeen, and might have become very rich in the 1970s and 80s. [L] A lost opportunity, clearly!

IM: Or you might have been a writer writing even more about the North East than you actually have, which is quite a lot. Were you happy at school?

AM: On the whole, yes. I had occasional moments of misery, which I think most children have from time to time, but on the whole I was happy, probably. I was in those days quite shy, even timid and therefore conformist, and if you're a conformist at school you tend to be quite happy. [L]

IM: Was your brother there as well?

AM: He was there, yes. He's three years older than me, so he left when I was fifteen or so.

IM: So then you had the question of university. Was it a question?

AM: No. It wasn't a question that was asked me, anyway! [L] No; it was assumed at Glenalmond, as at the other Scottish Independent schools, that if you were regarded as one of the more clever people, you would try for Oxford or Cambridge, and I went to Cambridge on a History exhibition to Trinity. That was more or less decided for me: - nobody asked me about it. [L] This was the nineteen fifties: you didn't ask young people about things like that: you told them what they were going to do, more or less.

IM: Would it always have been history, do you think?

AM: Probably, yes. I was never an exact enough Classicist to do Classics at university, and I'd been in the History Sixth; - there wasn't an English Sixth at Glenalmond, because everybody did A level English, and so there wasn't a separate Sixth – the others were History and Classics, Modern Languages, and so on. And I was in the History Sixth, so yes, I think it would always have been History. And I'm very glad I did History at university.

IM: You've made good use of your historical expertise! [L] Do you think of yourself as essentially a historical novelist?

AM: No. I think of myself as a novelist, and I don't actually make any great distinction between the *historical* novels and the modern novels. And there are some I think of as modern novels, the three that deal with mid-twentieth century Europe [*A Question of Loyalties*, 1989, *The Sins of the Father*, 1991, *and Shadows of Empire*, 1997]. I think of it as a loose trilogy because the theme is similar, I think of those as contemporary novels, but I'm quite well aware that even to my children, who are in their twenties, they're historical novels. And it is quite a thought that we're now as far from the beginning of the Second World War, pretty well as Scott was from the 'Forty-Five when he wrote *Waverley*.

IM: But we have much more material to hand.

AM: We've much more material to hand, certainly.

IM: And are in a sense more limited in what we can do, because the facts are too clear.

AM: Yes. The facts are too clear, and you can have too many facts. We're probably going to talk about *A Question of Loyalties* later, but this novel set in Vichy France which I wrote in about 1988, I suppose – I now know far more about Vichy France and France in the Second World War than I did when I wrote that novel. And I rather think I couldn't make a novel of it now, because too much knowledge can get in the way of imagination. I think the people who do research for a novel usually write rather bad novels as a result of it, because the research overweighs the imaginative element.

IM: So you don't consciously do research?

AM: I think if you're doing a novel which is set in the past, or in a foreign country, that's the sort of thing that you might do research for. If you do research, it should be done quite a long time before you write the novel. That gives it time for it to settle in your mind, and you forget quite a lot of it in detail. If you 'get up' a subject for a novel, then you're in danger: the factual element of it becomes too prominent. You can see this in some of Scott's later novels, when his imagination is flagging – something like *Count Robert of Paris [1831]* – what he is doing is just fictionalising the sources just, without bringing much of himself to it.

IM: It's interesting in a big, general sense, - I'm not talking about the novels individually just now – that you wrote your prose history of the Caesars such a long time before you produced the Roman trilogy, which turned into a quartet, which became a sequence of Roman novels. Did you not really have to go back to the history in between?

AM: Not a lot. You go back to check that you aren't making too many mistakes, but otherwise no.

IM: Let's think about this young man who did History at Cambridge. What I'm interested in is how this young history graduate moved at some stage to Italy, doing some teaching, I think, and at what stage he decided he wanted to write.

AM: I decided I wanted to write long before I published anything. When I was at Cambridge I was saying I was going to write novels, but people didn't believe me. Then I taught at a Prep School in Scotland for ten years. [1960-1971]

IM: Back to Drumtochty?

AM: Yes. In that time I wrote a number of short stories, and in the long holidays that teachers get and that are supposed to give you the opportunity for creative work if you want to, I started two or three novels. I think one of them, which was a Jacobite novel, got to about thirty thousand words, but it was all derivative stuff. It wasn't until I was over thirty that I started writing anything that was publishable. The first things I published were one or two short stories in the *London Magazine*, which was edited by Alan Ross as you know, and like an awful lot of writers I owe a considerable debt of gratitude to him, not only for publishing me, but for encouragement and advice, because he was certainly the first person – other than myself! [L] – who believed that I was trying to do something worthwhile.

   I moved to Italy when Drumtochty got into financial difficulties – went bust, in effect – and closed, and I went to Italy about a year later, simply because I was at a loose end, and I'd been to Italy on holiday two or three times and I liked the place, and also I thought well, if you're going to be a writer, Rome is not a bad place to go. I didn't actually write much when I was there, one or two more stories, one or two pieces of journalism. I got married. I'd known Alison for years: in fact she was the daughter of my ex-employer-boss at Drumtochty. She came out to Rome and we decided to get married .

IM: When was that?

AM: That was in '73. We got married there, and our first child was born while we were there. Then I found I was having to do so much teaching that everything else was being squeezed out. And we'd lost the flat we'd had in the centre of Rome, and had to look for another one, and couldn't find anything we liked, so we came back to Scotland and Edinburgh. That would have been '76 or so.

IM: So, was it during that period that you came across or got to know Muriel Spark?

AM: No. I never knew Muriel when we were in Rome. She would have moved in very much richer circles. [L] That was her Grand Period, you know, when she had her apartment in Rome, with cardinals paying court. We didn't move in those circles: lower Bohemia, not upper Bohemia! [L]

IM: Can you just tell me now when you did meet her?

AM: I was asked to write a little book about her by Norman Wilson, who ran the Ramsay Head Press and who had this series of short critical studies of Scottish writers. I was asked if I'd do one on Muriel. I must have reviewed her last couple of novels for *The Scotsman*, so I said yes. So I wrote the book [*1979*], and she was actually very nice about it, and seemed quite to like it. So I met her after that. I think she probably liked it because it didn't go into too much inquisitive biographical stuff. She was very much against that, at that time.

IM: I think she still is, unless she does it herself.

I'm curious about the fact that your first novel was so unexpected, and so different from everything you've written since [L]

AM: The first novel, *Change and Decay in All Around I See* [*1978*]. As I say, I'd written short stories, and published short stories, and it started as a short story – and went on. And it is a very loose, episodic novel, which could almost stop anywhere. I think part of the reason was that I had attempted three or four novels which hadn't got very far, and so I wrote the kind of novel which could stop at any point. As to construction, although it all takes place in London, it is a sort of picaresque novel.

IM: Dominated by conversation.

AM: Yes. Some of the conversation which I thought was technically adroit now seems to me rather silly. There's one scene in an Indian restaurant, as I remember, where there are perhaps half a dozen characters and you have four pages of dialogue, little of it more than one line long, and I knew who was speaking all the time, but I doubt if many readers would have realised who was speaking. I thought this was terribly clever and interesting to do. Now I think the reader should have been given a little more help. But it was influenced in that way by people like Henry Green, and I suppose probably Firbank. The starting point was this chap who has come out of prison and is living in a Turkish baths in Jermyn Street. It happened that in the early seventies I had spent a few months in London – when I had some redundancy money after the closure at Drumtochty actually, and I was living very much hand to mouth, and drinking too much; and I did spend quite a number of nights in the Turkish Baths in Jermyn Street, because they were cheap, convenient, comfy. However drunk you were, you could go in when the pubs closed, and have a Turkish Bath, and a massage, and sleep – and they'd bring you a cup of tea in the morning. And it cost, as I remember, something like a pound.

IM: [L] I would never have dreamt of asking you whether that had roots in real life!

AM: That was a starting point. I did pick up the book quite recently, and I still think bits of it are rather funny, but it was no great success, despite getting lavish praise from Robert Nye. [L]

IM: And indeed me! [*In* The Scotsman, 27/5/78]

AM: Yes, yes indeed. For years after, Robert kept saying on the reception of another novel, yes, this is all right, but I wish you'd write something else like *Change and Decay*! [L]

IM: I was very struck in reviewing it by the influence of – or the references to – Waugh in particular, but also Graham Greene. I think I described it as 'marinaded in Waugh'.

AM: Yes, and I think probably Eliot as well. It's a very literary book of low life. [L]

IM: And it was very appropriate therefore that as an academic I should have been reviewing it, because I recognised some lines that I don't think many people would have done. But you didn't really write anything else like that ever again.

AM: No. I did start one at one point, a sort of sequel to it I suppose, but it never got very far. I'd still quite like to try it, but I suppose one's now so far from the voice one had then that it might be rather difficult.

IM: So you didn't immediately go on in the same vein because something made you want to write about Scotland in *The Last Peacock*. [*1980*]

AM: Yes. I can't remember what made me, except that this was after all the late seventies, and I was living in Edinburgh when there was all the excitement about the '79 Devolution referendum, and quite a lot of political excitement in the two or three years before that. One was mixing with people from newspapers, and I was writing for newspapers myself; but especially meeting people like Neal Ascherson and Tom Nairn and Colin Bell and so on, who were all engaged actively. That is probably enough to suggest why one wrote a book that was set in Scotland, but also I do remember that it actually just started one day. I was working for a research institute at the time as an editor.

IM: That was the Nevis Institute. [*A short-lived literary/political affair, with Board Members like Ritchie-Calder, George Bruce and James S Grant*]

AM: That was Nevis Institute: it never got very far, not even to the foothills. [L] I remember one day when there wasn't much to do in the office, I started writing about this old woman lying in a bed, and a girl looking out of the window at rain coming down on rhododendrons, and the old woman's obviously dying. That was the starting-point of the novel; it just went on from there. When I started writing it as I remember I didn't know who the girl was, who the old woman was.

IM: But the family and the scene must have meant quite a lot, because in a later novel you went back to the same group of people, except taking the girl out, which confused me at first when I read it. [*These Enchanted Woods 1993*]. I've been here before, but where's Belinda?

AM: Yes. Well, she's in Rome. [L]

IM: But she was so much a central kind of voice.

AM: She was, and the reason for going back to it – well, one of the reasons for going back to it – apart from the fact that things had moved on in Scotland as well, was that I thought that in *The Last Peacock* I had been rather unfair to the other sister, Fiona, by seeing her entirely from the outside, from a hostile point of view and that it would be interesting to turn it round and show her as she saw herself. For some years I had it in mind that some day I would do that. I think the parts of *These Enchanted Woods* that deal with Fiona and her former-and-   would-be lover are actually very good. I think there are other things in the book which spoil it. The American novelist that I bring in was a very slack bit of imagination in retrospect – the sort of sub-Compton-Mackenzie-Highland-farces -type characterisation. I think that's a great pity, because I think her introduction spoils what might have been one of my best books.

IM: It is very definitely a kind of curate's-eggy book. Another thing; I was disappointed for example that less was made of Colin than I had been hoping for; because he had become very interesting at the end of *The Last Peacock*, but he kind of melts away, fades out.

AM: Yes. He simply becomes a comic character, yes. I think that's fair comment. I think there are amusing scenes with him in *These Enchanted Woods*, but again with this delightfully sexy dumb blonde who's not quite so dumb he's given a too-easy get out, as it were. The best bits in the book are those dealing with Fiona and Tony Lubbock, her would-be lover, and her husband, and there are some scenes that I like. The scenes in the imaginary gentlemen's club in Perth, I think, are rather good, but it is as you say, a mess, a curate's egg of a book.

IM: I don't entirely agree, because I found it very enjoyable when I went back and reread it recently, but it just doesn't fire on so many cylinders as some of the others.

AM: I think you could make a rather good novella out of it, by taking out quite a lot and republishing it like that, simply concentrating on the Fiona/Tony Lubbock/Gavin situation.

IM: Might you go back to the place or the people some time?

AM: I have actually written a novel which hasn't yet found a publisher, which has Belinda in it, but it's set in Rome, and it's about alcoholism and not drinking and murder.

IM: It sounds very tasty! [L]

AM: I think it's rather good, but Sceptre that it was sent to, decided they couldn't sell enough copies of it: they made nice noises, but said they thought they couldn't sell enough, so at the moment it's sitting in my agent's office while we think what we should try to do about it. And I'm afraid I accept they were right.

IM: You mean that it's not commercial?

AM: Yes. I think it's good, but I think that it would only give them what they would consider a reasonable return if it won some prize, and that's always a gamble. So I can't blame them for saying no.

IM: I can!

AM: Well, yes. [L] Shall we say I understand why they have said no.

IM: Right. If I can skip over *The Death of Men* [*1981*] for a minute, I wanted to ask about the way in which *One Night in Winter* [*1984*] connects both with the factual murder trial of the time, and with these *Last Peacock* characters. There is an overlap, isn't there?

AM: Yes. There's a very small overlap of character. Mansie Niven … He appears in *The Last Peacock* and *These Enchanted Woods*, and briefly I think in *One Night in Winter*, which I haven't read for years.

IM: Is he based on any particular M.P.?

AM: There is, shall we say, a certain resemblance to the late Sir Nicholas Fairbairn. [*1933-1995:lawyer: flamboyant and outspoken Conservative MP.*]

IM: How interesting! [L]

AM: But I think Mansie Niven is a more interesting character than Nicky Fairbairn was. [L] And I think he's also a nastier character. Mansie Niven is a shit, whereas Fairbairn I don't think was, in that way. Fairbairn was somebody of whom you might genuinely say, he was his own worst enemy, whereas Mansie Niven had many enemies, much worse than himself. [L]

IM: So: the Garvie trial?

AM: Well, I was living in Kincardineshire, at Drumtochty, at the time of the Garvie trial, it was just over the hill; and he did use to drink sometimes in some of the pubs. And of course there was enormous excitement there. [*High-living landowner Maxwell Garvie was found dead in August 1968. After an Aberdeen trial that thrilled Scotland, Garvie's widow Sheila and her lover Brian Tevendale were found guilty of murder in November that year.*] Quite obviously, there are close parallels between the real life trial and the other one, although certain characters, the wife and the lover, are very different. And there's the other girl, in *One Night in Winter*, who is very important in the novel, who has no parallel in the Garvie trial. I suppose Fraser Donnelly bears *some* resemblance to my idea of Garvie, but he's a more flamboyant and I think more dangerous character – perhaps a more melodramatic one. His rather crazy mixture of Scottish Nationalism and Californian counter-culture: I don't think Garvie ever articulated anything like that, though he may have lived it a little.

IM: So what do you think made you do it? I'm particularly interested in the Garvie trial – I don't mean in detail – but because it led Paul Harris to start publishing, because he had to write his own book and publish it himself. [*Student Harris, greatly interested in the trial, founded his own publishing company, Impulse Books, initially in order to publish his account.*] And it sent you off on to a genre that you haven't really revisited.

AM: It was one of the most dramatic trials, and it did also seem to indicate a shift in morality as well. It was the nearest thing Scotland – or the North East of Scotland – had to what is conventionally known as the sixties. Revolution of consciousness and so on. North East Scotland was still in most ways, and certainly in sexual morality, pretty strait-laced. Even for a girl to be pregnant before marriage was something that mothers were immensely ashamed of, and embarrassed about talking about, and so on, let alone the notion of having a child without being married! [L] – Things that are now absolutely commonplace. So this sexual license, which was the motif really of the Garvie trial, caught the attention and the imagination, in a way that other trials didn't.

IM: Did you have a problem at all about closeness to fact, about the law? Did your publishers read it very carefully?

AM: I don't think they realised! [L] This trial was up in Aberdeenshire, and they were in London, and the resemblances I think are not close enough. The only person who might consider himself libelled was Max Garvie, and he was dead! [L] The other overlap with these two other books is that the narrator is a member of the old, or fairly old, land-owning class in Scotland, who has lost his purpose – just as they have, for the most part, and in that he resembles the people in *The Last Peacock*, and by the time he writes the book he is looking back twenty years, and he's a rather disillusioned, mildly depressed antique dealer in London. And I think quite a successful character.

IM: I'm very interested in your narrators. Some extraordinarily successful, very often in the sort of situation you're just describing, looking back over a distance. In *A Question of Loyalties*, for example, he's really quite of an age by the time he starts investigating his father, isn't he? But this ability to look back, and the voice of somebody who is himself disappointed and empty.

AM: Yes. And one most people consider a failure. And he considers himself a failure too, of course. I think there must be something in myself [L] – I can't imagine really having a successful, vibrant narrator, although I suppose the nearest I come to it is Augustus. [L] One thing is that people who are outward-going and successful tend not to look back. When people actually cast back over their own lives, it tends to be because of things that have gone wrong, because they've realised that they haven't done what they thought they would do, and the hopes that they once had have dimmed, and they regard themselves as to some extent failures. I think successes, if they do look back - the autobiography of a successful man is much less interesting than the autobiography of a failure.

IM: Said the man sitting there, who's got a happy house, and a lovely family, and lots of dogs, and all the rest of it! [L]

AM: That's all very true, yes, but nevertheless –

IM: You and that narrator are a bit like Graham Greene and his: I don't mean that there's a similarity, but it's almost a natural voice for you to use to convey what you want to convey. Greene does the same sort of thing, only he's being Greene.

AM: Yes, I think so. The question comes up here, what is worth doing: this is something that all my narrators have to find an answer for, and probably don't find a very successful one, or a very convincing one. But in some ways it relates to this: Enoch Powell says it of political lives, that all political lives end in failure, unless they are happily cut off in midstream. And I think that most human lives end in failure. One of the things that's quite often struck me in recent years: when one's younger, and more romantic about literature and being a writer, I sometimes thought, if I could write one thing that was really good, that would justify everything. But then you come to realise that whether it's good or not, once you've written it, it no longer belongs to you, and it doesn't matter to you, in a sense.

IM: It does matter to you in other senses.

AM: Yes, it's something that you're pleased to have done, and if a book is reprinted, you're pleased to have it back in print, but it's not as important as what you're trying to do next, which in its own way will be a failure, because the book that you write is never as good as the book that you were going to write. You're back with Plato's theory of Forms. The ideal book is out there somewhere, particularly at one time just at the back of your head, and what's done, however well it is done, is less that it was going to be.

IM: And beside all these philosophical questions, you have been, I imagine, plagued all the time through your writing career by the question of, will things sell, and how much money will they make.

AM: Yes.

IM: You haven't been the kind of gentleman writer who has plenty dosh, and can just take time. . .

AM: No, that's perfectly true: I've quite often thought it would be very nice to write a novel, put it away for a couple of years, take it out and take a blue pencil to it, and cut. But since I'm nearly always late in delivery [L], and I need the money, I can't do that. But you nearly always find if you go back to a book bits that seem redundant, and sentences that don't ring right, and so on, and it would be nice to be able to have had that opportunity. I think it would actually make for better books. We talked about *These Enchanted Woods*: I think if I had been able to put it aside for a couple of years I'd have taken out the American novelist.

IM: Yes. I hadn't thought of her as being the devil in the business, but I can see it as soon as you've said it.

AM: Her being the reincarnation of Mary Queen of Scots: that's what I mean by sub-Compton-Mackenzie-Highland-farce: it's too stale. [L]

IM: I'm interested in the general question of how much making enough money affects what you choose to write, the subject you choose, or the way you choose it; because it has to be there. Or are you of the 'No man but a blockhead ever writes except for money' school?

AM: Sometimes, yes. [L] It all depends what you mean by blockhead, of course, and I think people generally write better when they need money. No doubt there are exceptions, but the dilettante writer who doesn't need money, or the writer who no longer needs money, often loses an edge. I don't know that it's made very much difference to me. One obvious difference: I would probably not have written six Roman novels if the money had not been a consideration. Though I've enjoyed writing them, and I think they're good. I wrote *Augustus*, and then a paperback publisher came along and said he'd like to commission two more:

so it just grew, and the other thing that I've been conscious of ever since *Augustus* was that the Roman novels sell more in the way of foreign rights than my other novels.

IM: That's interesting.

AM: Well, it makes sense, you know. The Roman Empire is something of interest to everybody, and so that has been a consideration in my writing. But on the other hand, because I enjoyed writing them, and because in a sense they are easier to write, I probably would have gone on. The only reason they are easier to write is that you at least have the outline of your plot. You don't have to think up a plot. You've got to think up incidents, of course.

IM: And most importantly, you've got to decide who's going to be the narrator, and at how many points in their life: to have two books, or whatever, so that you can take two bites at it.

AM: Yes, absolutely. Technically they've been very interesting to write. But it is a help not having to think up a plot, and to know for instance that you've got to get Caesar to the Theatre of Pompey on the Ides of March, 44 BC.

IM: Shamelessly taking advantage of Mr Shakespeare as you go! [L]

AM: Yes, although it might also be the case that Shakespeare had read an earlier version of the narrative of Decius Brutus. [L] [*Massie chooses Decius Brutus as his narrator.*]

IM: Yes, but... When Brutus and Antony talk over Caesar's corpse, they don't half use strangely reminiscent words, reminiscent of Shakespeare.

AM: [L] Well yes, but the point I am making is that Shakespeare, who as we know, got a lot of his Roman stuff from North's version of Plutarch's *Lives*, may well have come across an earlier version of this manuscript, and stolen from it! This is one of the private games one can play with these novels, which you hope some readers will spot. The best example, and also the best game, is the narrator of *Nero's Heirs*, who is this imagined Roman noble living in exile on the Black Sea, and who is asked by his friend Tacitus to supply him with his own memories of the last year of Nero and the first years of the Flavian emperors, as material for the history Tacitus is writing. Tacitus is half a generation younger. So he does this, but some of the book is sent to Tacitus and some is not, but one of the pleasures was that this allowed me to steal Tacitus' best lines, give them to my narrator, and allow my reader, I hope, to suppose that Tacitus stole them from my narrator. [L] A silly joke, but fun.

IM: Absolutely. I can see that you maybe got a bit trapped with the Roman novels, but I'm not sorry. Why didn't you do Claudius, too?

AM: Two points – no, three points about Claudius. The first is that Graves has done it.

IM: That isn't a good argument!

AM: Well. The second is that I don't find him interesting. And the third reason is that he does actually appear in *Caligula*, and just in *Tiberius*, I think, and that's enough of him. [L] I think the fact that Graves has done him is quite a good reason; one could set out to do him in a different way. And probably not with Claudius as a narrator.

IM: Yes; well I imagine you would.

AM: But then I didn't actually mean to do *Caligula*, because I thought: what does anyone know about Caligula? He was mad, and he made his horse a consul: how do you make a novel out of that? [L] I think it was a German publisher who said they would take *Nero's Heirs* if I did *Caligula* as well.

AM: So I then had to go back to Sceptre and say well, I think I'd like to do *Caligula* after all: what about it? So I did it: whereupon the German publisher decided they didn't want either of them [L], having already paid the advance, of course, which I didn't have to pay back because they drew out of the contract. *Caligula* still hasn't found a German publisher. [L]

IM: This comes out of the Roman novels, but applies more widely.

In general terms, one of the things, I can't think of a female narrator.

AM: No. There isn't one anywhere. And there are not many conversations in the novels between two women without a man being there. There are one or two in *These Enchanted Woods*, and maybe in *The Last Peacock* as well actually, and one or two in this novel which is sitting in my agent's office. I don't think I could convincingly get a woman's voice to be the narrator, to carry a novel. As for conversation between two women, it's quite difficult to know what they talk about when they're alone. It's often been remarked that Jane Austen has no conversations between two male characters when there are no women about.

IM: Except when Anne overhears. . . [*A tacit reference to the denouement of Persuasion*]

AM: Yes, which is the exception that proves it.

IM: So it's a very traditional sort of ruling, that you write best about what you know best and are closest to, and that's men.

We're not talking, really, because there's not enough time or tape, about all the books that weren't fiction that you were writing up till about 1989. There were quite a lot!

AM: There were quite a few.

IM: Was it usually because somebody suggested it to you?

AM: Yes, usually because someone got in touch with my agent and said, would Allan write a book about such-and-such? And I'm afraid I said, how much? And if the answer was satisfactory, said yes. And actually the only one I think which is really of my own choosing was *Byron's Travels*. [*1988*] It's the only one which I would ever like to see back in print.

IM: I don't want to seem repetitious, but what about *The Caesars*? [*1983*]

AM: *The Caesars*, yes. It's been in and out of paperback once or twice. Yes, I forgot it. I did want to write it, and in fact, what happened with it was, at that time I had no agent, and I put it up to Bodley Head, who had published a couple of novels, and they said no. Then Giles Gordon called to see me one day in Edinburgh, and I mentioned this to him, and Giles said, oh, I could sell that for you, sell it in a week! I think it took him ten days. [L] So Giles became my agent.

IM: So that was in about '81 or '82? And until his death he was your agent.

AM: Yes, he was, and a very good one. I miss him a lot. [*Giles Gordon died, aged 63, in 2003*]

IM: Both the man and the agent. Pretty irreplaceable. But you have another agent now?

AM: Yes, well, I'm still with Curtis Brown. Handled by John Sadler now, and that's fine.

IM: I also felt up to a point – and this is very, very unacademic, that you were interested in *Ill Met By Gaslight*, interested in the murders and the evil of it. [*1980*]

AM: Yes I was, and I forgot it too. Yes, that was my idea.

IM: Was it? Ah!

AM: Yes. It's five Edinburgh murders, and two or three of them I think are actually genuinely interesting. One or two – I think it was written in a rather too what? A style that's at once a bit sort of ex cathedra and a bit sententious. Which is something that writing about murder quite often prompts people to be. I've only just glanced at it occasionally over the years; I don't know whether it's any good or not, but I've taken to quoting [L] what I think is a very true remark of Bron Waugh's. Bron said that there were only two possible reactions to reading something that you'd written a long time ago: the first was, God, this is awful tripe; how could I have perpetrated this? How shaming. And the second was, this is absolutely marvellous; I can never do anything as good as this again. [L] And I think he's right! [L]

IM: I did wonder whether having written *Ill Met By Gaslight* might have 'brought on' *One Night in Winter*, if you see what I mean.

AM: Yes. I think it's quite likely, yes. One's been thinking about murder, but it's difficult to remember exactly.

IM: We'll leave that to some future PhD student, to decide whether the murders in *Ill Met* connect better with Aldo Moro or with Maxwell Garvie! But having marvellously managed to get back to *The Death of Men* [1981], can I ask you about that? It was a book that very much impressed both of us at the time.

AM: Well because of this new edition I did read it again recently, and in fact Joe Farrell had arranged last month that we gave a talk or conversation about it at the Italian Institute in Edinburgh. [*Canongate Classics, 2004, Introduced by Joseph Farrell*] It was obviously the result first of all of living in Rome. It's a political novel, but it's also a novel about my ideas of Italy, and the city of Rome, and the Italian family, and politics. And reading it again now, it also seems to be a fairly timely novel, or a novel that is relevant again now because it is also about terrorism, and what you would do when somebody is abducted, kidnapped and held prisoner.

IM: And what makes the Tomasos of this world. [*The main terrorist.*]

AM: And what makes the Tomasos, yes. One remark which hadn't occurred to me as being [L] especially effective, was drawn to my attention last year by my son Alex. He'd read it some years ago, and thinks it one of my two best books, but he picked a copy in a second hand book shop in Washington. It was published in America – it's one of my few books that have been published in America – somewhat strange, as reading it again I thought it was a very anti-American book. He picked on one passage when the narrator says, terrorism has changed; terrorists used to have an achievable purpose, like a free Poland, or a united Italy: Now they don't: they want something which is vague, like a just society. You can't negotiate with people who want that sort of thing, because you've got nothing to offer. [*See pp 188-9.*] I think that's probably true.

IM: I wonder why your books haven't been published in America. Not perhaps the Scottish ones, because if London doesn't notice Scotland, it's quite possible America doesn't.

AM: Well, one or two of the Roman ones have been, and *The Sins of the Father* was, but they were all published by a very small press in New York, and *crept* out [L]. America's got an awful lot of novelists.

IM: How important are things like winning prizes?

AM: I think quite obviously winning one or two particular prizes does give or may give a novelist much wider public notice, and will achieve a lot of sales for that novel. Whether that's carried on subsequently is much more doubtful.

IM: Did you find it was? You got the Saltire Prize for *A Question of Loyalties*. [*1989*]

AM: I'm sorry to say, I don't think the Saltire Prize makes much impression. I think the only British prize that does is the Booker. The Whitbread, perhaps, to some extent, but I still think the Booker gets far more attention. Because there is only one Booker, while the Whitbread I think are giving five prizes at the same time, the Whitbread interest is clearly divided. But there again, I think it's only that particular novel will sell, but if people don't enjoy it, they're not necessarily going to buy later novels. I think prizes are like reviews, you know –

IM: [L] That's just what I was going to ask about! How important is networking?

AM: Networking?

IM: I mean among other writers who are also reviewers?

AM: I don't know, because I don't think I do any networking. [L]

IM: I don't mean anything bad, but I'm sure you're one of the people who's always reviewed, aren't you?

AM: Yes. I'm lucky enough in that way. But whether that's because I review myself, I don't know: I don't think so. To what extent do reviews sell books? Since one sees that the bestseller lists are always full of books which are not reviewed... I've quite often quoted Rupert Hart-Davis who was asked if a good review would sell a book, and he said, no, but a concatenation of them may. [L] It must help: if you're not reviewed, nobody probably even knows the book is out, which is a problem. If you are reviewed, at least some people have a chance of knowing, and some will buy it on the strength of the review. But the best way is still word of mouth, people telling their friends.

IM: And radio – important?

AM: Well, it's terribly hard to judge these things. Again, I think, if you are on the radio often, a great many times with the same book, then you must do something for sales because it lodges in the consciousness. One or two things, even if they are at much greater depth, probably don't make much difference to sales. People listen to radio because they like listening to radio. People read reviews in newspapers because they like reading book reviews. I don't think many people read book reviews to see what they're going to buy. Some do, I dare say, but I'm sure for fifty people who read a book review, two or three are doing it thinking of what they should buy. I think at one time people probably did it with a view to what they would take from the library.

IM: Yes: that has to have made a great difference.

AM: But of course library sales are now way down, and the kind of libraries that bought huge numbers of books were popular circulating libraries: they no longer exist. Boots must have taken say a thousand, fifteen hundred copies of any novel from a reputable publisher. Because people were paying a subscription they didn't want to wait for a book, so for the same library you might have to buy six or seven copies - changed days! On the other hand, in those days, only a small minority of books went into paperback. There was virtually no what they call vertical publishing, with the same house selling hard back and paperback in print: you were relying on Penguin or Pan to buy it. They were really the only paperback publishers in Britain at that time.

IM: Yes, hopeless. It gives an enormous power to Penguin, of course.

AM: It did.

IM: Do you worry about your publishers, and how big they are, and how conglomerated they are, and things like that?

AM: I've had several publishers, which is not necessarily a good thing, although it always seems a good thing at the time. And for instance Sceptre, who are part of a conglomerate, are nevertheless run very much independently, because Carol Welsh, who's run it for years, has a good deal of autonomy, and so I've never felt there that it really was part of a conglomerate. But I've had one or two books published by imprints of Random House, and have been fairly disappointed by the way they were published. In one case it was because the editor who had commissioned the book had disappeared, by the time it went in: I wasn't even late with that one! [L] I think ideally one would like to be back in the kind of publishing there used to be, where you stayed with one publisher all your life, and he eventually brought out a collected edition, but that doesn't happen now, of course. Even far more successful novelists than myself have never been to a collected edition.

IM: I think Greene was probably about the last, and that was done in bits, rather than as a whole. But I can't see that happening any more.

Even in your very first novel, we talked about the importance of conversation. Have you thought ever of writing drama, or film, or television?

AM: Well, I have done a couple of plays. One was a one man play about Scott, which was commissioned for the Borders Festival, and I did a comedy for Pitlochry, nine or ten years ago, which was rather an old fashioned, well-made play, and which I loved doing. [*First-Class Passengers*, 1995] And I realised that for a writer to hear your own lines being spoken well, by actors, and hearing an audience respond to them, gives a satisfaction that you don't normally get in other ways. I think if somebody else had wanted to take on that play afterwards, I might have written more plays by now. But I don't think I really understand the modern theatre. [L]

IM: What about the idea of televising or filming some of your novels?

AM: Nobody has ever come to me.

IM: That's interesting.

AM: It's depressing! [L]

IM: It's something to look forward to. Imagine a television series of the Roman ones.

AM: Yes. Some of them would be very difficult to film, or even televise, because of the time-shifts – very difficult to do on television, because you're tending to do things in episodes. And most of the books I'd count as my best books do actually have time-shifts in them.

IM: Just in brackets there, can you tell me what your best novels are? Today.

AM: Today. I think the ones that I think most highly of are the three of the mid-European trilogy, *A Question of Loyalties*, *The Sins of the Father*, though it's a rotten title, and *Shadows of Empire*; *The Death of Men*; and I have a high regard for *The Ragged Lion*. I wouldn't like to disown any of the Roman ones, but...

IM: No. That's interesting, and worth having a think about. I've often wondered about the title, *The Sins of the Father*. [*Quoted from* The Book of Common Prayer's *version of the Second Commandment:...I the Lord thy God am a jealous God, visiting the sins of the fathers unto the third or fourth generation of them that hate me...*]

AM: Ah yes.

IM: And why is it just singular, *The Sins of the Father*?

AM: [L] Well, the title of the novel should have been "Eichmann's Children", because at one point in the novel a character says, we are all Eichmann's children, because we live in the shadow, of the consequences of the Holocaust. I was very keen that that should be the title, and the half-witted marketing people in Random House assured the editor that nobody would ever buy a novel with the title "Eichmann's Children". I can't remember why we accepted *The*

Sins of the Father, but I agree with my son Alex who said, that's a rotten title, Dad, it's a Jeffrey Archer title! [L]

IM: There's that, but there's also the strange way in which everybody knows the phrase, "sins of the fathers", even if they don't know where it comes from, I don't see why it should be cut off down to one side, given all the ambiguities of the Jewish fathers: did somebody do it to you?

AM: No, I can't remember. I think I may have said I wanted it in the singular, simply because I'm sure there are other novels with it in the plural. [L]

IM: It's fascinating how the Eichmann thing has drawn novelists, from Muriel Spark to Robert Shaw, for instance. Do you know *The Man in the Glass Booth*?
[*Robert Shaw, film actor and novelist, published his novel in 1969*]

AM: Yes, yes.

IM: I think it's very fine. There never is going to be an end to writing about the Holocaust, the trials.

AM: No, I wouldn't have thought so.

IM: Have you got to the end of your writing about it?

AM: For the moment, certainly. In that I don't have an idea for another novel dealing primarily with that theme.

IM: How far ahead do you tend to see or plan?

AM: One likes to know what one would like to do next, and beyond that . . . Subjects occur to you, and they sometimes come suddenly. You may have a notion, I might write a novel with that sort of setting, that sort of theme, but until you actually have a character, or a moment, or a voice, or a sentence, or an image... Something has to happen to crystallise it, and it may be any of these things.

IM: How soon does it have to be found? You've just finished, met a contract, so is the next contract lined up?

AM: Well, I've been doing this Dark Ages trilogy, and I've the third one to write, the Charlemagne one. But I've also started a Scottish novel which is meant to be a sort of episodic thing, covering about a hundred years – bit more than a hundred years actually. It's set in the North East, with bits abroad.

IM: *The Hanging Tree* is out on the edge somewhere. [*1990*]

AM: Yes. I can't remember how that even came about. It is, it came about partly from going to live in the Borders, certainly, and reading again the Border Ballads and reading Border legends. I think a publisher asked if I'd like to do a medieval Scottish one, but I'm not even sure about that, and it's unlike anything else I've written. I think bits of it work very well, and bits of it probably rather badly. But I do keep meeting people who have read it and enjoyed it.

IM: Might you write more about the Borders?

AM: I have in mind at some point a sort of sequel to *The Hanging Tree*, but it would actually probably move out of the Borders, though it would deal with members of that family, the next couple of generations down. I would quite like at some point to do a novel set in the French wars of religion; you've got the same divisions, you know, and probably one would use a couple of Scots as the main characters, probably cousins, or something of that sort. That could be a sort of sequel to *The Hanging Tree*.

Day Two

IM: Having listened overnight to the first tape, I want to start by asking some biggish or general questions, because I don't want the whole thing to turn into a step-by-step process just through all the novels, although no doubt we will do a bit of that. The first big question comes out of what we were just saying off-tape, which is that Allan doesn't use a computer, or email, or anything like that. How do you write?

AM: I write on a typewriter.

IM: A typewriter? That's new-fangled!

AM: Well, it is an electronic typewriter, [L] which is a step up from a manual: I don't think you can get manuals now. I keep wondering how much longer I'm going to be able to get electronic ones. No, I'm not a very good typist – I'm not as bad as Iain Crichton Smith was, but I remember Giles suggesting that now that Iain Crichton Smith was dead, I was probably the worst typist in the world. [L]

IM: How about when you're writing: how private is it?

AM: Completely.

IM: Alison doesn't see it what you're doing? You don't talk to her about it?

AM: Absolutely, no.

IM: There are protective walls around you, and she protects you from everybody else?

AM: Yes, yes. The exigencies of publishing, whereby you want to have a contract usually for a book before you've written it – obviously you've had to give some indication of what it's going to be in an outline - but apart from that, no, and I never consult anyone, and haven't for a very long time, about novels in progress. Obviously once the novel is finished your publisher or editor may say, such-and-such needs to be changed. It doesn't often happen, whether that's because they think it's just right, or [L] because they don't have that much interest in it, I'm never sure!

IM: I don't think people have the time to take the vocation of real editing the way they used to do.

AM: Yes, I think that's true. On the other hand, it is also the case of course that an awful lot of authors, novelists, were never edited much, because the assumption was, which on the whole novelists themselves share, that the novelist knows best. It's often not the American assumption, of course, but it is or was the assumption here.

IM: Yes, but it's always handy, I think, to have someone to point out that you've repeated this, or, you know.

AM: Yes. One or two people who've handled my books have made useful suggestions in the past: Euan Cameron certainly did when he was at the Bodley Head.

IM: So it's a very private activity. Do you find that you write more or less easily as time goes on?

AM: I'm not sure that I can answer that [L].

IM: Oh good, go on. Just talk about it.

AM: It certainly doesn't get easier. What I think also is, the more you've done, the more you start wondering whether you're actually doing anything new. Graham Greene has the thing that the novelist becomes the prisoner of his method, and I do feel that sometimes, that you get into a way in which you can write novels, and that is in a sense restrictive. So it doesn't become easier, and it doesn't become easier to think of subjects, because you've used them up. [L] And again, Waugh has the remark that novelists probably only have half a dozen novels in them, and the rest is professional trickery. This is one reason why I've always thought it was not necessarily a good idea for people to have a success when they were young, because before you become a published novelist you store up material unconsciously, and you draw on that for your own writing life. Because once you have actually become a professional writer, a full time writer, you don't collect as much material unconsciously. Obviously some comes, but you spend most of your time not collecting material at all, but using it. And inevitably you do use up a lot of your material, and then you sometimes find the case of people who are having to hunt for material for novels. One very good example is James Kennaway. I remember when I read *The Kennaway Papers* which his wife Susan published, you see this man actually struggling to make his life into material for the novel he wanted to write. And it's partly because, if Kennaway hadn't written anything up to that point, he would have had a much deeper well to draw on, but he had already exhausted his well; and you see the same with Scott Fitzgerald.

IM: But you don't very obviously use your life at all. I mean I know for a fact that you've got grown up and by implication reasonably well adjusted young, but you don't deal with children much in the books at all.

AM: Not at all. Or practically not at all. I've never thought of that, but it's true. There are one or two children – there are some children in the Roman novels.

IM: Because they have to be there, and they have to die! [L]

AM: Yes. Some of them grow up: Caligula starts as a child.

IM: True, true!

AM: There are one or two things about children – not small children but adolescent ones - in the three modern European novels. But relations of parents and small children, no, there's nothing of that.

IM: Is that deliberate?

AM: Never thought of doing it.

IM: Did your children go to boarding school?

AM: Yes.

IM: Maybe that's got something to with it, that you didn't have –

AM: Well, they didn't go off to boarding school until they were thirteen.

IM: But all the same, it meant you didn't have so much day to day contact

AM: Yes, that's true.

IM: New subject: did you find that all that carry on about literary theory and the author being dead, and all that: did it make any impact on you?

AM: No.

IM: Well, you were talking yesterday about whether novels were old fashioned, so what are you looking for in a new fashioned one?

AM: I was talking about certain novels being old fashioned, yes, I don't mean so much that they were old fashioned when they were written, although they might have been considered that by some. The Linklater novels we were talking about off-tape obviously were not trying to do the same sort of things that Joyce and Virginia Woolf were trying to do, and they weren't even trying to do the sort of thing that Hemingway was doing; but the ones I was saying were old fashioned now sound dated. Obviously some dating, some sense of being dated, occurs even in books that survive, because they do belong to their period, and you can't entirely divorce them from that period, either the period in which they are set, or that in which they are written, or sometimes both, of course. But if they're good enough they transcend that thing of being dated, whereas other ones simply get stuck in the period they were written. I don't know if that's very clear.

IM: Are you conscious that what you might write in the next book, which is the Charlemagne one, might do things you've not done before?

AM: I think that it's unlikely, in the Charlemagne one. There are three Dark Age novels: there's a certain amount a novelist will gain there. They are also in a sense not novels, but romances.

IM: Yes: the word picaresque for the first one, particularly! [L]

AM: Which was also something we talked about yesterday with *The Hanging Tree*: I did actually subtitle that "A Romance". I was using the word as Stevenson did in his essay "A Gossip on Romance", when he talks about romance as the poetry of circumstance, and drama as the poetry of character. And in the Dark Ages novels circumstance is more important than character, whereas in twentieth-century novels character and circumstance, I think, I hope, are so interwoven. There is a sense, obviously in which when you're writing as romance it is less serious, because you can do almost anything you want. If you want to kill somebody and bring him back to life, you can even do that, as Scott does in *Ivanhoe* And *Ivanhoe* is of course the supreme romance. You don't take the characters seriously for a moment, but the glitter and the story and the mood can carry you along at enormous speed. And the other master of romance is Dumas. Coming up here in the train, I took with me to read one of the later D'Artagnan novels, *The Vicomte de Bragelonne*, and it's wonderful! I hadn't read it for years. About a year ago in *The Scotsman* I said it was a novel I meant to read over Christmas, but I never got round to it, [L] so this Christmas. . . And it's wonderful! Stuff about the kidnapping of General Monk, and taking him in a box over the North Sea: you don't take it completely seriously, but it is irresistible, and one can see why it was Stevenson's favourite novel too.

IM: So do you think it was interesting or significant that you started writing this trilogy of romances?

AM: I don't know if it was interesting or significant: it was one of these enterprises which was suggested by the publisher. Anthony Cheetham wanted a series on the Dark Ages, and I'm not at all sure that the kind of books that are eventually emerging are the kind that he wanted, [L] but they dangled a large cheque in front of me, and it's taken me much longer than I thought, because I started writing the first one, and I wrote about thirty thousand words, and I thought, this is terrible, and I set it aside for two or three years, rather hoped the publishers would forget about it [L]. But then when I got going I thoroughly enjoyed writing it, and I thoroughly enjoyed writing the Arthur one, and I expect to enjoy writing *Charlemagne*. I've started it, so I am enjoying it, yes.

IM: How intimidated did you feel when you did *Arthur*?

AM: Because so many other people have done Arthur? Yes. Intimidated? Probably not quite the right word. Conscious of what others have done. The device I was employing of having the story told by Michael Scott to the Emperor Frederick II I think made it a lot easier to tackle something that lots of other people had done, in the same way that *Charlemagne* is depending quite a lot on the *Chanson de Roland*. Because that's the aspect of Charlemagne that Michael Scott would know about, so it's depending on the *Chanson de Roland*, and Ariosto, and drawing on that, so it is, even more than *Arthur*, probably the most literary of the three. And like *Arthur*, of course, it's an anti-papalist one, because Frederick was on the Guelph and Ghibelline side [L]. He's on the Imperial side against the papacy in the twelfth century, and so it's obviously anti-papalist. Not in the Knoxian way, but. . .

IM: I'm not going to let you talk about it any more, because I am superstitious about books still unwritten.
But if somebody was trying to do a dissertation or answer a big exam question on your work, I can't imagine a question that

wouldn't have the word 'Empire' in it. Is it an important word for you?

AM: Well, clearly, since so much of the stuff is written in one way or another, yes. I'm not quite sure how [L]. I think of myself obviously as a child of the Empire in some sense, and I feel or think that for several generations of Scots, I won't say it's the thing that gave meaning to their lives, but the Empire was a justification of the Union, and in that way it is important too. Obviously the Roman Empire is something rather different.

IM: And really the 'message' of your Roman books is that Empire doesn't work, unless you've got a dictator-cum-tyrant, that even Augustus had to become that, and that you can't restore the Republic.

AM: You can't restore the Republic.

IM: And this is a very depressing message.

AM: Yes, it is. And obviously in the end the British Empire hasn't worked. I think there's an element of pessimism that runs through most of my work, in that I think that most human activities do end in failure. Even glorious lives end in failure, and even where there is a success it is bought at a cost of other failings. You mentioned Augustus. One of the fascinating things in dealing with Augustus was this question that he does seem to be arguably one of the comparatively few people improved by power. Ronald Syme in *The Roman Revolution* has this question: how did the icy and blood-stained Triumvir turn into the benign Father of his country? Which is a good thing to say to yourself, trying to do it in a novel. But of course in becoming, in restoring the Empire with this Republican façade, Augustus behaves absolutely ruthlessly to his own family. And he kills quite a lot in himself, as I have Maecenas, his friend from childhood, point out at one stage: the boy that I knew and loved, he more or less says, has vanished, has gone, has been swallowed up in Empire.

IM: This kind of difficulty between public and private is perennial as well.

AM: Yes it is. The private life is I think for all of us much more important than public life. It matters in a way that public events don't. I've always liked the story of Balzac turning away from some political discussion to say, now let's talk about something important: who should Eugenie Grandet marry? [L] And the question of who you marry is far more important than the question of who becomes Prime Minister. To all of us. But the condition of having – or the possibility of having – a decent private life depends on there being a decent public life. Because when the state breaks down or falls into the hands of a tyrant private life itself is immediately corrupted, destroyed, even. If you take Stalinist Russia, children were encouraged – as of course is happening in Britain at the moment – where children are encouraged to report on their parents.

IM: It's happening in Britain at the moment?

AM: Yes, it's happening in Britain at the moment .

IM: Go on.

AM: In a small way [L] Where the state tries to interfere too much in private life too. Private life becomes corrupted as the state itself is corrupted. So that's where the tension between public and private comes. And also of course in both of them, in the question that matters to almost all novelists who regard themselves as serious, it's a question of right and wrong behaviour, of what actually is the right thing to do in these particular circumstances.

IM: Right and wrong is a good way back to this other general point.
I think our generation very roughly was maybe the last to take very seriously the possibilities of religion, especially Christianity, in youth.

AM: Yes.

IM: Have you had or changed your world outlook over time?

AM: Yes. I think what you say about Christianity is absolutely true, and I sometimes think I would like to have religious faith, but it seems less and less possible the older one gets. I have friends who are church-goers, and who do take their Christian faiths seriously, and don't seem to have doubts about it, but the older I get, the less probable any of it seems to me.

IM: So there was a time when you were a believer, as it were?

AM: A sort of believer, anyway. As an adolescent I was never actually confirmed in any church, but I certainly thought very deeply about it, and I also have a respect for churches: I think churches are quite a good thing [L]. I'm not one of those who says, Christianity would be all right if it wasn't for the church. I would say that Christianity is probably all wrong, but the church has historically on the whole been quite a good thing. And I can also feel a nostalgia for the austerity of Scots Presbyterianism, you know, the Stevenson lines about where among the graves of the martyrs the whaups are crying, My heart remembers how. [*"Blows the wind on the moors to-day and now,/ Where about the graves of the martyrs the whaups are crying,/ My heart remembers how!" from 'To S R Crockett'.*] That makes the hair on the back of your head stand on end. I suppose that goes back to some race memory. I think actually that the extreme Covenanters that he was talking about were all wrong, [L] and I think Scott gets it about right in *Old Mortality*. We were talking about terrorism yesterday, but Scott's pages where he has Balfour justifying the murder of Archbishop Sharpe, they are absolutely early twenty-first century, how the Lord delivered them into his hands, and so on. Osama bin Laden would not disagree.

IM: That's the frightening bit. When we interviewed Naomi Mitchison, she ended up her interview by saying, and even if the Russians and the Americans all hugged each other and were happy, there would still be the Ayatollahs [L]. She was really afraid of what she called 'the religions of the Father God', which could make people fanatical.

AM: Yes, well, indeed they could, and when one talks about having a nostalgia for Scots Presbyterianism one has to remember that other side of it, and the minister of the Kirk who reported after Philliphaugh, when the Covenanters were massacring the Irish women who had been following Montrose's army: "The Lord's work goes merrily on." [L]

IM: Religion-wise, I think an awful lot of people in our generation, both of us included, have found it less and less satisfactory as a way of understanding life, although not necessarily chucking out ideas of good and evil, or right and wrong. I know we're not talking about your journalism here, but as regards politics, have you changed where you were, from when you started?

AM: I'm not sure: I swither about politics. I think I was more hopeful at one time, but I think on the whole politics are two steps forward and one back at best, and when it comes to the real crisis points at the moment, I think making the right decision is so very difficult, because it's very rarely a matter of black and white. And I do find it easy – this may be a character fault, but I think it is an asset as a novelist – [L] I do find it easy to understand why people join what history determines is the wrong side. I can see the attractions and the sense of it. Most obviously in *A Question of Loyalties*, Vichy turns out to have been the wrong side. But it didn't necessarily seem that in 1940.

IM: No. And Lucien's motives don't seem . . . bad.

AM: No, no. And I can see in the same way why people became devoted members of the Communist Party, and I can even see why people were attracted to Fascism. Even people who later turned against it were attracted to it. One of the more honest things in

Compton Mackenzie's novels is in the huge *Four Winds of Love* sequence of novels, I think it's in the *South Wind* – or is it the beginning of *The West Wind*, he has a lot of words about a young Fascist with whom the hero's daughter falls in love in the very early years, 1921 or 22, and he does show why at that moment Italian Fascism seemed attractive. And I think that was very brave of him, considering he was writing this in the 1940s. But if you are a novelist trying to write about public events or politics, you have to give both sides the best arguments you can muster for them.

IM: Yes, absolutely. I think the novelist has to have a range of sympathy that makes it fairly impossible for him to be a zealot in a particular line.

IM: Yes, absolutely. I think the novelist has to have a range of sympathy that makes it fairly impossible for him to be a zealot in a particular line.

AM: Yes. Even the characters that you regard as the villains of your novels have to be given some redeeming qualities.

IM: Yes, or you can't believe in them. I was interested that so far after your Roman novels there's a big gap, and then there's the Dark Ages, and we don't go to people like Marcus Aurelius, do we?

AM: No. Marcus Aurelius might make a subject for a novel. You asked about Claudius, and I said no, Graves has done him, and some other people who are interesting are also blocked off in the same way, I think. Julian, which Gore Vidal did, and Constantine, who is the subject of a very good novel by Colin Thubron, called *Emperor*; and Hadrian, most obviously of course, because one wouldn't want to try to compete with Yourcenar. [*French novelist Marguerite Yourcenar published her* Memoires d'Hadrian *in 1951*] Marcus Aurelius might be a possibility, but I feel quite comfortable, if that's the right word, in the Rome of the late Republic and the first century of Empire; less so the further away one gets from that. The first of the Dark Ages books, there was no pretence of accuracy about the Roman element in it.

IM: Yes; it's a different kind of writing altogether.

I was noting things last night that I wanted to ask about. Obviously this comes into the Roman novels, but very much also into the modern world ones, a lot of homosexuality, compared with other writers, a great deal.

AM: Some other writers, yes [L].

IM: Clearly in the Roman world one has to accept how it was, and try to understand it, which you do, but is it because you have found so much bisexuality and homosexuality in modern life, that . . ?

AM: I think so, and certainly in the circles that I am writing about. If you take the Vichy novel, the number of French writers of the first half of the twentieth century who were homosexual or pederast is quite remarkable! [L]

IM: In *Shadows of Empire*, for example – you almost fall over it; if it's not a female reporter, it's an old friend from school, or. . .

AM: No: in *Shadows of Empire* there is certainly the female reporter, yes, the American lesbian, who I think is rather a good character. One brother is, the one who's in the Foreign Office, who is not promiscuous.

IM: No: in fact he more or less decides to be chaste in order to get on.

AM: And one of his school friends is, an Etonian of that twenties, Brian Howard generation. And the narrator himself has a platonic thing at school, then has this affair with a French boy at the end of the war. He also says, in that, that he doesn't want to – next time he comes back to Paris, the boy comes to him and says he's got this girl, and the narrator says of him he doesn't want him to be trapped in homosexuality.

IM: And is that something that you think happens?

AM: I think it can happen, yes. And the narrator sees this affair himself as being something which is almost a return to his own adolescence, at a time when he is feeling that almost everything else in his life is fallen apart. I think he regards it in himself as being something which is evasive, almost. It's an escape, a temporary withdrawal. And there is also of course the Tory MP who marries his sister, in what will turn out to be a *mariage blanc*. But again, there were one or two Tory Cabinet Ministers of the time who were in such relationships. And obviously one of the people one had in mind not as a model, but as the same sort of thing, was Chips Channon, who married a Guinness, but was predominantly homosexual. [*Henry 'Chips' Channon, 1897-1958. Through his marriage to Honor Guinness in 1933, became Conservative MP and eventually Lord.*]

IM: There isn't, as far as I can remember, - having read all of them recently, it's diabolical – (L) a hint of serious disapproval?

AM: No.

IM: Any disapproval?

AM: No, I don't think so.

IM: I suppose, if the boy's young enough, there might be?

AM: Yes, it would depend on the age and the willingness. Obviously there would be disapproval of the seduction. But there would be disapproval of the seduction of a girl that age too.

IM: Yes: grooming is not good! (L)

AM: Yes. And actually the expression of that disapproval comes from Tiberius: there's this German boy whom he's attracted to, fighting in the arena. He saves his life, and he says he's not going to force himself on him, because the boy could not resist, and it would be unseemly. Which I think is a sort of reasonable attitude.

IM: Yes. It is: I have a soft spot for Tiberius! (L)

AM: He's my favourite character in the Roman novels, the one with whom I have most sympathy, certainly of the historical characters, the genuinely historical characters, as opposed to the invented ones.

IM : Part of the reason, though, that I was asking about homosexuality is that if one were still working inside the believing Christian mode, it would be a difficult and different matter, and end up to be a protest, so it's interesting that it doesn't.

AM: Yes. My attitude to it is more that of the ancient world (L).

IM: Yes, yes. And sort of pragmatic. What about patriotism?

AM: Ah. 'What sins are committed in thy name!' (L) Well, I think love of country is something that is natural to people. And equally of course it can be natural to people to come to hate their own country, which is a form of self-hatred, I suppose, because the idea of the country is an extension of the self. I think patriotism, fine. Patriotism and Nationalism I think are different things. The problem, of course, is to know what is the patriotic thing to do. In certain circumstances the answer may be clear, but in others it isn't. If you happened to be a Ukrainian this week, what is the patriotic thing to do?

IM: Vote? (L)

AM: Vote: but vote for which?

IM: One of the Victors. [*Both candidates for the Presidency had the first name Victor.*]

AM: [L] That's a sort of Talleyrand reply.

IM: I've never been accused of that before: thank you!

AM: Hearing the crowd in the street when the Revolution is going on, and Talleyrand holding up his hand and saying, listen, we are winning! And somebody saying but who are we? And Talleyrand saying, I will tell you in the morning. [L]

IM: Well, perhaps at this stage we could go back a bit to the books. I wanted to open up some of these things, because it's quite important to be thinking freely: if I'm going to ask you questions that twenty-five years from now somebody will wish I had, we have to do it both ways. But we were roughly started on the modern trilogy, *A Question of Loyalties*, *The Sins of the Father*, and *Shadows of Empire*.

AM: I suppose they're written over a period of about ten years: I think *A Question of Loyalties* was out in 89, and *Shadows* in 99, or 97. [97]

IM: I still think that *A Question of Loyalties* is one of the best things you've ever written, [L] besides being on the Saltire committee that gave you the prize. I thought it was extraordinarily inventive in its narrative form, as well as extraordinarily good at teasing out ambiguities and difficulties, and what you were saying a minute ago – it's easy when we look back, to see that one shouldn't have been a Fascist, or a Communist, but it wasn't easy then.

AM: No, it wasn't. I would agree with you about the structure: I like the structure. The structure makes it a much more complex novel than a straightforward narrative one would have been. In a sense of course, the structure is forced on me by the choice of the narrator, who is dealing with telling about many events quite a long time before the time of its telling. He's telling in the 1980s about things that happened in the 20s, the 30s, the 40s. I hadn't read the book again for ten years, I suppose, until a French edition at last came out, and one of the things that actually struck me then was just how much of the book is not set during the Second World War, or the years leading up to it, but is actually the narrator's own story. I'd forgotten just how much of it - the first hundred and twenty pages or something - are his story, taking us up to the time when he, who knew very little about his father, discovers that because of his father's wartime record, his own first really serious love affair with this absolutely delightful girl Freddie –

IM: She's one of your best!

AM: Yes, - is to be broken. And that is what turns him back in on himself in a sense. So one of the themes of that book, as of the next, is the consequences of what the fathers have done. Yes, I think the Normandy section in that book, dealing with the love affair between Etienne and Freddie, is the nicest thing I've ever written! [L] One is not usually supposed to use the word nice in connection with serious fiction.

IM: It's an idyll which works.

AM: It's an idyll which works until it's broken. And I think because you have that idyllic element in the book, even if the idyll is broken, the cruelties and deceptions and compromises and so on, the shabbiness of much of the war period is relieved by that. At least I think that's what the effect should be.

IM: Yes. It's also basically educational, because I fear that we don't as a readership know or, unless we are made to, care very much about Vichy France, for example.

AM: Well, yes. I don't greatly admire Nabokov as a novelist, because I think he's too tricksy for my taste, but in his lectures on literature, things he gave at American universities, he says at one point that the novelist is three things, he's a story-teller, he's a teacher, and he's an enchanter. And I think that's what the novelist should be, I don't say one consciously aims at it, but I think all these three elements are there in the novelist; and teaching, the teaching side of it, telling people things, may be moral truths, or it may simply be factual things, as about France in the Second World War.

IM: And demonstrating the moral complexity.

AM: Yes, indeed: that is part of the teaching side. And the enchantment: it's a matter of luck if you ever bring that off: you can do the story-telling and the teaching consciously, but the enchantment either comes or it doesn't; it's when Kipling's demon sits on the hand of your pen, or something like that.

IM: I think I want to go on to *The Sins of the Father*. Was it partly inspired by the Freddie/Etienne thing? The sort of Romeo/Juliet thing?

AM: Yes, that's there. *The Sins of the Father* is in one sense the odd one out of the trilogy, in that the idea was suggested to me. Richard Cohen, who was the editor at Hutchinson's at the time, who had published *A Question of Loyalties*, had the idea. He hadn't edited it: that was Euan Cameron, but he had the idea, and was looking for a novelist to write it [L] And his story, he said it came from a newspaper, was how Eichmann had been identified in Argentina because his son had fallen in love with a girl whose father had been in the camps, and who recognised Eichmann. Now I believe that Richard was wrong, and it was some other Nazi of whom this was true, but that doesn't matter. And he wanted a novel written from that, and I thought about it, and I realised yes, that's a way into this subject. So yes, the Romeo and Juliet aspect is based on what was suggested to me, but I think probably also yes, there is in a sense a continuation of Etienne and Freddie, if Freddie had said no, I'm not going to be guided by my father: I love you: I'm going to go my own way. Which is what the girl Becky in effect says. The novel starts in Argentina, then goes to Israel. A lot of people didn't like the third part of the novel, which is a sort of epilogue, which introduces a first person narrator. I felt that was necessary. It happens later, and it tells of what happened to Franz and Becky after, and I felt that was best done by another voice. He's a sort of cousin of Becky's. One leaves them in Israel, so determined that they're going to marry and live together, and if it stopped there, the reader might think there was a chance of a happy ever after. But I show how what happened to them made it impossible for them to be happy ever after. As a novel, it's almost entirely about consequences.

IM: Yes, absolutely. One of the consequences is that Becky develops a sort of sexual willingness, as it were.

AM: Yes.

IM: Do you regard that as something not to be blamed either, but just understood?

AM: Yes. Both their lives are broken in different ways by the same thing. Becky I suppose chooses to live for the moment, which turns out to be unsatisfying, as it usually is, I think, if you live just for the moment.

IM: As well as the young lovers, I'm interested in both the fathers. I think they're very interesting figures.

AM: I hope they are! [L] One of the things about the character who bears a resemblance to Eichmann, Franz's father, that one has to get over, is his ordinariness. The fact that somebody can do terrible things, his role in the Holocaust, and afterwards live the life of a conscientious engineer working on projects up in Argentina, building bridges.

IM: With no private life.

AM: With no private life, but retaining a sense of responsibility for his son, being to that extent a conscientious father. It's if this evil has been shut away in him, and there's a sense in which the trial and the waiting for execution are a release, so that he can now talk about it.

IM: He becomes a real character once he's in Jerusalem and things are happening. He's so mysterious before that.

AM: Yes: whereas the blind economist who is the Jewish economist, he is an example of somebody who's gone to Argentina to escape Israel, he has this line – why don't you go to Israel? Too many bloody Jews! [L] Partly he feels guilt, because he collaborated with the Nazi regime as long as he was able to, as some few very privileged Jews did, he was an economist working with Schacht in the Reichstag, so he has a certain guilt about that, but he is also the anti-Semitic Jew, sometimes called self-hating Jews. But when the moment comes when he recognises this Nazi, and he has the choice: do I get in touch with Mossad, the Israeli secret service, so they can snatch him, or do I put my daughter's happiness first? Do I say, it's a long time ago: Franz and Becky seem well suited and happy: they will live a comfortable bourgeois life in Argentina?

IM: He doesn't spend very long on that one.

AM: He doesn't spend very long on it, but put it this way: we don't know how long he spends on it.

IM: We more or less feel he's picking up the telephone as we leave the room! [L]

AM: Yes, but because we see him from outside, we don't go into his mind at that moment, as I remember, we see the results of his decision, rather than his actual deliberation, which may have cost him a sleepless night at least. And of course in doing this he also destroys his own marriage. Because his English wife is a very Home Counties schoolmaster's daughter, who I think is one of my more sympathetic characters actually, because she lives in the world of private lives rather than public lives. She finds it cruel and wicked that he should have put this abstract idea of justice ahead of his duty to Becky, the daughter.

IM: It's also putting revenge before love.

AM: Putting revenge before love, and revenge is a kind of wild justice.

IM: It's a very inescapable book. But I should move on, because there are two books more that are both very different, but they haven't come into chats about anything else. The first of them is *The Ragged Lion*, about Sir Walter Scott.

AM: Yes. And the other is?

IM: *King David.*

AM: Yes. *The Ragged Lion*: well, again I was asked to write a novel about Scott.

IM: There's a bit at the beginning of the book that explains that you wrote the play first.

AM: Yes, I wrote the play about Scott, and it was suggested when I was doing a two-book contract with Hutchinson. The first one I wanted to write was *These Enchanted Woods*, and then they said, would you like to do a novel about Scott? Just the sort of vague notion that publishers have. So I said yes, but how to do it. I didn't want to see Scott from outside, so I employed this device, which is at least characteristic of Sir Walter, the fake manuscript, and with a slightly tongue-in-cheek Sir Walterish introduction about how this manuscript came into my hands, and the manuscript is the sort of memoirs – detached memoirs – that Scott writes in the last six years of his life, in parallel with the Journal. I think it was just convincing enough, and I may say that one of the nicest things about the experts mentioned in the introduction was Eric Anderson's. He who had edited Scott's Journal, said that he was fooled by the introduction till half way through. [L] There is a good deal of invention in it, and there is a good deal which is simply pastiche of some of the things Scott himself wrote, and some things which are lifted pretty straight from the Journal, with the suggestion in an end-note that probably Lockhart had seen a copy of this narrative, and used parts of it in his biography. Spending some months as it were in engagement with Scott was a very enjoyable experience, and I also liked to take the opportunity to try and write some verse. I can't write poetry: because everything I write in verse is a sort of pastiche or imitation, but it was agreeable trying to do that. And some of it I think works quite nicely. It's a very personal book, but I think probably one of the two or three that I most enjoyed writing.

IM: I was very interested in his supernatural experiences. Did that come from anywhere, or Massie?

AM: It doesn't come directly: it comes indirectly from Scott himself. The thing about Scott is that he is a puzzle: the book is trying to elucidate that puzzle. He himself says at some point in the Journal that he is known as a sociable man, but that his happiest hours have been spent alone: 'on a braeside with a book and a bannock and my ain company'. He also has this very interesting observation: when a friend of his youth is involved in a scandal, a homosexual scandal. He is caught with a stable boy or a guardsman or something of the sort, and he has to flee the country. Noting this in his diary, Scott first of all says 'our passions are wild beasts', and I can't quote from memory but he says, fortunately we are able to lock them up in our own breast. He also then says, if at our social table we could see what passed in each other's breast, we would shun human society, and take refuge in dens and caverns. That is not the sort of Augustan, sociable Scott: it's the dark side of him.

IM: And you get the feeling, in his account of his marriage to Charlotte, for example, that that bit of him is so locked away, it as good as doesn't exist.

AM: Yes. But it comes out of course in the novels in places. And the way he uses the supernatural in the novels, which just stops short of asserting, this actually happened, and his fascination with it, which is of course partly simply the commercial thing, this is good stuff to put in, but it comes from something deep inside him too, I think. I think he was very much aware of a capacity for evil and self destruction, which is in him somewhere and which he suppresses, but it's suppression and not repression. Repression is when you don't admit something is there: suppression is when you know it is, and you say no.

IM: He's half way to being Dr Jekyll.

AM: Yes. The supernatural bits in the novel: he's never sure if he's imagining them.

IM: He can't leave them alone.

AM: He can't leave them alone, yes. It's like playing with images of cruelty in your mind, which some people can't leave alone, and yet they suppress them, they wouldn't act on them.

IM: Pre-figuring Dr Jekyll, and all that that's going to entail.

AM: Yes; it's the duality, the old Karl Miller's doubles, and of course the Justified Sinner.

IM: It's a very interesting business altogether.

AM: Yes. One of the things I wanted to do with Scott. People who don't read Scott, and who just dismiss him, as a sort of Tory reactionary, think of him as a dull man, because he is a reserved man.

IM: Look who's talking! [L]

AM: I wanted to suggest that he was a much more interesting person.

IM: Yes, absolutely. So what precipitated *King David*? [1995] Don't tell me somebody asked you to write it?

AM: No. No: I wanted to write *King David.* Two reasons. Or three, I suppose. First, it's a wonderful story. Second, I think David is the most fascinating character in the Bible, and I also find it fascinating that he is obviously the hero, to the writer of the Book of Samuel, and yet all his evil deeds are presented to us just like that! He is the beloved of God, the Chosen One of God, who is also an adulterer, a murderer – by proxy at least - and a ruthless king. It's almost a parallel to Augustus. And also he's a poet, of course, too, if we assume, and I think we're quite happy to assume, that the Psalms are written by David. So he is such an immensely complicated person, capable of magnificent behaviour and the meanest behaviour, and I just wanted to try and explore him. You might also say that another attraction is that Scots Presbyterianism is so absolutely steeped in the Old Testament, and until quite recently, until the middle half of the twentieth century, the New Testament was almost irrelevant to the Church of Scotland! [L]

IM: Is there any other part of the Old Testament that has the same kind of attraction? Because one go at the Roman Emperors and you're hooked: one go at the Bible and you might go there again.

AM: There are obviously other characters who might be interesting to deal with - Joseph is the most obvious, but that means competing with Thomas Mann! [L] And Moses, I suppose. One of the attractions about David and Joseph and Moses would be that you actually have a pretty full narrative life story in the Bible that you're working from, whereas if you took some of the later interesting moments in the Old Testament, Ahab and Jezebel and Elijah, for instance, there's actually quite a shortage of incident; you'd have to invent a great deal: which of course could be done, but it might take it further away from the Bible than one might want to go. In the case of David, you're actually able to keep quite close to the Bible, while also getting quite a long way away.

IM: Yes. One of the questions that the reader keeps pondering is, does he always really believe that he is the Chosen of God? Or is he just doing what he wants to do?

AM: He doesn't know, is the answer: *my* David doesn't know. He thinks he is; but he is aware that he may not be. Most of the time he thinks he is, because what has happened to him in his life justifies him in that belief, just as a dictator, who has risen to power by the favour of the crowd, a Hitler, say, or a Mussolini, can very easily come to believe that he is the incarnation of some will, beyond himself. Because everything that has happened to him justifies this. If you rise from sleeping in a Viennese doss-house to be Chancellor and dictator of Germany in twenty years...

IM: Somebody must be on your side.

AM: Yes. Even if you don't believe in a God, you incarnate the national will, or something. So David has that feeling too, I should think.

IM: I would love somebody to do an account of Paul.

AM: Paul, yes. All the fictional accounts of Paul are written from the side of admiration.

IM: That's not the one I was looking for! [L]

AM: No. Gore Vidal did a sort of jokey one in *News from Golgotha*. It's one of the I find rather tiresome things when he's playing about with modern technology as well, so things come up on computer screens. It's the same sort of method as *Myra Breckinridge*. I prefer Vidal in his more sober fictional mode.

IM: Like *Julian*?

AM: *Julian*, and the sequence about the American Republic, particularly the earlier ones. I think that's where he's at his best: *Lincoln*, and *1876* and *Burr*.

IM: I suppose it would be reasonable at this stage to ask you which modern novelists you most admire. Today!

AM: Living, or?

IM : I mean you're not committing yourself forever!

AM: [L] I see what you mean. Some of them are dead, of course, and some of them are obvious, like Waugh and Greene: and I do admire Vidal's American historical ones immensely. I think the best living Scottish novelist is Willie McIlvanney. One of the tests for a novelist of his colleagues and rivals is, would I have liked to have written that book? I would love to have written *The Kiln*. I couldn't, but I would have loved to have written it: I think it's a wonderful novel. I cannot understand why he is at the moment so often forgotten when people start talking, why he's out of fashion.

IM: It's a question of the number of years, the fashion; but I don't think he's so out of fashion south of the border. His sales are probably still pretty good, which is good [L].

AM: But when people are talking about the renaissance in Scottish writing –

IM: I'm sure that's a question of age: you've got to be under such-and-such.

AM: Yes, but Alasdair Gray is older.

IM: Yes, but look how old Robin Jenkins is! And people want him to lie down properly and get buried [L]. [*Sadly, Jenkins died in 2005.*] Alasdair Gray hasn't really produced anything very exciting for a while.

AM: No, he hasn't. He just seems to – perhaps he has more disciples. Willie doesn't. Willie's is a more solitary path, perhaps.

IM: It's a long time since *Docherty*.

AM: But it's not that long since *The Kiln* – seven or eight years.

And those are I suppose his two best, but certainly *The Kiln* I would like to have written.

IM: Any by women?

AM: Women? Well, Muriel, [*Spark*] yes. Would I have liked? – yes I would like to have written some of her novels, but I couldn't have, again. There's a certain up-and-downness there, I think, but there's always something there. I still like some of the early ones best, I'm more likely to re-read *Memento Mori* than some of the later ones.

IM: *Memento Mori* and *Girls of Slender Means* have totally survived their time: I've been teaching them both recently, and they go down a bomb.

AM: What about *The Bachelors*?

IM: I haven't done that for ages, as it happens.

AM: Then there are these very strange ones which she was writing at the turn of the sixties and seventies, like *The Hothouse By the East River*, which I think is wonderful, but I'm never quite sure what to make of it [L], which I'm sure would delight her!

IM: I would put in a bid, if we were talking Best Living Scottish Novelist, for Janice Galloway.

AM: I haven't read enough of her.

IM: The question I should have asked is, have you read her and disliked her, or have you not read enough of her?

AM: The latter

IM: What about A L Kennedy?

AM: Can't read.

IM: Jessie Kesson?

AM: Yes, she's OK, yes, yes.

IM: I've just been teaching – almost the last thing I did, was a course on Scottish Women Novelists since the War. You wouldn't think there were enough, but. . .
And I included lots of people like Elspeth Barker: I think her *O Caledonia* is one of the. ..

AM: My sister-in-law, Elspeth.

IM: Is she? [L]

AM: Yes, she's Alison's elder sister.

IM: Well, I think she's wonderful: why doesn't she write another one?

AM: The new novel has been going to be finished in about six weeks for the last ten years at least!

IM: She mustn't do an Archie Hind!

AM: Yes, I know what you mean, yes.

IM: I do think *O Caledonia* is wonderful – and I said that totally unaware that you're related. [L] That's blown my mind.

Books by Allan Massie mentioned in the interviews:

Fiction

Change and Decay in All Around I See, 1978
The Last Peacock, 1980
The Death of Men, 1981
One Night in Winter, 1984
Augustus, 1986
A Question of Loyalties, 1989
Tiberius, 1990
The Hanging Tree, 1990
The Sins of the Father, 1991
Caesar, 1993
These Enchanted Woods, 1993
The Ragged Lion, 1994
King David, 1995
Shadows of Empire, 1997
Antony, 1997
Nero's Heirs, 1999
The Evening of the World, 2001
Arthur the King, 2003
Caligula, 2003

Non Fiction

Muriel Spark, 1979
Ill Met By Gaslight: Five Edinburgh Murders, 1980
The Caesars, 1983
Byron's Travels, 1988

James Robertson

I was aware of James Robertson's stories in Scots, The Ragged Man's Complaint, *and his first novel* The Fanatic, *but I found myself paying really serious attention to his work when the novel* Joseph Knight *was nominated for the Saltire Book of the Year, and I found myself in agreement with the whole panel that we had a winner here. When he came to read at Aberdeen's Word Festival, I lay in wait for him, and he agreed to be interviewed, though we had endless difficulties in arranging the dates.*

IM: This is the 25th of October 2005, and we are recording at Isobel Murray and Bob Tait's house in Aberdeen, where James Robertson has very kindly come up to save us the trouble of coming down! He lives not so far from Coupar Angus. Could you start, James, by telling me a bit about your youth, your background, your education.

JR: Okay. Well, I was born in Sevenoaks, Kent, in 1958. My ancestry is three quarters Scottish, you might say. My mother's parents were both Scots, and my father's father was Scottish, but all of those grandparents had moved south for various reasons in the early twentieth century. So my father and mother were born in England, and so was I, and so were my two siblings – my older sister and my older brother – my sister's six years older than me, and my brother's three years older. So I was the third of three. I was born in a small-ish detached house in a quiet cul de sac in Sevenoaks, actually born in the house; my Mum was allowed to have me there. We lived there until I was five, then we moved to a slightly different area a few miles down the road. We were only there for about nine months, and then my father got an offer of a job in Scotland. He'd worked in various capacities: he'd worked for British Oxygen, and he'd really worked in sales, and he got offered a post with John G Stein, a business that made bricks for lining steel furnaces, blast furnaces, in Bonnybridge, in Stirlingshire. So we moved north when I was six and three quarters, and settled in

Bridge of Allan, in the more salubrious bit of Stirlingshire, (L) right at the northern end of Stirlingshire: Perth-shire was only two miles up the road. So we were a reasonably well off middle-class family, coming from the south of England, but always with quite a strong sense of being Scottish in some way.

IM: Is this the whole family; not just you?

JR: I think all of the family, but my sister was that much older: she'd spent that much longer in England: she was twelve by the time we moved up. My brother was nine, and I think I was young enough – I hadn't quite had that amount of southern-Englishness impressed on me. Also my mother's parents moved back north. They'd always wanted to move back to Scotland, and they moved north at the same time. One of my aunts also came north. So the family re-emigrated, and came back to Scotland, and I certainly remember thinking, as we came up overnight on the sleeper, that it was like coming back, even though obviously I'd never been here before. Even though I hadn't any real definition of what it was, I certainly felt Scottish from the outset.

IM: Did your brother and sister develop Scottish accents, or did they remain English?

JR: My brother and I have got Scottish accents: my sister doesn't, particularly, and I think that was probably an age thing more than anything. The other factor involved in that would have been probably the education that we got, because we all went to private schools. So we were not as exposed to the voices of our peers as we might have been if we'd just gone to the local primary and secondary schools.

IM: Was sending you to the local schools just not considered?

JR: I don't think so. My father had been to Public schools in England, and he probably thought that's what should happen. My brother and I went to a very small school in Stirling called Hurst

Grange, which took about a hundred boys from the age of seven to thirteen. It was situated on the edge of the King's Park in Stirling, and it was I think a very good school. The education was very good: I think the teaching was good: the food was good (L) – I remember the food being fabulous! It gave you a good grounding in a load of different aspects of life - the sort of things you would expect maybe of that kind of Prep school. Lots of games and outdoor activities; your day was filled up with activities, and I tend to think, looking back now, that that's where I got my real education – not at the next school. The Prep school was run by a headmaster called Tim Brown, who ruled it very very rigorously. He could be incredibly fierce and incredibly strict, and sometimes unfairly so, we thought, in the way he meted out discipline, and the way that the whole community of the school would be made to suffer for the misdemeanours of one or two – that kind of old-fashioned attitude towards getting children to observe some kind of moral code. When I think about that now, I think there were all kinds of things there that I would now thoroughly disagree with and disapprove of, but when you're going through that system at the age of seven, eight, nine, ten, you just accept that that's what happens, and you just get on with it. For all his faults, as I see them now, I was very lucky, because I was academically quite bright, and he favoured boys who were academically bright. He didn't have time for the ones that were struggling a bit in the class, but if you were able to cope with the work you got on okay there. One of the subjects he taught at the upper end of the school from the age of eleven, twelve, thirteen, was English, and he gave me a very good grounding in English, and the way the language works, and he made us read widely. When I think back, I think that's where the real basics of my education came from. Most of us went on to 'Public' school. Some of the kids went on to Stirling High School, but very few. I went on to Trinity College, Glenalmond, as it then was.

IM: Did your brother go to Glenalmond too?

JR: My brother went to Glenalmond too, and that was quite a different experience. Although it was in some respects separate,

Hurst Grange always felt to me part of the local community, very much part of the town of Stirling. Glenalmond is stuck in the middle of the moors, north of Perth, and it doesn't feel like it belongs to any community except its own. Again, Hurst Grange always felt very Scottish to me, and Glenalmond felt English. I think I genuinely did feel and notice these differences. I wasn't unhappy at Glenalmond, again because I was able to cope with the academic work, it was okay, and I was also quite into sport. If you weren't into rugby and athletics and all the other things, it must have been an absolutely hellish place. And there were kids there that really suffered because they weren't. So I survived Glenalmond, and couldn't say that I hated it, at the time: I think I just got on with it. But I was always aware that there was something strange about it: it was different from the kind of system that most people were going through.

IM: The system that you were going through at Glenalmond was inevitably going to lead you on, I think, to Oxford or Cambridge. That's what as I understand it, any bright boy from Glenalmond would do.

JR: Absolutely. If they thought that you were good enough, then you were schooled to go to Oxford or Cambridge.

IM: So you automatically went for that?

JR: It was made clear that I could and probably should sit a separate Oxbridge exam, so I did. The other factor was that my father had been a student at Cambridge, so he was quite keen. My brother had gone to Edinburgh University to study Agriculture, so I think my father was quite keen that one of us should go to Cambridge. I sat the exam and went down to Cambridge for the interview, which you were always summoned for as well. This was to read History at Downing College.

IM: Had you decided it was to be History?

JR: Yes. The subjects I was best at were English and History, and I didn't want to do English because I had already been writing for a long time, writing fiction, poetry and other things, and I knew instinctively that I didn't want to study English for three or four years, because I was afraid it was going to put me off, and that I would just have a surfeit of English Literature and Language of various kinds, and I didn't want to do that. History was the other subject I was equally good at, and I thought History was really enjoyable. It was one of the subjects that was taught quite well at Glenalmond. A lot of the teaching was terrible at Glenalmond, absolutely appalling.

IM: Did they teach any Scottish History?

JR: Virtually none. The only Scottish History would come as an appendix where it had to be fitted in to English, to British History.

IM: Where did James VI come from, sort of thing?

JR: That sort of thing. How do you explain Montrose's involvement in the Civil War? I don't suppose it was that different from any other school: I don't think it was particularly peculiar to the private system. Anyway, I went then to Cambridge for the interview at Downing College, and they told me that my exam results were not actually that great. They were okay, but they were nothing exceptional. So there was a question mark I think over whether I was good enough to get in, and I was sent for another interview where I was interviewed by three History dons, which was quite intimidating for a seventeen year old, one of them standing behind you and the other two sitting in armchairs. They asked why I wanted to go to Downing College, and I said I'd only chosen Downing because my father and my uncles had been there. Their eyes lit up and their faces changed and they said, oh well, we'll find a place for you then. (L) I got home, and something inside me just went – I really don't like that at all. And I'd also been aware, in the couple of days I spent there, that Cambridge could be seen almost as another dose of Glenalmond writ large, with a lot of the same kind of kids hanging about. I didn't want to do that any more. So when the letter came offering me the place, I wrote and turned them down, which I think was just not done. (L) I got a letter back, which I've still got, which opened, 'Dear Robertson, we note that you're not coming, and have removed your name from the list'. It wasn't even signed. (L) I knew that I'd done the right thing, and I went to Edinburgh instead.

IM: Was it Edinburgh inevitably?

JR: No: I'd thought about St Andrews as well. I don't know why I thought these ones. My brother was at Edinburgh, and I'd been over there a couple of times when he was a student, spent the night there, and he'd shown me around the town, and I thought, this is an exciting place; so really Edinburgh was going to be the first choice.

IM: Having gone to Edinburgh to study History, are there names of people that you'd want to put on the record as having been particularly important?

JR: As teachers and lecturers? Edinburgh had then and I think still has a very large History Department, and there were some important people teaching when I was there. I was taught by a woman called Frances Dow, who was a very good teacher and lecturer, and I ended up doing a course on the English Revolution with her in my final year. There were other modern historians like Paul Addison, who I did a course on the First World War with: there were other names that I didn't get taught by, but there was a good body of serious historians. There were a lot in the medieval field, but I didn't particularly enjoy medieval History – you had to do it in second year, but I did what I had to do and then moved on. I was more interested in slightly later and modern History. Seventeenth century, and then there was a gap, then twentieth-century History. But again, Scottish History was pretty much a ghetto. It was there, in the Scottish History Department, but you had to more or less do Scottish History and nothing but, in order to do any Scottish History at all. As an undergraduate, I didn't do Scottish History. I did a lot of American History, mainly in my third year, when I was on an exchange scheme to the University of Pennsylvania, I went to Philadelphia and obviously studied a lot of American History. That was the first time that I'd ever really been out of the country, so that was an eye-opener. Culturally, and for all kinds of reasons. It was a wonderful, wonderful experience, a great year. It also made me step outside Scotland and reassess it from another point of view. Interestingly, when I became involved in various ways in the movement for some kind of self government or parliament for Scotland in the Eighties and Nineties, I found that pretty much all of the key players in that movement had at some time spent some time outside of Scotland. I think that's very important, because it's a maturing thing, and it makes you see your own country and its issues and its problems and its strengths and its failings in context and perspective in a way that you can't see unless you've actually spent some time somewhere else.

IM: So when you came back, you had just one year to go. Did you have 'Big Bang' Finals still then, with all the exams at the end?

JR: Yes, most people did, but I was fortunate because of the exchange scheme in America: they accepted the results that you got in your third year in the American system, and you were able to carry them forward towards your degree, so at the end of fourth year, when most of my fellow students were having to sit seven exams on two years of work, I only had to sit four exams on one year's work.

IM: Jammy! (L)

JR: It was jammy, and it made life a lot easier as far as I was concerned. I ended up getting a First, and I think that was a big contributory factor, because it really took the pressure off, in terms of revision, while everyone else was struggling to remember stuff from two years previously.

IM: So, looking back on the student experience generally, what do you think were the valuable things?

JR: Probably the most valuable thing of all was going to America for a year. I think that was immensely valuable to me in many different ways. I remember distinctly, for example, and this is something we may come back to, more or less on the day that I flew to Philadelphia, Hugh MacDiarmid died. Now I had never heard of Hugh MacDiarmid, or if I had, it was only in the vaguest of terms. There were obituaries here and there, and I think I was buying *The Guardian* weekly in Philadelphia, and there was a review of his *Complete Poems*, which were published posthumously. I don't know how much notice I would have taken of all that had I still been in Scotland, but somehow because I was outside of Scotland I homed in on this and thought, why don't I know about this man? Why don't I know about his work? And I was determined that when I got back I was going to find out. In fact, even before that I went downtown to a very strange and esoteric bookshop where I managed to find a volume of Hugh MacDiarmid's poems, which I bought. I think the bookseller was amazed that somebody had finally decided to buy this. That started me off on the MacDiarmid trail. That year in America really gave me a perspective on Scotland that I hadn't had before. In other respects, I had a lot of fun as an undergraduate, which was great, and I don't regret it at all. I made a lot of good friends. I probably didn't make the best use of my time. (L)

IM: Who does?

JR: I could have been a more conscientious student, but that wasn't really what being a student was like in the late Seventies.

IM: What about the family back in Bridge of Allan? Did you feel anyone looking over your shoulder?

JR: No. My Mum and Dad are amazing people. They do that really difficult parental thing, and they've always done it, of enabling you to make choices and take responsibilities, and standing back and letting you do it, which I think must be one of the most difficult things to do as a parent. They've always been very good at that, but they've also always been very good, when you make the wrong choices and make the wrong decisions, at coming back in and supporting you. So long as I seemed to be getting on fine, they didn't interfere: they didn't ask too many questions; they didn't pressure me in any way. They just wanted me to get the most out of it and perform as well as I could. When I got the chance to go to America they thought that was the most fabulous experience, and I couldn't possibly not do it: and when I got a good result in my Finals they were obviously pleased with that. They were absolutely there all the time, but in no sense did I ever feel any pressure.

IM: Excellent. That is very important: other people's experiences can be so different. The expectations that are laid on one can be pretty hard. You went on some time later, James, to do a PhD. Did it not occur to you when you graduated?

JR: No. When I graduated in 1980, the last thing I wanted to do was more studying (L). It was suggested to me that I could: the First opens doors, and if you want to do postgraduate work you can do it. I thought about it and thought no, I don't want to do that. Also having been in America for a year had given me a bug, to want to see some more of the world. There was a class prize which I won, which was worth quite a lot of money – I think £600, which was a lot of money in 1980. I spent that on buying an air ticket to Australia, and I went to Australia for a year on a working holiday visa. I went with a friend who'd graduated at the same time, and we both had decided we weren't going to just jump into careers.

IM: Taking your year out at the end rather than the beginning?

JR: Yes. We just picked up what jobs we could, and bummed around Australia, and that was again another great experience. Then I went on down to New Zealand for another two or three months. I came back through America. I was away for about a year and three months. But I guess there was that little Protestant work ethic thing sitting in the back of my head (L) that was going, this is all very well but – you should be earning a living, boy (L). I thought I'd better go home and find myself a job. I arrived back in the very beginning of 1982, which was the height of the Thatcher recession.

IM: Can I just interrupt here to check that you were intent that you were going to be a writer at some point- a published writer, I mean, because you already were a writer.

JR: I had intended to be a published writer since the age of six.

IM: Yes: so you hadn't deviated from that.

JR: No. Again you may want to come back to that later. I had written many books by the time I was eighteen or twenty. I'd completed manuscripts and sent them off to publishers. They had not, thank God, been accepted. (L)

IM: Have you got any of them still?

JR: I do, I do. They're buried, and nobody else knows where they are, and I shall decide what to do with them in due course. (L) I wrote a lot of Westerns (L). I was very into the Wild West as a kid, and I did finish one of those, and I wrote another couple of novels. One of them was about boarding school. And I wrote another one which was really a loose collection of short stories that ended up being a very surreal novel, because I was very into Surrealism at the time. All these different influences were happening right through my teens, and yes, I believed I had to come back and get a job, but at the back of my mind was the idea that I would at some point be a published writer.
I came home at the start of 1982, and the recession was really biting, and unemployment was shooting up, and I stayed with my parents because I could not get a job. For six or seven months. Of any kind whatsoever. It's the only time in my life when I've actually been on the Broo. I used to go into Stirling and sign on every

fortnight. You forget now what it was like, but there were queues of people out the door at the Labour Exchange. It was incredible. And I was one of the lucky ones, because at least I had a family home where I was going to have warmth and food on the table, but there were a lot of people who were not in that position. At that point I wrote another novel! (L) I didn't have anything else to do at the time. Again luckily that's never seen the light of day. The rest of that year was weird: I did get a job eventually, in Edinburgh, a very low paid job working for a wholefoods shop, and I was working there for three or four months, but I was earning less than the rent cost. It just wasn't going to work out in the long term. I went back to America at that point; I'd saved enough money. I went because I'd an old girlfriend there, and we thought we might make a go of it, but we didn't. I came back, and at the start of 1983

JR: I got a job as a sales rep for a publisher, Cassell, who had once been a very renowned and important publisher, but in their latter days they were not in the same shape as they had once been. The main thing I was doing was selling Berlitz travel guides, and I did this from a large yellow transit van, and I travelled round the whole of Scotland and the north of England for about a year and a half, doing this job, which was okay in its way, and once I'd got on top of it wasn't that intellectually demanding, so I had time to do other things. I was beginning to get very politically conscious of things, partly because of length of the dole queue, Mrs Thatcher's government was in power and to my mind was doing all the wrong things, and I felt that Scotland was being particularly hard done by for various reasons. The Devolution Referendum of '79 had happened when I was out of the country, and I felt very aggrieved that I had been denied a vote in that. I'd tried to get one and they wouldn't give me one, because I'd left the country voluntarily; and apparently that meant you couldn't vote (L). I was reading a lot more as well: I'd begun to get into MacDiarmid in the last couple of years, and I was beginning to read – I'd realised that there was this whole field that I had not known existed, which was Scottish literature – and Scottish history as well - in spite of having studied for four years I knew virtually nothing about them.

My self education began at that point, and I read and read and read. And I read magazines like *Cencrastus*, and *Chapman*, which gave me access to what was going on in the contemporary Scottish literary scene. And I began to write my own poems and send them in to *Chapman* and *Akros* and *Cencrastus*.

IM: And *Lines*?

JR: *Lines* was one I didn't get into at that point: I don't know why I missed out on it. For some reason it didn't attract me in the way that some of the others did. I think the others were wearing their Scottishness a bit more proudly in their sleeves, and I was in a very Nationalist phase at that point. There were a number of good magazines around, and Alan Bold produced a book, *Modern Scottish Literature* (1983), which the passage of time has made a wee bit out of date, but at the time there was nothing much of the kind around – that I knew of, anyway. I was able to read about authors I didn't know about, and then go and buy their books, or get them out of the library. So it was an important time.

IM: But you've still got to decide to do this PhD.

JR: I think I'd always had it in my head that I might go back and study at some point. And this intervening period convinced me that I wanted to go back and learn more about Scottish History and Scottish Literature and culture generally. The only way in which I was going to have really enough time to do that would be to go back into fulltime education. I decided to go back to Edinburgh because I knew the city, and I quite fancied going back to live in Edinburgh. I applied to do a thesis with the vaguest of titles – it was something like 'Aspects -

IM: That's a good start! (L)

JR: (L) 'Aspects of change in Scottish historiography ' – or something like that. But Nicholas Phillipson, who was a specialist in the Enlightenment period in Scottish History, agreed that he would supervise me, and I got the offer from the university that I could do this on the same day that I got offered a job to be the sales rep for the AA, for their publications, and I looked at them both. My mother was through, and we talked it through, and one was going to earn me a reasonable amount of money, and the other was not going to earn me any money, and was going to be a hard graft, and there was no obvious outcome at the end of it in terms of career and so forth, because even then I knew I didn't want to be an academic full time, permanently. And my mother said, which one do you want to do, in your heart? And I said, there's no question: the PhD. So she said, that's what you've got to do. That's pretty good, because a lot of mothers would have said, take the safe option! So I went back, and started reading up on this vague, vague historical subject, (L) and I was reading about different interpretations of Scottish History, and how over the years in different centuries, different historians had reinterpreted Scottish History, particularly in its relation to British History, and particularly in the way that Scotland was or was not perceived to be a separate country or part of a wider union. Here I came upon Sir Walter Scott. First of all, some of his non-fictional writings, his essays, and his views about history, and then of course I started reading the Waverley novels.

I realised that this was what I really needed to do my PhD on, Scott. Because Scott seemed to me to be the key to some kind of understanding of why Scottish History was perceived in the way that it is – or was, in the late twentieth century. Scott was the architect of how people looked at Scottish History, but I also felt that there was something else going on there as well, that to some extent Scott had been wrongly blamed for the tartanisation, the shortbread tin effect on Scottish History. I thought, if I read Scott, and read enough about him, I'll maybe be able to understand how that had come about, how those two views of Scott and Scottish History had come about. So my thesis was really about how Scott devised a system of – patriotism, if you like, which enabled Scots to both take pride in their own history and their own country, but also to operate within the British Empire. Something that had been done before by other people in many ways – David Daiches had done a lot of work on this – but it was new to me, and I wrote I think a perfectly adequate thesis on this subject, but I didn't think it was going to break any major new ground as far as the outside world was concerned. But it certainly broke a lot of ground as far as I was concerned.

IM: Far more important!

JR: That was exactly why I did it, and also it meant that I was back in Edinburgh from 1984 to 1989, and that enabled me to continue to build up my own knowledge and interest in what was going on culturally.

IM: Is that when you started having to do with *Radical Scotland?*

JR: I'd begun to get things published in magazines – poems, mostly, and I think I sent a poem in there and it got published. And then I was approached by the editor, a man called Alan Watson, who asked me if I would be interested in joining the magazine team to look after the arts and culture section at the back. The reason he asked me was because Alan Riach was doing that job, but he was about to disappear off somewhere else –

IM: To New Zealand!

JR: Alan is now back of course as professor of Literature in Glasgow. There were a lot of interesting people got involved with the magazine round about that time. I moved in, without really knowing what I was doing, but I got a lot of support from Alan Watson, who was an excellent editor. He could be a very stormy and impatient man, but knew exactly what he wanted to do as an editor, and I learned a lot about writing and editing articles, and commissioning things. I worked on the magazine, purely on a voluntary basis - it was all done because we believed in what the magazine stood for, which was to find some common ground between Nationalists in the Labour Party and Socialists in the SNP, and other like-minded people from other parties and from no parties, to build a campaign towards getting a parliament. I must have been involved in the magazine for about five years, and I think we did make a bit of difference. Although it had a very small circulation, it was very much used as a mechanism for getting people to talk to each other. It was an incredibly important thing to do, through the Eighties, to galvanise people to talk to each other and actually work together, rather than fight each other. Eventually we got where we wanted to be. It folded in 1990 or '91, and we decided that there was not much more that we could do, that the Sunday papers and other media were now doing it. I feel very privileged, now, that I had the chance to work on that.

IM: You were Deputy Manager of Waterstones in 1992?

JR: Yeah. It took me four years to do my PhD, and the first three years I had a grant, but didn't quite make ends meet, so I got a part-time job at the first Waterstones to open outside London, which opened in Edinburgh's George Street, and I worked there, and when my grant ran out I worked full time there, and then when I finished my PhD I got transferred through to Glasgow, to be Deputy Manager of the new branch they were opening there. I worked for Waterstones for about eight years altogether. This was again interesting, because it gave me an insight into the book world, and how the book-selling world interacts with the publishing world. It also in a way gave me access to my first publisher, because a very small Edinburgh publisher caller Black and White Publishing was setting up at that time, run by two guys called Campbell Brown and Steve Wiggins. Steve worked in the Edinburgh branch where I had worked, so. . . They started off by producing walking guides to Edinburgh, which were quite successful, and then they began to look around and think, there are Scottish titles out of print that we can reprint, and they started with John Buchan, who at that time was out of copyright. They published *Sick Heart River*, which I think is a really fascinating novel, and that seemed to do quite well, so they began publishing more Buchan, and then they took on some other authors. They managed to start reprinting old Nigel Tranter books: he had said he'd quite like to have some of them back in print. Slowly they began to build up a list – not the most exciting or innovative list, I would have to say, but it was quite a worthy list. At this time I was writing quite a lot of short stories, and they said they would publish a collection. So I was lucky that through that Waterstones connection I managed to get to a publisher. They published this very small book of stories called *Close* in 1991.

IM: This is the book of short stories which is now so rare that I haven't been able to get my hands on it. (L)

JR: Yeah: I've got one in the house now. It was a print run of a thousand copies.

IM: I didn't know B&W had done any new books of a literary kind.

JR: Mine was about the only one. And it actually sold pretty well: I think it was sold out in about eighteen months. That in itself was a good milestone for me, because having had the book published meant that I was eligible to apply for things like Arts Council grants, and writerships in residence.

IM: So you were no slouch when you went to Brownsbank. You've written about how you didn't at all expect to get it, but they clearly weren't going for the best known person. [*See 'Becoming a Writer' in Spirits of the Age: Scottish Self Portraits, edited by Paul Henderson Scott, 2005, p 352.*]

JR: No, they weren't, and I think it was deliberate on their part. Brownsbank was bought by Biggar Museums after Valda Trevlyn died in 1989. I'd met her once, very briefly, when she came to the launch of Alan Bold's biography of MacDiarmid, which was held in Waterstones in Edinburgh, and was a very drunken affair. Valda came to that, but she was really quite frail, and she didn't last much longer. When she died, the Museum was run by a man called Brian Lambie, a wonderful, wonderful man, who thought, this is a priceless piece of our national heritage sitting on our doorstep, and if we don't do something about it, it'll probably fall into disuse. So he negotiated with the farmers who owned the cottage – MacDiarmid had had it rent-free off the Tweedies since the nineteen-fifties – and the Museum bought the cottage, and then restored it. It needed a lot of work doing. They took the contents out and stored them, and then repaired the house and put them all back in again, so that it really looked as it had done when Valda and Chris were there in the late sixties and early seventies. Then they had to decide what to do with it. It's off the beaten track, and it needs to be lived in and heated, because it's very susceptible to damp and mice and everything else. They thought, let's put a writer in residence in there, and they managed to persuade the Arts Council that this was a good idea, so they came up with some of the money; Strathclyde Regional Council as it then was came up with some money, and they advertised the post. I had seen this advertisement and thought, I'm not even going to apply for that, because I thought it would go to a big name. Then I heard through Robert Crawford, I think it was, that they had had a number of applications, but they were still looking for more, because they were quite keen not to give it to a big name. They wanted someone who was just starting out ands needed a helping hand. So I applied for it, and was offered it, and this was fabulous. It was important for me as well because I was living in Glasgow at the time, and I was married by this stage, and my marriage was really on the rocks, and it was important that I made changes in my life. Here was a job that I wanted to do, living in the former house of somebody who was one of my literary heroes, and it gave me a roof over my head and a stipend for two years: this was just the most brilliant opportunity to change direction and go in the direction I'd always wanted to go all my life, which was to be a writer. Half of your working time there was to be spent in the community, working in schools, with writers' groups, etcetera, and the other half was yours. It was just wonderful. Suddenly there I was with ostensibly three or four days a week to write, which is what I did.

IM: Excellent. Your output during that time was quite impressive, really, and it probably doesn't cover all the things you were preparing.

The *Close* stories came out before you went, but *The Ragged Man's Complaint* was 1993, and the anthology of other people's Scottish stories, *A Tongue in yer Heid*, was '94, and then your first book of poems in '95. All that must have been happening while you were there.

JR: All happening there. And in addition to that I edited two volumes of the writings of Hugh Miller, whom I'd become interested in. I managed to persuade Black & White again to put them back into print, so I edited *My Schools and Schoolmasters* (1993) and *Scenes and Legends of the North of Scotland* (1994). Oh, and I wrote new introductions to two Scott novels for them, and a couple of Buchans as well. (L) So there was a lot going on. I had written about half of *The Ragged Man's Complaint* before I went there. But it was the most fabulously productive time, and I've said elsewhere in a poem that MacDiarmid changed my life. In two ways. When I'd read his poems, he opened up a whole view of Scotland, literature, writing and politics: he revolutionised my ways of thinking. The other way he changed my life was by having had Brownsbank, and letting me in there for two years: hugely important.

IM: So what happened when you eventually had to shoehorn yourself out of Brownsbank? (L)

JR: (L) In '95 I finished at Brownsbank and moved back to Edinburgh. At this stage I was in a relationship with Angela Cran, and had been for some time.

IM: You know, I guessed that! (L)

JR: We worked together for the next year or so. I had a commission to write a book called *Scottish Ghost Stories*.

IM: That interests me: who commissioned that?

JR: That was commissioned by Little Brown and Company, who are now part of Time Warner Books. The reason this came about was another connection from my time at Waterstones. I knew a lot of the sales reps, obviously, and one of them was a really nice guy called Stuart Creighton (sp), and he was from Time Warner Books. I bumped into him one day, and he said, do you fancy writing a book of ghost stories? I've always said that we should have a book of Scottish ghost stories on our list. Things went a bit further and they told me what they were looking for, and I said yes, because I had to do something to earn some money after Brownsbank. So I researched this for about four months in the summer of 1995, going round the country visiting old castles and other places where hauntings were supposed to take place, and retelling them, more as real as opposed to fictional ghost stories, digging around, trying to find stories that were not so familiar. And as soon as I began, people said, you must speak to so-and-so: they've got a ghost in their house. So I wrote this very rapidly, because there wasn't a huge advance involved.

IM: On the one hand there was research to do; on the other hand there was hardly time to do it. I rather wondered who it was written for, although it's obviously been very successful. You see it in every Oxfam bookshop.

JR: (L) It's been unbelievably successful. I wrote it really for the general reader. I thought, I'm not going to try to be too highbrow about this. I went in as a sceptic, thinking, I don't know whether I believe in ghosts or not, but let's go and do it. I knew I didn't have the research to do it properly, but I also thought, well it's an opportunity to turn some folklore into history. In that sense it was my most populist effort, if you see what I mean. It came out in 1996, and I think it's been reprinted about seven times; it just goes on selling. It sits a bit oddly with the rest of what I've done.

IM: Except that one or two names keep coming up, that have indeed come up again this summer with the gentleman whose name I can't pronounce. *Life Beneath the Shadow.* (2005)

JR: Oh, Cai Guo Qiang. That's right: these names do keep coming up. (L) Thomas Weir came up in *Scottish Ghost Stories.*   And subsequently I went, that was really interesting; I wonder if I really found out as much about him as I could have. And I went back and researched him and found there was a huge amount more about Thomas Weir, which led to *The Fanatic*. And yes, in the work I did this summer with Cai Guo Qiang in the Fruitmarket Gallery, they wanted thirteen little ghost stories, one page ghost stories to be written, so yes, I revisited that territory again, so he keeps cropping up: it's an odd one. Because as I said, I'm a sceptic in the most literal sense: I neither believe nor disbelieve this stuff. I think most ghost stories can be explained by other means than ghosts. There are all kinds of cultural and social reasons why ghost stories exist, but I also have to say that I've met people who I have absolutely no reason to disbelieve who have undoubtedly experienced things that you can only describe as hauntings. I remain pretty open-minded about that.

IM: Can I just have a little more on *Life Beneath the Shadow*? It's an interesting concept. The guy starts out by wanting to paint or create pictures of a number of Scottish characters, and you and – is it the head of the Portrait Gallery? – suggested some names to him. Was it his choice after that? Or did you lean on him? (L)

JR: Pretty much. We led him towards names. I think we had a short leet of twenty names, and of course Cai didn't know much about these people at all. Cai is a very impressive man, who lives in New York but is originally from China, and who has many exhibitions going on all over the world. To my shame, I was not familiar with his name or his work at all, before I was asked to be involved in this project, by the Fruitmarket Gallery. He has a deep interest in spirits and other worlds, and he was interested in bringing some of that to this exhibition in Edinburgh, and he then thought, Edinburgh is a city which is quite well known for some of its ghosts, so he thought that would be a useful thing to tie in to the exhibition. This is when they brought me on board to say, here is a local writer who can maybe guide you in the direction of local ghost stories.

IM: So you and he as it were chose the characters, and then he worked his magic with gunpowder, making pictures of them. Who wrote the little potted biographies at the end: was that you?

JR: No: the Fruitmarket Gallery compiled them. I did see them, and I tried to kind of fine tune some of them, but they compiled them.

IM: I've seen them do things like that before: Anne Bevan and Janice Galloway did *Pipelines*, about the Edinburgh water supply and sewers and drains [2000]. The idea is that, with you telling him about these people, he creates these pictures, and then from the pictures – and obviously your knowledge of the folk they're meant to be of – you create a little story for each one of them. But they don't have to relate directly.

JR: No. Basically once we'd decided on the thirteen names, then the Portrait Gallery and the Fruitmarket Gallery supplied him with as many images as they could of these people. But of course with some of them there were no images. There are no images of Thomas Weir, for example, or of the Brahan Seer, or James Kirk, the minister who wrote the treatise about the fairies.

IM: That was Robert!

JR: I beg your pardon, Robert Kirk. (L) So he had to use his imagination for these ones. Meanwhile, while he was off thinking about these portraits, gunpowder portraits he was going to make, I was writing the stories.

IM: Oh, you were writing them separately?

JR: I wrote them separately. They were not specifically related to his portraits, and not necessarily to the characters. Well, one of the figures was James Hogg, and the story that I wrote was about a shepherd being guided in a snowstorm back to safety by a mysterious figure with a light. That was the ghost element, but it wasn't about James Hogg. So I was using the people and the names as a jumping-off place to write other stories.

JR: But when I saw the portraits, when the exhibition opened – I was just amazed by them, because he seemed somehow to have worked in elements of my stories into these portraits. But as far as I had been aware, he had not seen my stories. (L) Then it transpired that I had written the stories just in time before he started making these, and his translator had got the text, and as he was making the portraits she was reading the texts out to him, and so he was able very cleverly to work in some little elements of my stories into these portraits. So it was a weird circular effect, which I think worked really well.

IM: It's a very interesting book, but I would hate to have to write a treatise upon it's composition! (L) Meanwhile we go back to the *Scottish Ghost Stories*, wasn't it? And then an introduction with Angela Cran to Dorothy Haynes?

JR: That was another collection that came out of Brownsbank. Dorothy Haynes was a writer whom I'd admired, her short stories. I'd come across her occasionally and really liked what she was doing. One day at Brownsbank – quite early on, actually, I couldn't get any reception on the little television, so I got the local electrician to come up to sort out the aerial on the roof. When he knew what I did, he told me, oh, my mother used to be a writer. I shuddered a bit: I thought, oh here we go, and he went on, she's dead now, but she had lots of things published. I said, what was her name, and he said, Dorothy K Haynes. This turned out to be a man called Leonard Gray. This is too good an opportunity to miss! He had masses of manuscripts of her stories, most of which had appeared in magazines, and in things like *The Pan Book of Horror Stories*: she had a lot of things in those anthologies. But he also had original copies of books she'd written, a couple of novels and one book of stories in the nineteen-fifties.

IM: *Thou Shalt Not Suffer A Witch To Live?*

JR: That was the first one, which was illustrated by Mervyn Peake. He said he'd love to see his mother's work back in print, so we put together an anthology, which consisted of most of the stories from the original *Thou Shalt Not Suffer A Witch*, plus some more which we thought really deserved to be back in print. I'm still proud of that book: I think there's some great stories in there, but I have to say sadly it did not sell, and it was remaindered, and it's gone again. [*Thou Shalt Not Suffer a Witch To Live*, edited and introduced with Angela Cran, *1996*] And Dorothy K Haynes is one of those writers who has just not been taken seriously. I think she's a fabulous writer, and when she's on form her stories are excellent.

IM: Latterly I knew about her, having great difficulty in publishing anything: it's very sad.

JR: It is sad. She wrote a huge number of stories over the years.

IM: But I fear being female didn't help. Can I take hold of that, and also your collaboration with Angela Cran on the *Dictionary of Scottish Quotations* (1996). This absolutely fascinates me, partly because you talk in the introduction about giving women their place, (L) but then I didn't know whether that was you or Angela Cran, or a meeting of minds.

JR: I think that was a mutual meeting of minds: we were very aware that that had to be done. We had to try to redress that imbalance, if we could do it, without being too artificial.

IM: How successful has it been in staying in print?

JR: It's out of print, and I had some negotiations with Mainstream, the publisher, about a new edition, but it requires a lot of work: there's a number of mistakes which really need corrected, but having seen that first edition, which I was very pleased with when it came out – it broke new ground, in some ways - now I would go back to that and do it quite differently. I would take out quite a lot, and I would put in a lot of other things, which is in the nature of that kind of thing, but at the moment it's such a huge task to take on that I've basically said that I can't do that. Angela and I are no longer an item, although we're still friends: she's got her hands full with bairns, and just now it's not on.

IM: I'm interested in the whole idea behind it, because actually it's not like any dictionary of quotations that I've ever used, and I do use them a lot. With most dictionaries of quotations, the main point is that if you get hold of half a quotation or half-remember it, you can look it up and get it right. But an awful lot of the quotations in your dictionary will be completely new, I suspect, to most of your readers. It's almost like, these are the quotations we think you ought to know (L). I went right through it, and it was enormously interesting and fun, but where some of them came from and who is expected to know some of the quotations – I dearly love Naomi Mitchison myself, but that twenty-seven of her sayings should be as immortal as all that implies (L). . . whereas only seventeen of Muriel Spark, and twenty-nine of Dunbar, does seem a little strange. I'm flying a kite here: I think you get a certain social, not party-political, a social message, a kind of, what is Scottish identity? Feed some of this into your backbone, my friends.

JR: I think that's a fair point, actually, and I think that's where we were coming from. I think we were aware in the early 1990s that there were an awful lot of building blocks of books being produced that were part of what we could call the regeneration of Scottish identity, people being more aware of their country and its cultural and literary inheritance. For example, there was Duncan MacMillan's book on Scottish art; there was John Purser's book on Scottish music; there was the *Concise Scottish Dictionary:* Trevor Royle and Mainstream produced a companion to Scottish literature –

IM: And Daiches did his *Companion to Scottish Culture.*

JR: There were others as well.

IM: There was a Gaelic one.

JR: That's right: there was Derrick Thomson's *Companion to Gaelic Culture*. There were a whole range of these, and these were really important books, and I had them on my shelves and I used them all the time, and there were a whole lot of other people. Ah, brilliant: that's another book for the Scottish reference section. And the one that we thought was missing was a dictionary of Scottish quotations. Why do you need a dictionary of Scottish quotations? We felt that where Scottish quotations appeared in British works – for example, if you look up William Dunbar, there's very few. The quotations of MacDiarmid that you get in them seemed to me to be absolutely not the ones that struck a chord for whatever reason in Scottish terms. Those books seemed to me to represent Scotland in a certain way, and we thought you could produce a book of quotations that represent Scotland in an utterly different way. And we thought that was an interesting and an important project to do. I take your point: I think that was really it. We're maybe not actually saying, you ought to know, but there was a point at which we were saying, look at this wealth of material, and use this book as a jumping off place to go and find out more. I think we were trying to do that, and it served that purpose at that time, but now I think if I was going to do a revised edition, I would look at it in quite a different way.

IM: Or indeed, you might want to set a couple of young people with computers into the other kind of dictionary of quotations, the often-used ones, the ones we all get wrong, because with computers, so much of the back-breaking work you two must have done –

JR: Now you can do it on the internet. That's true, and it was (L) back-breaking work. It's unbelievable when I look back, that we did that whole book in about fifteen months, while we were both doing other things – in Angela's case holding down a full-time job, while I was doing lots and lots of other work, including all kinds of things to earn money.

IM: Can I ask you a possibly insulting question? Does either of you speak Gaelic?

JR: I can speak a little bit of Gaelic, and I can read it pretty well. I did a crash course in it. One reason was because I wanted to be able to read Sorley Maclean's poetry, and also because I wanted to be able to pronounce mountains properly (L). I couldn't claim to be fluent in any way, but I do have a limited knowledge and understanding of the Gaelic, and that was another aspect of it. We thought, a Scottish Dictionary of quotations should include it. To some extent it could be seen as tokenism, because we could only put in a certain amount of Gaelic quotations, but I still thought it was important that Gaelic was represented in such a book. It's interesting that now, ten or eleven years down the line from that, it's very difficult for Gaelic to be left out of these things. I think we were on the right lines there. To some extent we were at the mercy of our Gaelic adviser, John MacInnes, (L) and that meant that to some extent we had to defer to what he thought should be in, although we had some discussions about this, because I don't think that John had quite got hold of exactly what we were looking for sometimes. So the Gaelic quotations sit slightly oddly against what else is in the book. Again, if I was going to do a new edition, I would be looking probably for a younger Gael to revamp that part of the book completely. No offence to John MacInnes, but we don't need to do that that way next time.

IM: I hope you don't have to do it at all, because I'm hoping you'll be too busy with other things. It was tremendously worth doing once, and it's a document of its time, but it has its idiosyncrasies, which make it fun – like ten quotations from Jessie Kesson (L). . . Now I do want to ask you about two things: take them in whatever order suits you best – Kettilonia and Itchy Coo.

JR: Well let's take Kettilonia first. I said that for ages I had sent poems and stories off to be published in small magazines, *Chapman* and *Cencrastus* and *Akros*, and *New Writing Scotland*, and all those kinds of anthologies. I made it a rule to myself from about 1982 when I seriously began to want to get things published, that I must always have something out there, and I did get quite a lot published over the years. But one of the things I felt increasingly as we moved into the 1990s, was that magazines were getting slower and slower at responding, and the final straw was when I think I sent a story to *Chapman*, and Joy Hendry took eighteen months to reply, saying that she might use it, but she couldn't tell me when. The same thing was happening with poems and so on. I'd now moved from a typewriter to a PC, and I thought, it shouldn't be that difficult to produce a pamphlet, and get it printed within a relatively short space of time. I knew there were things that I wanted to get published within a reasonable length of time, and I also knew there were other people out there as well, that had good work that just wasn't going to see the light of day, possibly for years. I'd had a tax rebate, of about £500, so I stuck that into a new account, and added another £500, so I had £1000.

I set up a new imprint, to publish new and different, and interesting and unusual writing in pamphlet form. I started with five pamphlets: one of them was a series of poems that I'd written that were loosely based on the films of Alfred Hitchcock; because I was a great Hitchcock fan, and 1999, the year that I started this, was the hundredth anniversary of his birth, and I wanted to produce these as a group. I thought they worked as a sequence, so I had to do it as a pamphlet. And Matthew Fitt, whom I was very friendly with, and who succeeded me as writer in residence at Brownsbank, was writing what would eventually be his novel *But n Ben A-Go-Go* (2000), and he'd written quite a lot of it in bits, and he gave me sections of this amazing futuristic novel in Scots, and we published that as a pamphlet called *Sair Heid City*. There was a young Fife bloke called Andrew McNeil, whose poetry I knew, and I published some of his poems, and the other one was extracts from another forthcoming novel, a man called Hamish MacDonald, whose novel was eventually published by 11/9, called *The Gravy Star*, and it was one of the best books that 11/9 published in its relatively short time. For the fifth one I translated an entire eighteenth-century poem called *La a'Bhreiteanais*, The Day of Judgment, by Dugald Buchanan, into Scots, which is a bizarre thing to have done (L), but again nobody else in their right minds was going to publish this, so I'd have to do it myself. So these five pamphlets were brought out in 1999, they've taken quite nicely.

IM: How did you circulate them?

JR: I did the layout myself on the computer, printed it out, and went to a fabulous little printers in Glenrothes, called the Dolphin Press, who specialise in A5 pamphlets, and they were able to do these for a price that I could afford. I built up a mailing list of people I thought might be interested. I managed to get the manager of John Smith's bookshop in Byers Road in Glasgow, a guy called John Cairney whom I'd previously worked with in Waterstones: he agreed to launch these, and take quite a large quantity for his shop: that was a big plus. By and large most bookshops just do not want to know about pamphlets, and I thought, I'm going to get my sales by running readings and events, and by mailing people. These ones seemed to go quite well, so I did another five the next year. One criticism was levelled at me by I think it was Janet Paisley, quite rightly, that there were no women in the first batch, so the next year I got Ellie McDonald in, and I also then resuscitated Muriel Stuart, a really interesting poet –

IM: Who was not Scottish!

JR: Who is not Scottish at all, but MacDiarmid claimed her –

IM: But he was wrong! (L)

JR: But nevertheless, she's a great poet. I just kept finding interesting people – Iain Macdonough, a really interesting poet who lives in Edinburgh but originally came from Sutherland: Angus Calder's translations from Horace, *Horace at Tollcross*; a woman called Helena Nelson, who comes from England originally, but has been in Fife for years and years, and wrote a really interesting pamphlet called *Mr and Mrs Philpot on holiday at Auchteraw*. Over the years as I've got ever busier with my own work, I've not been able to do this as much: I think I did five the third year, but then it's dropped to two or three a year. It's mostly poetry: I've done a little bit of fiction, but in the pamphlet form poetry sells better: people don't believe you can actually put fiction into a little pamphlet – they want a proper novel. Poetry goes really well in pamphlets, and given that it's so difficult for people to get published in book form in poetry, this seems to serve a dual purpose. It gets people into print quickly. The optimum print run is about three or four hundred: we're not talking about large numbers here, but I can sell three or four hundred pamphlets over the course of two to two and a half years, and I know that they're reaching people who really want to read this stuff. And some people can go on and get books out.

IM: There have been one or two of these things, haven't there? Clocktower?

JR: Clocktower Press, which Duncan McLean set up.

IM: Which he did on something of the same basis to start with. It was more prose.

JR: He did more short extracts, and that was where I partly got the idea from, because Clocktower Press was breaking new ground. They were much more samizdat than what I do, but they published extracts from the novel that would become *Trainspotting*. I have a copy of that sixteen-page pamphlet, which is worth about two hundred quid (L).

IM: And Hamish Whyte?

JR: Hamish Whyte and Mariscat.

IM: And John Herdman's started doing some.

JR: More recently he has, *Fras*. Tessa Ransford started an award, the Callum Macdonald Memorial Award, specifically for poetry in pamphlet form. This had a huge effect in generating people to produce this stuff, and produce it well, and I think they get fifty or sixty entries a year now, which is really quite impressive. [*JR won this award for* <u>Stirling Sonnets</u> *in 2002*] It's rather rejuvenated the Scottish poetry scene, and I see the pamphlet now as replacing what the literary magazines used to do, in the sense that I'd rather get a really good swatch of somebody's work in 24 pages than just read one poem here and one there. The good poetry magazines still do very well, - I'm thinking of Gerry Cambridge's magazine *The Dark Horse*. I think the circulation is tiny, but it's a great magazine.

IM: And there's one called *Northwords*?

JR: *Northwords* has just gone online. They've stopped producing a paper version. That was a good magazine. Although it wasn't producing stuff specifically from the Highlands, it had a seriously north look to it. But it filled a gap.

IM: It filled more a need in the writer than a need in the audience: the audience don't know about the need – it's like the dictionary of quotations. (L) If you manage to persuade them that they need it, that's great. But a writer should at least be able to have half a dozen people saying, we really liked that one. But why did you put in the next one? – I hated it!

JR: That's very interesting: I think you're right, in a way; it does fulfil a need for the writer, and it provides new ways for readers to access people, who may go on to do more. I'm thinking of people who've been published through Kettillonia, and who've gone on the do other things. I'm not saying that wouldn't have happened without Kettillonia, but these are stepping stones, in the way that for me, in the eighties, *Chapman* and *Cencrastus* were very important stepping stones. But if it takes two years, you can't do that, and that was really why this whole thing came about.

IM: Okay: from the sublime to – the childlike. Itchy Coo. What prompted that?

JR: The idea came first. Matthew Fitt and myself had become good friends, subsequent to his being at Brownsbank. We got along very well, and we shared a lot of interests. We come from utterly different social backgrounds, but we had a shared interest in Scottish language, and we fundamentally agreed about some of the things that needed to be done to raise the profile of Scottish language in education. We had had to discover all this for ourselves. It wasn't just about the literature: it was about the language as well, because it was in the guidelines for the curriculum, the five-to-fourteen, that children should be encouraged to use the language they bring to school. This is a complete turn-around from punishing them.

IM: Is Matthew a teacher?

JR: He is a teacher. Matthew was aware of all this. He's a qualified teacher. Also involved was Susan Rennie, who was a lexicographer, and had a wide knowledge of Scottish language. The three of us had talked about what we might do to produce some good quality Scots language materials for schools. We were aware of things that had been done in the past: worthy efforts, but mostly one-offs. The people had done it purely for the love of it. Very often they hadn't had the money to produce good quality stuff, so it hadn't looked that great. They often couldn't afford to do reprints. There were all kinds of issues, and no continuity. We wanted continuity, and to produce a set of texts that would effectively take a child from pre-school right through to upper secondary. At every stage, there would be some material in Scots that they could access, and if we planned it properly, there would be links between these texts. When they got to reading Robert Burns for their recitations on the 25th of January, there would be a connection there between the language they used every day and this slightly strange and old-fashioned poem they were having to learn.

IM: Can I have a date in here?

JR: We were talking about this in the late 1990s, roughly 1997 to 2000.

IM: Well, we have reached the 26th of October, and the second tape with James Robertson, who has come to Aberdeen very kindly to do it, and we left him talking about the Itchy Coo project, which does everything from *A Scots Parliament* (2002), which I found actually very instructive, as well as pleasant, to *Eck the Bee* (with Ann Matheson, 2002), (L), which is not so instructive!. Say some more, James.

JR: In the year 2000 we went to the Arts Council, and they said they would run with this project if we applied for Lottery funding, and also if we went into partnership with a publisher. So we went into partnership with Black and White, publishing in Edinburgh. They supplied the expertise in terms of production, marketing and distribution of the books, and Matthew Fitt and myself primarily provided the editorial side of things, and Matthew was also going into schools, doing a lot of classroom and in-service work, so there was back-up support for the books: we didn't just bung them out into the ether and leave them to fend for themselves: we backed them up with quite a lot of teacher support, because that was very much required. The project started at the beginning of 2002, and ran for two years initially, and in that time we produced sixteen books –

IM: That's amazing!

JR: Which was an unbelievably ambitious number, and nearly killed us. (L) We were writing quite a lot of them as well as commissioning: we were doing everything. It was a very steep learning curve! Also I'd never been working with illustrated books, so there was a whole other dimension there of working with illustrators: it was exciting, but it was incredibly stressful as well. Somehow we managed to keep it on track and make it a success, and we subsequently had a bit more funding, so we managed to keep it going, and produce a couple of books a year. They range from very, very simple illustrated ABCs and counting books, these obviously aimed at the younger age groups, then working our way up to slightly more challenging ones, books with more words and fewer pictures. There are books of short stories and a couple of novellas, by the time you get to secondary level. The idea is that at each stage of schooling there are Scots language texts available to children, so that their language fits into some kind of continuum, and they don't come to the likes of Robert Burns and find it doesn't bear any relation to anything they've done before. Nobody would teach another language like that: let's learn French: here's Baudelaire. (L) There's a big anthology waiting for them at the end: it's called *The Smoky Smirr o Rain*, an anthology of Scots prose and poetry over six hundred years [*Ed Matthew Fitt and James Robertson, 2003*]. The idea is that this opens up the literature that by and large is closed to most people going through the Scottish education system. Things are better than they were, as far as access to Scots in schools is concerned, but you're still very dependent on the enthusiasm of individual teachers. We've got quite a long way to go before it becomes part of the structure, and inevitably it's problematic, particularly in secondary schools: they have to squeeze so much into the curriculum that they really are hard pressed to find space for this, but it's made a difference and we're pretty pleased with what we've managed to achieve so far.

IM: It must be hard sometimes to limit the amount of your energy you put into it.

JR: Certainly in the first two years, that was what I was doing for 75% of my time. Now I've managed to limit it to about 15 or 20% of my time. It's under control, and I'm determined that there is a limit as to how much time I can give that any more. But we've set something up that is not going to disappear again. There is now a body of work out there that the publishers and the schools want to keep. Whereas other Scots language books in the past have been one-offs that were around for a while and then disappeared, I think Itchy Coo will remain in print for the foreseeable future.

IM: Before we leave the topic completely, as I said, I found the book on the Scots parliament extremely useful, and I was going to ask how you came by the job of the three-day writer in residence to the Parliament.

JR: That really came from an approach by Scottish Book Trust. Mark Lambert, the director, was somebody I had worked with indirectly in the past. He was taking Scottish Book Trust into the Parliament for three days, under a scheme where charitable organisations can set up a stall so MSPs can see what they do. He thought they should take a writer with them, and the Parliament agreed, so he asked me, I think because he thought that the work I had done at various levels, particularly the Scottish historical side of things, would tie in with the start of a new phase in Scottish politics and history. I delivered three half-hour talks on the relationship between politics and literature, past and present, particularly in the Scottish context, and relating where the Parliament is located to that literary context. Basically I was trying to give MSPs and their staff some basic background on how Scottish literature has reflected politics over the years, and how politics has reflected literature, and so on. The three talks became three essays which became *Voyage of Intent*, and I also wrote this little series of sonnets as a result of the experience of being in the Parliament for three days. [*Voyage of Intent: Sonnets and Essays from the Scottish Parliament*, Scottish Book Trust with Luath Press, *2005*]

IM: And they were illustrated or decorated with some of Miralles' designs.

JR: Yes. I spent a lot of time with various people in the Parliament when I was there. I went in with an open mind about the Parliament building, the press had been so full of negatives, and I came away really feeling quite positive: this is actually a pretty amazing building, and it works! There's eleven hundred people working in there, and everyone I spoke to said this is the most incredibly brilliant building to work in, and it's got all kinds of interesting and elegant features: quite a stunning piece of architecture. So I came away thinking it was maybe time to be more positive about it. So the book is quite a positive take.

IM: Do you think there will be another writer in residence?

JR: I think there probably will be. I think everyone thought this experiment had been pretty successful. Next time it might be six months, rather than three days.

IM: Good. Well, let us turn the clock back, because when we start looking at your fiction, it is a question, to some extent at least, of going back to the history. The first of your books that I read, the first I came across, was *The Fanatic*. Tell me a bit about that, and what made you write it in two layers, from two different centuries at the same time.

JR: The reason for the two stories going on at two different periods is twofold. I'd started writing the nineteen-nineties story, about somebody who was a kind of misfit In the present day, but I didn't really know much more than that about what I was trying to do – creating a loner in Edinburgh, but I didn't know why he was a loner. And then while I was researching the Scottish Ghost Stories book, I came across the story of Major Thomas Weir, and decided that what I'd written about him in the *Scottish Ghost Stories* was only scratching the surface, so I went back and found out a bit more about Thomas Weir, and through Thomas Weir, I found out about James Mitchel, the Covenanter who is the principal character in the old story, the would-be assassin of the Archbishop of St Andrews. Mitchel seemed also to be an outsider, a loner, somebody who doesn't really fit properly into his own period in the seventeenth century. So I was juggling with these two misfits three hundred years apart, but also three hundred yards apart, in the sense that they both inhabit the same territory, which is Edinburgh's Old Town. These parallels began to emerge, and then these two parallel stories, linked by Major Weir, began to take shape.

IM: You say that James Mitchel is the main character in the historical bit: what does that mean for John Lauder?

JR: (L) Interesting, isn't it? John Lauder is the mechanism by which the story gets told, in a way, through the strange process by which his missing journal is located by this mysterious librarian who may or may not exist, Mr MacDonald. In some respects he's a mechanism to enable the reader to get into that story, but he does have a role. Part of it is to say, here I am, in the late seventeenth century, on the cusp of something old, an old world moving into a modern world. And he wants to be in that place where he can see back into the past and see into the future. So in a way John Lauder is somewhat playing the role that I as a writer was playing by joining these two stories up. To my mind John Lauder kind of plays the role that Archie Jamieson would play in *Joseph Knight*.

IM: I think you're grossly unfair to both of them, (L) because they're both a lot more than mechanisms, but I see what you mean. Does Lauder enunciate a very central question, when he's coming to this business about religion? He still believes, but his friend, whom I can't pronounce –

JR: John Eleis, pronounced Ellis.

IM: His friend doesn't believe, and he knows that, and he's really worried because you seem to either have to be a fanatic or an unbeliever. Is that a central question in the book?

JR: I think it is for John Lauder, and I suppose yes, in a sense that's one of the big questions in the book: can you be a moderate believer? (L) Or is it all or nothing? And I suppose that question keeps coming up in a whole range of different ways. The title, *The Fanatic*, doesn't just apply to James Mitchel: it can be applied to a number of characters for different reasons. I remember in a late stage of drafting, my editor, Leo Hollis of Fourth Estate, homing in on that conversation that John Lauder has with John Eleis, saying this is the crux of the book. He made me go and write that several times, to try to get that right. Are you obliged to take sides, or can you actually occupy some sort of middle ground? I think John Lauder wants to be able to occupy that middle ground, and needs to try and find out how to do it. So that is a big dilemma.

IM: It's almost as if he represents the twentieth century, which he knows is going to fall away from religious belief. This is a subject we come back to quite a lot in other books. And whether the absence of religion makes everything empty.

JR: Yeah. That's the sort of thing that occupies my mind quite a lot as well. If you take religion away... I didn't grow up in a particularly religious family background, but my schooling – the primary school – was intensely religious, so I grew up quite a devout wee Presbyterian, and then rather lost it in my teens. But the question is, if you don't have that religion in there at the start, can you still lead a life with certain moral standards, or does it all begin to fall away and go to shit? We are living pretty much in a post-religious age, or post-Christian age, and you wonder what effect that has on the way society conducts itself. Personally I would like to believe that we don't need religion, but I also worry sometimes that maybe we do.

IM: Or something.

JR: Or something, yes.

IM: Your twentieth-century characters don't lead spectacularly meaningful lives, do they, in *The Fanatic*?

JR: No, they don't.

IM: Hugh Hardie, that runs the ghost tours, and Jackie Halkit, who's a kind of lightweight publisher, and the amazing Andrew Carlin, who –

JR: Is very lost in the late twentieth century. Yes. It's almost as if they don't really know what they're here on this planet to do, whereas if you go back to the seventeenth century, people had a very definite idea (L) that they were here for various purposes. You could argue that these were all delusions, all manufactured purposes and hadn't any real basis in reality, but if the reality is that actually our lives are fairly meaningless, that's also a rather (L) depressing prospect.

IM: I think it would be perfectly possible for somebody to read *The Fanatic* and assume that the author is a religious believer.

JR: Ye-ah: I suppose it might (L).

IM: With some such message as, we really do need religion: we've just got to find a much better formulation.

JR: That's interesting: I suppose with all the books I try not to say, this is the message of this book –

IM: Oh, sure!

JR: But you're right; somebody could take that message out of *The Fanatic*. Hopefully they would take the message that religion as practised in the seventeenth century in Scotland was not a model we should necessarily follow (L), because of all the appalling behaviours that grew out of it to some extent. The very conclusion to *The Fanatic*, though: I did try to have a chink of light at the end there, when Andrew Carlin, having gone through all these various traumas in his own life, goes down to the beach at Portobello and almost learns to accept that he can actually let go of many of the things that have traumatised him over the years. And that all there is is himself, where he is, on planet earth standing beside the seaside, and that's OK. It's all right not to have the sense of purpose and so on that the Covenanters had in the past, and that he somehow felt he ought to have, but doesn't have. I suppose I was trying to say at the end, it's OK just to exist. But maybe that was more because I felt that Andrew Carlin needed that kind of therapeutic ending (L).

IM: I suppose the sceptic wonders how long it's going to last. So, why do you think, you by-passed Major Weir, for all that you give him a good run for his money, and concentrated much more on James Mitchel?

JR: James Mitchel became more interesting to me because he has this particular thing at the centre of his character: rightly or wrongly, he decides that he is going to take action, and he decides that he is going to kill somebody, because he believes that that is what he should do. Just as part of a fiction, I thought that was interesting, but of course this was based on historical fact. Let me go and investigate what would make somebody turn himself into an assassin in 1666, or whenever it was. Partly because that sort of stuff goes on all the time, and has gone on all the time in history, and is still going on. But that seemed to me to be the absolute turning point in Mitchel's life: he tries to kill the archbishop, and he fails, and everything in his life seems to have led up to that point, and everything subsequent to that point is bound up with it: the rest of his life is about how he will or will not escape punishment for that attempt. As for Major Weir: he had acted in many ways in the past, but he seems to me to represent more other people's fears and infatuations with witchcraft and other worlds and so on, and I rather feel he was more acted upon in some respects, although he himself obviously has acted upon his sister. What Major Weir does, it seems to me, is much more a series of private deeds, that until he bursts into the public scene are kind of contained within the relationship he has with his sister, whereas Mitchell's act of attempted assassination is very much a public political act. I suppose in a sense what Mitchel was trying to do interested me more. But then Weir's perversion, and the way his nature has become so twisted and horrible, is a manifestation of another way that somebody of his beliefs could go.

IM: He becomes a very evil kind of Deacon Brodie character. I half-thought that James Mitchel is capable of doubts and fears, and having human reactions to what he thinks it's his duty to do, whereas Weir sometimes seems not really human, not susceptible to my understanding.

JR: I think that's true up to a point, and then I think Weir begins to realise, particularly when he's languishing in prison, that he is actually equally susceptible to fears and doubts about what he'd done. When Mitchel's lying on the Bass Rock in prison, he's also remembering his former mentor Major Weir, and remembering where Weir went, as it were. I think he's frightened of going the same way.

IM: You have created them both as fully rounded characters, so they don't just stand for things. It's interesting that this is a historical novel: was your whole Scott reading and everything predisposing you to that?

JR: Definitely. Having done all the work on Scott, and having read Hogg and John Galt and the others, particularly those three, in relation to the Covenanters, I don't think there's any doubt that that's what made me start to write a historical novel. I suppose my historian's penchant for research got hold of me (L), and I did spend a long time digging up the most astonishing facts about Covenanting ministers and so on. The book was much longer than it is now, and fortunately my editor Leo Hollis forced me to remove some of that material, and I think there's still actually probably a little too much of it in there at times, but I was reluctant, having got hold of these wonderful stories, to let go of some of them. But there's no question at all that the novel is not so much a homage to Scott but a revisiting of the territory that Scott visits in his historical fiction. Particularly looking at the relationship between past and present, which I think is central to Scott's fiction, and I was trying to ask, is there any kind of relationship between these dark and strange days of the late seventeenth century and Scotland in the late twentieth century? There is, and I was trying to see what the relationship would be: how does the past still echo down to the present? And also, how does the present, if you like, influence the past, because the past only looks the way it does because of the way we see it.

IM: Tell me a bit more about your relationship with the editor, Leo Hollis. When did you get him on board; is he still on board, and how big an influence is he?

JR: I think I started writing the book about '96-7, and I finished an early version of it in about 1998, but I couldn't find a publisher. It did the rounds, and people said it's interesting or it's weird (L), but I couldn't persuade anybody to publish it. It ended up on the desk of an editor at Fourth Estate, who happened to have been a student at St Andrews University and who read the opening section of James Mitchel on the Bass Rock and said, ah, I know what this is about. So he read it, and he bought it, but passed the book on to a young, upcoming editor, and Leo and I got on very very well. Leo was from London or the south of England, and had no working knowledge of Scottish history, literature or anything else, and because he was coming from an outside position, I think he was able to see the wood for the trees in some of what I had written, because it was a mess at that point. I'd tried to include everything – this is the one book I'm going to write - so he was able to start unpicking it, and we had long conversations, and worked on it a long time. A lot of whether that book works or not is down to him. He enabled me to cut out some of the stuff that was extraneous, and to bring out the real main themes of the book. He then worked with me on *Joseph Knight*, almost up until the end, and then he left to go to another publisher, and I've not worked with him since, although I still keep in touch. So he was very important, certainly crucial as far as *The Fanatic* was concerned, and we worked well on those initial stages of *Joseph Knight*. But I think *Joseph Knight* needed much less editorial intervention, because I'd learned an awful lot from that first experience.

IM: Yes: without being at all rude to *The Fanatic*, there's such a huge leap between it and *Joseph Knight*. Perhaps we should turn to *Joseph Knight*, which after all won the Saltire Prize and brought you to the attention of all three of the Scottish reading public (L). I don't suppose it has sold enormously, has it?

JR: This is really weird. *The Fanatic* has actually sold much better than *Joseph Knight*. For some reason it was taken up and sold really well outside Scotland, which really surprised me. I think it has probably sold about fifty or sixty thousand copies. *Joseph Knight* hasn't sold anything like that number. But there's all kinds of factors there. Fourth Estate by that stage was part of Harper Collins, and I think the book was not pushed and sold as hard as it might have been. Part of the reason why I moved to Penguin was that it was a great shame, because *Joseph Knight* seemed to me to be eminently more saleable than *The Fanatic*. You're right: *Joseph Knight* has had the critical attention, but not the widespread readership that I would have hoped. But it's maybe a sleeper: I think the book will last, and hopefully reach that readership over the years.

IM: Oh yes. If it was coming out in a new edition, who would be doing it?

JR: That's an interesting question. It's still in print, and therefore at the moment it still belongs to Fourth Estate. We'll see what happens.

IM: What made you choose the case of Joseph Knight?

JR: I'd actually started writing the book that eventually would become *The Testament of Gideon Mack*. But then I got diverted, because somebody said to me, having read *The Fanatic*, have you ever heard of this court case of a slave fighting for his freedom through the Scottish courts? He handed me a photo-copy of a page out of a book on the history of Dundee, where Joseph Knight got a two-line mention. I'd never heard of this man, but I thought that does sound quite interesting. So I began to try and find out some more about the case. I couldn't find very much, but then I found references to it in Boswell's *Life* of Johnson, and I began to find one or two more references in a couple of books of histories of the slave trade, and then finally Angus Calder the historian, who knows a huge amount about African people living in the British Isles, and also about the history of Africa and its relationship to the slave trade, said, oh, Joseph Knight? You need to go here, here and here to find out more about this. So that opened up all kinds of doors.

JR: All kinds of doors, and then I discovered that in fact the record of the court case exists in the Advocates' Library. So I suddenly was presented with a whole wealth of material, and as I began to research this I thought, it was a story that was just there; I didn't even need to invent it, and it was to my mind the most fabulous story of somebody plucked from the West coast of Africa at the age of ten, taken across the Atlantic in a slave ship, and then uprooted from Jamaica ten years later and brought to Scotland. And this amazing man, about whom we don't know much at all, was somehow able to say, I'm not putting up with this any more, (L) I'm going to find a way of winning my liberty from these circumstances. I just think it's the most incredible story. So it was tailor-made for me: I didn't have to construct the story.

IM: You didn't have to construct the plot, but in fact an awful lot of your story seems to me to take place inside the head of Wedderburn.

JR: Yes. I suppose the problem was, how do I tell the story, because the obvious thing was to tell it from the point of view of Joseph Knight the slave, but I felt uneasy about that for various reasons. I didn't think I would be able convincingly to get inside the head of an eighteenth-century African, and I also thought that that presented a possible problem, that I would end up making Joseph Knight this heroic hero, fighting against the forces of evil on all sides, and that seemed to me to be possibly going to falsify the story. It seemed to me much more interesting to look at his story in the context of the Scotland of the Enlightenment and its relationship with the plantations in the West Indies that were actually fuelling the economy at that time. That seemed the real historical context, and when I began to build up a picture of that context I realised that it's not about heroes and villains in that strict black and white sense – if you'll excuse that phrase. There are shades of good and evil right across the board, so I tried to approach it from the point of view of someone you'd immediately think of as the villain of the piece, the slave owner, John Wedderburn. When I discovered that he had been a Jacobite who'd actually fought at the battle of Culloden as a sixteen-year-old, I thought, there's another dimension to this story as well. So it became clear that you couldn't tell this story successfully in that heroes-and –villains way: you had to visit the shades of good versus evil behaviour that existed in all the camps. I didn't want Joseph Knight himself to be only a good man to whom evil had been done. When you actually meet him, he doesn't come across as being a particularly saintly guy: I didn't want him to be. That was irrelevant. He shouldn't have been a slave. That was the point, and likewise, whether he was good or bad, John Wedderburn as a slave-owner, occupied a role that in the twentieth century is seen as wrong, though not in his own perspective. I suppose the whole book is about the fact that when you have an economic system like slavery everybody gets dragged into it, and everybody gets tainted by it, but it doesn't make everybody evil.

IM: No indeed; or you couldn't have what happens toward the end, with Susan Wedderburn, having had all the ups and downs and horrors and all the rest of it about slavery, ending up cleaving to her father and therefore deciding not to care about Joseph Knight or anything to do with him. It's not wicked in her: it's human.

JR: No, it's not wicked in her: it's human, and also she as a young woman in the early nineteenth century to some extent has her liberty curtailed, and therefore she is not free to act in the way that she might otherwise have done. There are all kinds of versions of slavery within that book, people who are fettered in different ways.

IM: After all, it's interesting: she's relatively given her head compared with a lot of young women of her day, and she's allowed to read all manner of rubbish, according to her father, but she isn't really very well educated; she hasn't really had access, from what we see of her teacher, to any kind of clear or rational education.

JR: That's absolutely right. She's been given the run of the library, but she's not been given any education in how to read.

IM: What about Joseph's wife, since we're on the ladies?

JR: Okay, Joseph's wife Ann Thomson, as with James Mitchel's wife Lizzie Sommervile in *The Fanatic*, is a genuine historical character, but because of the way history happens, we don't know very much about these women, because they are women of a certain class, and not considered to be important in the historical record. All that we really know about Ann Thomson is that she had two children by Joseph Knight, one of which died. We don't actually know if the other survived or not, but I let that child survive, and I also gave her another child as well, so by the end of the book they have a son and a daughter. I've had to think for myself as to what kind of person she was, and like Joseph I suspect that she must have been a pretty strong-willed woman, because it does appear that she stood by him. She married him, which was in itself quite a bold act, I suspect, in late eighteenth-century Scotland, and she stood by him and appears, certainly at the time of the court case, to have been very much on the scene, supporting his fight for freedom. That was really all the information I had to go on.

IM: The ending-up at Wemyss: is that your addition to the story, or do we know that any of that happened?

JR: No, that's invention. I suppose one of the things I was trying to do in this book was to provide a solution to the mystery of what happened to the real historical figure Joseph Knight, because all the evidence stops, immediately after the court case. We know that he wins the case. We know that he is basically a free man in 1778 once the Court of Session has made its decision. And then he vanishes from history: we know nothing more about him. Where would he go, such a man? The Scottish miners were almost in slavery, but were also emerging from slavery at this time, and we know historically that the miners did raise funds for other slaves. I thought, this in itself demonstrated that there was a sympathetic relationship going on there, so that made me think that perhaps if he also had been in receipt of help from the miners of Fife, perhaps he would have decided that that was actually a place he could go with his family to live. That's why I had him end up becoming a miner, but it's pure fiction on my part.

IM: Very, very appropriate, though, isn't it?

JR: It seemed to me that that was a place that was appropriate. There's a big chink of light at the end of the book, which is that having been through the terrible experiences that he has been through and having finally got to a place where he is a free man, he effectively chooses to go back into a sort of servitude, but it's on his own terms. A good result for him.

IM: But we're in danger, I think, of making Joseph himself too central to the book. By the time you'd finished building up John Wedderburn and his brothers, you could almost have the book without the court case or anything else, just about this wonderful split way in which the family – the brothers – can go off to Culloden and then make their pile in the most ruthless and heinous kind of way, and then come back and live such beautiful, hi-falutin', posh lives thereafter. It's an astonishing picture, an indictment of a whole historical fact.

JR: And again in a sense all I had to do was try to illustrate that, because that was how it was, and there's been a fair amount of work done on this. Certainly a number of Jacobites ended up elsewhere in the colonies and made fortunes and came back again. But it wasn't just Jacobites: there were lots of people leaving Scotland at that time and going to make their fortune in the colonies, and usually that was on the back of slave labour, and then return. The Wedderburn case is particularly interesting because they have to get out of the country for political reasons. Twenty years later the politics of Jacobitism are effectively dead, and they are not any longer considered a danger to the country, whereas their father had been horribly and brutally executed immediately after Culloden. They can come back and re-establish themselves. It makes you sit up and go, what kind of society is it that can allow that kind of 'repatriation', whilst still endorsing the brutalities of the plantations? Not even giving them a second thought.

IM: James, for example, particularly, the brother who rejoices in the black flesh. At least John Wedderburn is too Calvinist – or something - to enjoy himself with his female slaves.

JR: In a weird kind of way I think James Wedderburn is a more honest character than his brother John. James just goes, this is the system we're in. We're running the plantations here. I am going to exploit and make the most of it. I'm not a particularly nice guy, but this is what I am going to do. John is more hypocritical about it. Again, shades of behaviour there. James is more reprehensible in many ways, but he abuses people more honestly. (L)

IM: John's got hang-ups that James doesn't have, but that makes him a more interesting character, really.

JR: Makes John more interesting? Yes, I suppose that's why I homed in on him rather than James. He's thinking back over the sixty years of his life since Culloden. He can't bring himself to say to himself, actually, you haven't behaved very well, but that's almost what's going on in his head. Particularly his treatment of Joseph Knight, but by extension his treatment of all the other slaves has actually been wrong.

IM: The shameful brother Sandy – I take it you made up the journal?

JR: I made up the journal. The brothers all existed, but I wanted somebody else's perspective on what was going on. Sandy is this weak, miserable failure of a younger brother, really, and his journal just came out of nowhere in a way. I don't really understand the processes by which something like that happens, but suddenly I found that Sandy was writing a journal, and that solved lots of problems for me, letting me show Joseph Knight as a young boy there in Jamaica. You mentioned one could almost write this novel without Joseph Knight appearing in it, and the reason why I went on keeping him back until the end was because I was trying to address that issue of how he had disappeared from the historical record, and so in the novel he only gradually re-emerges from history. Angus Calder said, while I was writing it, he is a figure of darkness, a disappeared person, and what you are doing in this book is making him reappear. He's an absent figure for most of the book; we only see him through other people's eyes. We read about him in Sandy's journal; we hear about how John Wedderburn remembers him; but we only meet him in the last twenty pages of the book. That was obviously quite deliberate. I got criticised for that. One reviewer said, once again the black man has to wait until all the white people have spoken before he gets his say, and I thought, he's really missing the point (L).

IM: When the book was discussed by the Saltire Prize panel, we had arguments, and some people thought he should have happened earlier, but not in that simplistic way at all: just because they'd got so interested in him. But really, it's John Wedderburn's need for him: his ownership is such a strange but credible central passion, isn't it?

JR: Yes. Again, Leo Hollis helped me with this. You're right; there's this need that John Wedderburn has for Joseph. All the way through the book when I was writing it, I wasn't getting a hold of what that need was. I knew that that was what was in the core of that relationship, but Leo and I talked it through, and finally I realised that there had to be some scene that I hadn't written which would try to explain it, and that scene is near the end of the book when Joseph remembers them on the crossing from Jamaica to Scotland, when Joseph gets very, very sick and nearly dies, and John Wedderburn nurses him. They are alone. The master/slave relationship has gone on this ship, in this cabin, and he nurses him, and he's desperate he doesn't die, because if he dies, he will never be able to get rid of his guilt around the whole slave thing. At that point, it's him and Joseph, and they are two human beings together on this ship, and that seemed to me to be the core of it. At that moment, the need for Joseph to live is the only thing that matters to John Wedderburn, because if he dies, then any possibility of John Wedderburn managing to live with his guilt about all the other wrong things he has done in his life will go. Then of course, when they get to Scotland and Joseph does survive and gets better, that all recedes again in John Wedderburn's mind, and when Joseph decides he doesn't want to be a slave any more, Wedderburn, instead of going, this is my chance to expunge my feelings of guilt, actually digs his heels in and says, no you can't go; you are mine. It's only another twenty-five years later that when he is ostensibly searching for Joseph to find out what happened to him that all this stuff is coming to the surface again. Complex feelings.

IM: Yes. I also think that Archibald Jamieson is a lot more than a mechanism .

JR: He becomes much more than that, but that's where he starts. He's an invented character, this 'detective' who has to find out the story, and as I was doing the research, I was being a kind of detective myself, because I was digging up stuff that I don't think anybody else had looked at for a very long time. I began to think, I need a fictional character to do this for me. But you're right, as the book progressed he became less two-dimensional. As he learned more about this court case, and as he learned more about slavery, which is something he's not thought about ever before, then he is affected by it, and it changes him as a person. And then of course it makes him go and rethink things like his relationship with his wife.

IM: Which is very moving, I think, and very good. I think on the whole, whether out of modesty, you don't tend to present many big female characters.

JR: No. In the books I've written so far, there hasn't been a really major female character. I guess that's partly because the male characters have been to the fore. I'm aware that actually it's a pattern. I'd like to think that in some of the books I plan to write in the future there are going to be big female characters. But you're right. Mrs Archibald Jamieson plays a very small role at one point:

there's a couple of pages near the end where she is dying when actually it is her words that make the scales fall from Archie's eyes. And so she actually plays a crucial role, but it happens in a very short space of time.

IM: We're talking very much in the old-fashioned terms that literary critics wouldn't like, about character and so on, but *Joseph Knight* is an extraordinarily devious work in how you set things out, and how we learn about things, and who is telling the story, and when you actually look to see where did you hear about this trial, as often as not it's Archie telling his wife, totally unrealistically, so that the reader is on the one hand right up there in what's going on, but removed from a narrator completely.

JR: Yeah. I don't know how that fits with contemporary literary criticism (L), because I don't read it! That's not what I do as a writer. I think you can tell sometimes when you read a novel – I'm going to make a hugely sweeping statement here – you read novels by folk who've been on creative writing courses, and they've actually forgotten, it seems to me, every basic element of a good novel. It should actually have some good characters in it, and should tell a good story. Very often I find myself putting books down because I'm bored, because they've forgotten those basic elements. Yes, the narrative moves around: I think that's really interesting, and it's not new, absolutely not. But I find that interesting. The way that I told the whole court scene is very artificial, in that if you deconstruct it, it's Archie Jamieson telling his wife, but you know that and then you forget it.

IM: It's quite extraordinary, given how fed up the justices on the bench are and how they keep on saying hurry up, hurry up, Joseph's lawyers going word for word through really long speeches: did any critics or readers complain about that?

JR: No.

IM: I didn't mind it at all, but –

JR: They are long, long passages, and what I did there was I looked at the records. We don't actually have records of the day in court, what we have records of are the informations and the documents prepared by both legal counsels and presented to the Court of Session before the case was actually heard. I use that as the basis for those speeches, and I hopefully took out some things and dramatised others, but they are long, long speeches.

IM: But I thought you brought it off: it was interesting that you brought it off.

JR: I was worried about that, but I hoped that if anyone had got as far as that in reading the novel, by that point, they would want to hear what the arguments were on both sides. Also, although people have probably worked out that he is going to win his case, it's not a foregone conclusion, so there is a certain tension in these speeches. It helps to put in context all that has gone before in the way that enlightened Edinburgh is living on the backs of slave labour, that contradiction of Davy Hume talking about human society being a progressive and developing thing. While drinking the coffee that is produced by slaves.

IM: I think that it worked extraordinarily well, but it probably wouldn't work so well if the whole story were told directly. In fact an awful lot of it is told indirectly, one way or another, and that makes it interesting; it creates or recreates the process of research that you underwent as an author for the reader as well, 'by indirections find directions out.'

JR: I didn't realise until later that there is a similar big court scene in *The Fanatic*, which also involves quite big long speeches of various kinds. This was not deliberate, but if you actually look at those two books, there are very obvious similarities in the way that those stories are told, certainly subconscious on my part. Those two big court scenes: I was quite concerned that they might be too much, but they seem to have actually worked.

IM: But you don't have them in *The Testament of Gideon Mack*. Which is my cunning way of moving on to that one. I should explain to the tape that I have read it in a more or less finished state. You said 95% as it will be.

JR: I think I said I started this book after I had finished *The Fanatic*, and then got sidetracked by *Joseph Knight*. I put it aside for three or four years and came back to it. When I started it, it was not about a minister of the Church of Scotland, it was about a school teacher. Originally it was going to be about a teacher who was having a crisis of some kind, possibly of faith but probably not. What it's now become is the story of a Church of Scotland minister having a crisis of faith but in a sense a reverse crisis of faith. It's not a historical novel, but there's a lot of history in the background. One reason for not doing a historical novel was I thought it would be quicker. (L) Because I wouldn't have to do the research. But this has proved completely wrong, because of course there are no perameters in the way that there were in the other books, and so it's taken me just as long to write this. I didn't want to be pigeon-holed, as was beginning to happen, as a historical novelist. In other respects a lot of the same themes are revisited. But Gideon Mack is a minister who has not believed in God for a very long time, and then things begin to happen which make him question his non-belief.

IM: In fact he didn't believe in God when he became a minister. He becomes a minister despite the fact that he doesn't believe in God.

JR: And he's able to justify that for a number of reasons. He is the son of a minister himself, and so in a sense there's a career path for him, and he doesn't want to go that way, but then he decides it's as good a route as any, and he is persuaded by his girlfriend who becomes his wife that actually it's a perfectly reasonable thing to do, in the late twentieth century, to be a minister who doesn't believe in God. In a sense a minister is a kind of social worker with an extra dimension, but that extra dimension actually doesn't have to be that strong. And it appears to be okay for a long time, that he can actually function as a minister without having to believe in God at all. But then things begin to go wrong when an experience that is outwith his understanding of reality occurs, when he – he's a runner - he goes running for his exercise, and he's running through the woods, and he finds this standing stone in the woods where there has been no standing stone before. How has it got there? What does it mean? Is he the only person that can see it?

IM : When he plans to take its photograph it doesn't come out.

JR: So he's faced with what to him is a big problem: if it's there, then what does it mean? Does it mean that actually I've got this wrong? Much further on in the book that leads on to the fact that he had a narrow escape from drowning in a river, and is rescued by somebody who it turns out to be – or it appears to him to be the Devil, and this of course (L) is very problematic if you don't believe in God. So it's quite a different book. And I suppose what I'm doing there is revisiting some of my own thoughts about what happens when you have left religion behind and then it comes back and hits you again. How do we in a post-Christian society live with the residue of Christianity, and how do we live with the absolutely fundamental thing of God, who to all intents and purposes doesn't actually affect our lives at all, but may actually be out there after all. I suppose I'm playing with all those ideas.

IM: Is it going to be a best-seller?

JR: I have no idea. If I'm honest, I'm prepared for it to be quite roundly slagged. I really don't know how this is going to take. I have no idea, and I'm slightly nervous about it, because it's taken me quite a long time to write it, and I just don't know how it's going to be received.

IM: I wasn't at all suggesting it should be slagged: I just wonder how attractive the subject matter is going to be. The book has to be what the book has to be, but Jenkins, for example, was writing round and round and round religious ideas for a very long time, until he eventually managed to write *The Awakening of George Darroch*, where he actually got a minister in the cast, but apart from the fact that it fell off a lorry and disappeared, the book wasn't a great success either. It's not the most obvious topic.

JR: No, but then to some extent the topics choose themselves, and *The Fanatic* was absolutely not the book that one would say was going to be a best seller, and ended up selling very well.
Robertson 6

JR: ...selling very well. *Joseph Knight*, to me was a much more saleable book. Looking at what *Gideon Mack* is, I would not say, this is going to set the heather alight, but who knows?

IM: Tell me about its relationship with James Hogg.

JR: There's more than a passing nod at Hogg here. There's a found manuscript, and in terms of the structure it follows very closely the *Confessions of a Justified Sinner*, with an Editor's Introduction, then the found manuscript, which is the bulk of the book, and then there's an Editor's Epilogue, in which some of the loose ends are tied up, but not all of them. There are some phrases of Hogg's that are in the book, although I haven't been explicit about that, and that's there for people to find if they want.

IM: People who've been teaching the Hogg for years and years (L).

JR: Will probably jump on them, and that's fine. I'm revisiting that kind of territory, and obviously in the *Justified Sinner* there's a Devil character, who may or may not be a figment of Wringhim's imagination, and in his manuscript the narrator is not altogether reliable: similarly in Gideon Mack's narrative, the narrator is not necessarily reliable.

IM: There's all sorts of things that come up, even in the Epilogue, that cast big doubts over his story as we've had it, for example and most particularly, I suppose, he says that he only once had this fantastic love scene with his best friend's girl, his wife Elsie, whereas she later tells Harry Caithness that -

JR: That it went on for months. Yes, there are a whole lot of contradictions there, and characters in Gideon's narrative that one assumes are straight, like Captain Craigie: but it then transpires in the Epilogue that they may not have been as straight as we thought they were. Yes, I'm questioning everything. The question likely to arise is, what are you trying to say in this book, and the answer is, I'm not actually trying to say anything, but I'm trying to throw up all these issues and dilemmas that people think about, perhaps not very consciously, about the relationship between their everyday existence and the possibility of an afterlife, and all those questions are in there, and I'm not necessarily providing any answers, but I'm asking the questions – partly because I ask these questions myself all the time, and I don't have the answers.

IM: Yes, it's very much more a questioning book than an answering book. Do you like Gideon?

JR: Up to a point, and then he bugs the hell out of me (L). I've written it that way to an extent deliberately, but to an extent that's the way he came out on the page. He's hopelessly inadequate in many ways. He will not face up to some of the things that he should face up to in his own behaviour, and he's constantly making excuses for himself, about why he behaves in certain ways. So he's not likeable in that sense, but in other respects I empathise with his situation and his dilemmas.

IM: I think his account of his childhood puts us on his side right from the start, doesn't it?

JR Yes. I think one feels quite a lot of sympathy for that, but one then has to ask the question whether he's really telling the truth. (L)

IM: And one doesn't start asking that until much later. (L)

JR: Yes, one assumes that most of what he is saying about his mother and father is true, and as the author I can say that it probably is true! (L) We do feel quite a lot of sympathy for him for that very loveless and cold upbringing, which clearly had an effect on the way he leads the rest of his life.

IM: And his father's absolute horror of everything American, all the adventures on television and all the rest of it: the father is a pretty revolting character, isn't he? Just so cold and distant. It is raised I think by the Devil later on, that maybe he was having a problem all the time – or was it by his wife? Or both?

JR: Both! Both of them raised that problem. His wife, Gideon's mother, who is still alive for most of the book, although having lost many of her faculties: she raises the possibility that actually he was deeply affected by things that happened to him when he was a chaplain in the army, and the Devil raises the same issue and says that he had lost his faith, and absolutely could not possibly admit that to anybody. And that might explain some of his coldness, but he's not a likeable character: he's not modelled on anybody particularly, but there are elements of him that have come from the headmaster in my primary school, but only very slightly, and it's probably unfair to say that he in any way was a portrait of that man. But there are bits of him in there. That very cold disciplinarian attitude, and the idea that anything that is not useful is of no consequence whatsoever – decoration, art – none of these things have any real use, and therefore they can be disregarded. He seems to have stripped his life bare of everything except what is necessary to function, and that's because he has fixed his vision on God, and the next life. It's almost that this world is the trial you have to get through.

IM: And do your best to destroy your wife and son in the process. Almost an imposition of silence on Gideon's childhood, which is awful. If you compare him to the other minister who comes to mind whose war experience is supposed to have done the damage, that's Robert Colquhoun in *A Scots Quair*. For all Robert goes a bit bananas at the end, he's a relatively sympathetic and warm character.

JR: Absolutely: he's totally humane. And interestingly he gets a mention in the book too, when Gideon goes for the minister's position in Monymusk he takes a leaf out of Robert Colquhoun's book as to how he might preach to get the job, but he himself admits that Robert Colqhuhoun a fictional character, is actually more principled than he is, and fundamentally a better human being.

IM: What about Jenny? Jenny is the wife of Gideon, who as you say helps to persuade Gideon to become a minister, although he doesn't believe in God. That's relatively easy for her to do, because she doesn't believe in God, and she doesn't think it matters, and she doesn't go to church. But do you think she's there enough?

JR: She may be another of these female characters that actually I should have pushed a bit further.

IM: It's a sort of courtship dance early on, when the two boys at university meet the two girls and Gideon basically fancies Elsie, but it becomes clear that Elsie and John are there for each other, so Gideon settles for Jenny, which is a very cold-hearted thing to do, but then he is a bit cold-hearted, isn't he?

JR: What we don't get in this book, we don't hear it from Jenny's point of view. We get some of Elsie's viewpoint on what's happening later on: we never hear what Jenny thinks about all this, and that's because she's dead. There's a level at which maybe that does her a disservice, because you're right, (L) she's there – I shouldn't say this before the book's even published – but she's the character that is least explained and least fleshed-out of all of them.

IM: That is not necessarily an important criticism, because her part is minimal and what we get of her is from Gideon, and this is both the advantage and the disadvantage of the first person narrative. I don't think she comes much into the Prologue and Epilogue.

JR: Not at all.

IM: So you don't get another voice about her at all.

JR: Elsie occasionally mentions her, and effectively says, Gideon's take on Jenny was not the whole story.

IM: But let's hear it for the Devil, because he's a rather more important character.

JR: When I started the book, if you'd said to me, and at some point Gideon's going to fall into a river and meet the Devil, I would have said, don't be ridiculous: this was absolutely not part of the plan (L). I suppose as the parallel with Hogg began to come out, I thought, where is the Devil in all this? And it turned out that he was living underground not far away from the manse (L). The Devil in this book is actually not a bad guy, really. I feel a lot of sympathy for him. (L)

IM: You even manage to feel sympathy for God! The Devil says he got fed up and walked off a while ago: poor chap! (L)

JR: Yes, and the Devil's left asking, what am I supposed to do now. I've sympathy for both God and the Devil because they're redundant. We don't know where God's gone to, but the Devil's still hanging about, doing petty things, and messing with people's minds by sticking standing stones up in woods, but effectively he doesn't have a role any more.

IM: He says, I could heal people just as well as Jesus, but nobody asks me!

JR: In *The Fanatic* the devil is a malevolent being who gets inside

Major Weir's head and plays with him, and he undoubtedly represents evil, but in this book he doesn't represent evil: he just represents a human being that is redundant.

IM: An immensely talented human being, like Marlow's devil in *Dr Faustus*. He had so much going for him, and here he is – redundant.

Main books and pamphlets by JR, or JR with another, mentioned in the interview:

Close B&W 1991
The Ragged Man's Complaint B&W 1993
Scottish Ghost Stories Warner Books 1996
Dictionary of Scottish Quotations edited with Angela Cran Mainstream 1996
I Dream of Alfred Hitchcock (poetry) Kettillonia 1999
La a' Breitheanais: The Day o Judgment translated from the Gaelic of Dugald Buchanan into Scots (poetry) Kettillonia 1999
The Fanatic Fourth Estate 2000
Stirling Sonnets Kettillonia 2001
A Scots Parliament Itchy Coo 2002
Joseph Knight Fourth Estate 2003
The Smoky Smirr o Rain: A Scots Anthology compiled with Matthew Fitt Itchy Coo 2003
Voyage of Intent: Poems and Essays from the Scottish Parliament Scottish Book Trust with Luath Press 2005
Life Beneath the Shadow twelve short stories by JR in book of the exhibition by Cai Guo-Qiang Fruitmarket Gallery 2005
The Testament of Gideon Mack Hamish Hamilton 2006.

Ian Rankin

*I had met Ian Rankin only on a few literary-social occasions before
I asked him to agree to the interview process: he did, happily. He spoke
fluently and fast, with little need for prompting. We did the interviews
in his Edinburgh home.*

*I had a problem reading or re-reading whole oeuvre and
distinguishing between them on the hoof, and hereby apologise for
perhaps unnecessary intrusions of bracketed dates in the text. I find
it often hard immediately to connect text and title: Rankin's titles are
often magic or poetic sounding, and frequently echo Rolling Stones
album titles, rather than reminding one instantly of the plot! It can
also be hard to pin down the specific order in which the novels are to
be read, or at least are presented. So dates are often added: I've tried
not to average more than one per paragraph! It may be an advantage
to readers that when I interviewed him he had just written the text of
Rebus's Scotland. For this task, he had read through the whole of the
Rebus output, seeing many as if for the first time. Given the extent of
the undertaking, he is remembering well here (much better than me!!)*

*The code '(L)' here often means IR is deadpan, and making IM
laugh by his delivery*

IM: 2 June 2005, at Ian Rankin's home in Edinburgh. Present, Ian
Rankin and Isobel Murray. I want to start today as usual, by asking
Ian a bit about his childhood, youth, education; that sort of thing.

IR: You want me to start at the very beginning?

IM: Cardenden.

IR: A very good place to start. But back in 1960, when I was
born, there were four villages, very distinct villages; Auchterderran,
Bowhill, Cardenden and Dundonald, which were known as the
ABCD. I was actually born in a prefab in Cardenden, but before I
was one year old, the families were moved out of the prefabs, and
there were new SSHA (Scottish Special Housing Association)

houses that were built in Bowhill. So before the age of one I moved into 17 Craigmead Terrace, Bowhill, and stayed there until I left for university at eighteen. I was in that one mid-terraced house in a cul de sac for all my early years. That's where my parents stayed until my Mum died, and my Dad died, and somebody else rented it after them. It stopped being home when I went to uni, to the extent that I only went back at weekends. Also, I'd only been at uni a couple of months when my Mum took ill, and then she went downhill rapidly, and she died before I started my second year. So it's not a place that's got happy memories.

IM: What did she die of?

IR: I was never 100% sure about that. She was supposed to have had a stroke, and after that multiple sclerosis, and when she eventually died they said it was lung cancer, so I think that the people at the Victoria Hospital in Kirkcaldy didn't have a clue. My Dad was looking after her all the time, and the bed getting moved downstairs into the living room, and a commode coming into the house. Every time you went back – without being too melodramatic about it, it was like *The Exorcist*, when you go back into the bedroom and things have changed for the worse. That was how I felt; that I'd go from being this literature student who sat in Potterrow Bar talking about T S Eliot and Shakespeare, and suddenly jump on a train and have to be a son again, by the time I got back to Cardenden.

That I also had mixed feelings about, because I always felt, in that terrible working-class intellectual way, that I was never going to be understood there. Although it was the place that had nurtured me in the early days, I'd sort of moved away from the town now, and I wasn't able to go back to Cardenden and talk about T S Eliot and Shakespeare: I'd to start talking about football and religious bigotry, and what my pals were up to in the factories, or Rosyth Dockyard, where they worked. I'd to subdue or hide all that other part of myself, which was the main part of my life at the time. We do have these multiple personalities inside us, and the me who sits down to write a book isn't the same me who sits here with you, isn't the same me who goes out for a drink with my mates, isn't the same me who plays with my kids. They're all different facets of the same person. We're a lot more complex and devious, I think, than we like to think.

IM: That's for sure. Were you a close family?

IR: Yes; literally. Uncles and aunties; it was like a big tribe. The family had moved there I think in the twenties or thirties, from the west coast of Scotland, I think Lanarkshire. It was when coal was discovered in Cardenden, and the mines opened. And they threw up all these rows of houses very quickly. They didn't even bother giving the streets names: they just called them One Street, Two Street, Three Street. My Dad's family were in Seventeen Street. But his Dad didn't come back from the First World War, so my Gran – whom I never met; she was dead before I was born - had five boys and two girls to look after, which must have been hellish hard. So it was leaving school at fifteen, and most of them went down the pit. My Dad was the youngest, and he didn't go down the pits, he went to work in a grocer's shop, a small Fife chain. There was one in Lochgelly that he ended up running, for most of his working life. Then still in various shops around Cowdenbeath, Co-op groceries and things like that. And eventually he went and worked in Rosyth Dockyard, getting the maps ready for the submarines and boats.

He'd been married earlier, and had a daughter from that marriage, and then his wife died. My Mum meantime had been married to a guy from Lochgelly, and then he died, and that was how my parents met – my Mum used to go into the shop in Lochgelly. So they each had a daughter from a previous marriage, so they were in their forties when they got married, and of course I came along soon after. My parents were a lot older than other people's parents, when I was at school.

IM: What about the ready-made sisters? Did they spoil you rotten?

IR: Not rotten. My oldest sister Maureen was married the year I was born, so there was a big gap between us, fifteen or sixteen years, and it was seven or eight years between me and my next sister, Linda. So when I was twelve, Linda got married and left home. We are pretty close: we phone each other up all the time. So we're fairly close, despite – or because of – the age gap, because there was never any competition.

IM: But it did leave you as the son of rather older parents, and the brother of rather older sisters, as a loner, from day one?

IR: I don't think of myself as having been a loner – I used to have mates: there were lots of kids around. But I always felt a wee bit different; going into my early teens, I would much rather spend time in my bedroom, listening to music and writing lyrics and poems, than hang around, but I was very good at looking like I fitted in. I would hang around the street corner, with the local gang, except when they said, right, we're going to fight the Lochgelly kids, we've arranged to meet them at the Brae to have a fight. At that point I would peel off and go home again. I was chameleon-like.

IM: So when you went to school, was that an enjoyable experience?

IR: Dunend Primary School was my first school – yes, it was. I loved it. I used to walk there and walk back, and both parents were working: my Mum worked in a school canteen, and then later on in a factory canteen, dishing up meals. The auntie who lived two doors away would give me my lunch, and then I would walk back to school again. Yes, I remember primary school being a lot of fun. The first two years of secondary school maybe not so much, because there was that two years at the Junior High, Auchterdearn, which was a school that only took kids up to sixteen, so they only did their O grades and that was the end of it.

At the end of the second year you got cherry-picked, so that a certain number of kids, who had the best marks, were told that they could go up to Beath High School, Cowdenbeath. It was a bus ride away; it was two towns further over, and it meant getting up a bit earlier, and it meant wearing a blazer. So ironically there were kids who decided not to go, given that choice. Brainy kids, brainy working-class kids, who said, I don't fancy that; I'm going to stay here with my mates. But I actually was looking forward to it, because by then it was clear to me that my interests were not necessarily the interests of the kids around me. I wasn't interested in going down to the park and playing football: I was interested in sitting writing song lyrics and listening to progressive rock music. I thought, if I go up to this other school, maybe I'll meet people who are more like me. And that happened. So it was a good move.

IM: Were you already reading, as well as writing?

IR: Oh yes! As soon as I could start reading I read comics, everything from the *Beano* and the *Dandy* when I must have been four or five, up through the *Topper* and the *Beezer*, to the *Victor* and the *Hotspur*. And my parents would buy me all those comics like *Look and Learn*, and *Tell Me Why*, that were supposed to be educational. I didn't like that: I wanted war and guts and glory. And I used to try to write and draw these comics myself. I'd get bits of paper and try and draw comic strips, but I was not very good at drawing. But right from the word go, I wasn't just interested in reading: I was interested in trying to create my own little universes, and play creator.

I went from comics to books quite quickly; we didn't have many books in the house, but come the summer holidays you always went down to Kirkcaldy, to John Menzies, to buy some books to take away on summer holiday with you. There weren't many kids' books that I remember: I went through the Ladybirds, and Bible story books: I did some Enid Blytons, but there was a big gap between Enid Blyton and teenage stuff. So what I tended to buy were TV tie-ins. And I would haunt the library – there was a library at Bowhill which had been set up with money from the miners – and I just haunted that place.

When I was at High School, they'd say, what are you going to be when you grow up? I had one 'uncle' who lived in Bradford and was a Chartered Accountant. My Mum had been born and brought up in Bradford. He had a car, and they owned their own house: they had a bungalow. I just thought, I want some of that. So I decided I was going to be a Chartered Accountant as well. I was going to go to Edinburgh University and study Accountancy.

IM: You were fancying going on with all your interests on the side, financing rather a fine lifestyle?

IR: Yeah - that's what the working class thought you went to university for, was to get a career. A profession. It was a weird sort of upbringing, to the extent that we were on the fringes of people who were in relative terms quite well off. The family my Mum's first husband belonged to in Lochgelly were actually the bees' knees in the town. The guy who ran the bank in Lochgelly was an uncle of mine: another uncle ran the local newspaper, *The Lochgelly Times*, and was a Justice of the Peace and a Freeman of the town, and all the rest of it. At weekends we would sometimes go up there, and they owned their own house, and they had a car. We were really uptight about it. My parents used to get really fractious about not making mistakes, and not looking like the poor relatives, really. It was a time of fur coats. Your Mum would wear a fur coat to go up to Lochgelly on a Sunday afternoon to sit and have a bit of cake with your Aunty Jenny.

One of the first short stories I ever had any success with was actually based on my Uncle Jack. He'd been an alcoholic, and probably still was when I knew him, I just didn't know. In the early twentieth century, taking all his clother off and walking through the streets, and because of who he was, everyone pretended this was quite normal practice. So I wrote a story when I was at uni called 'Walking Naked', which came first in a Radio Forth short story competition, and then my Aunt Jenny went absolutely ballistic.

IM: I'm not surprised! (L) What Highers were you going for?

IR: Let me think. English. I got about six Highers. In the summer I used to go and stay with my sister. I'd to go to the phonebox and phone my Mum to find out my results of my Highers. And I'd only got a C for my Higher Economics. So I went back, and I sat. I'd got an A for Geography, an A for English, a B for Chemistry, a C for German and a C for Economics. It didn't take me very long to realise, look, what I really like is English. And I'm really good at it. Why am I not going to uni and doing that? So it was getting that C in Economics that really made me think, why am I doing this?

IM: Good!

IR: Yes. So there was this sort of Road to Damascus moment. Then I had to go back to Scotland and tell my Mum and Dad. She'd bought me all these secondhand Accountancy books from somebody she knew at work. Then I had this huge empty timetable: I did Sixth Year Studies English, and I did Higher German and O level Latin, and that was all I did in my last year at school. I did love sixth year English, though. That was a nice bedding in for doing English at university. It was like doing tutorials. There were only five or six of us, plus this really enthusiastic teacher. But it didn't prepare you for lectures and stuff.

IM: (L) I don't think anything does!

IR: It didn't really prepare you for tutorials, now I think about it, because it's one thing to sit with your mates that you've been at school with your whole life, and sit talking about books, but sitting in a room with mostly English-educated students at Edinburgh, who're all very yappy, because they've been through the A level system, which makes them very confident and yappy. And all the Scots were sitting there, writing everything down, because that's how we went through school, we just wrote down everything anybody said, and then later on we'd maybe sculpt it into an essay. (L) So it was a very different way of being taught, and it took me a long time to come out of my shell at university.

At Edinburgh you do English Language and Literature, so that's your two main subjects.

IM: So what did you make of English Language?

IR: Ah, Jesus! Oh, God! (L) You did Middle English in first year – trying to read Chaucer in the original. And in second year I think we did Old English, which was even worse – thorns and things, oh, God! That to me was just-

IM: Just something you had to thole?

IR: Yeah, but English Literature was just something I had to thole too! Because what I was really interested in was modern literature. All the stuff I'd been reading – *One Flew Over the Cuckoo's Nest*, *Catch 22*, *Clockwork Orange* – these were mostly American books, and mostly post-war. In my last summer holidays I'd read Jack Kerouac, the Beat stuff, I loved them all. And then suddenly to go into English Literature 1, where you're doing a bit of Wordsworth, and a bit of Shakespeare, and a bit of Milton and stuff. And in second year you were only doing five authors: it was Pope, Wordsworth, Shakespeare, Hardy and somebody else. Oh my God, it was really, really tedious. I was desperately trying to get through this to get to third year where you get to choose, and I was going to specialise in American Literature.

IM: I notice still no Scottish stuff in the first two years?

IR: No, none. By that time they had just introduced a Scottish Literature 1, or they were just about to. So there was a possibility to do a year's worth of Scottish Lit. But there were precious few people teaching you who were actually Scottish! There was Ronnie Jack and Ian Campbell. But a lot of the guys we had – Geoffrey Carnall, Ken Fielding, Wallace Robson, and what was the Regius Professor's name? Was it Fowler?

IM: Alastair Fowler.

IR: Okay, he isn't English, but my God, he seemed it! (L) There was very little interest in Scottish, apart from really dry stuff like

Carlyle: you could get a very enthusiastic lecture on Carlyle if you wanted. Or Scott. (L) And I wasn't that interested. I was interested in American lit: I thought that was where all the good stuff was happening.

IM: So American was where you felt it was at?

IR: TV, films, music and books, it seemed all Americanised at that time. It seemed like a much more glamorous life than the life I was living in Cardenden. Or indeed in Edinburgh. So I was quite happy at the end of it at Edinburgh. I struggled through the first two years, doing stuff I didn't really want to do, to get to what I really did want to do, which was American lit, and then there was this great release when I got in, and suddenly you were studying stuff you really wanted to do.

IM: Like?

IR: We did a lot of people like Saul Bellow, and we did Heller, and we did Thomas Pyncheon, and we did Robert Lowell, and William Carlos Williams, who was my favourite poet at the time, and we did lots of older stuff. *House of the Seven Gables...*

IM: *Moby Dick*?

IR: As long as you skip the whale bits in *Moby Dick*, you're fine. (L) Just skip all the stuff about whaling and history, and get to the real meat of the story. They should have a condensed *Moby Dick*; that would be fantastic. We did the Great American Novel. The American Lit department was small and pro-active, and so Colin Nicholson, who was my tutor there, would introduce you to lots of writers, and you'd go to the pub after every tutorial, and you'd always end up talking to people from the History Department, the French Department; there'd be a few writers hanging around, a few poets.

I was in the Poetry Society at that time, and we got given money, basically to have poets come and talk to us, which was just fantastic. So every week you'd a different poet come along, talk to you, read out some poems, then you'd take him to the pub, and you'd get to quiz them, and grill them, and all the rest of it. And the other thing was all these wee literary magazines that were starting about that time: *Edinburgh Review* was undergoing a slight renaissance; *Cencrastus* came along at that time, and it published some of my earliest work. And Allan Massie was Writer in Residence for a year. The Writer in Residence changed every year, and most years it was poets, and by then I'd almost stopped writing poetry. I went to see Peter Porter, and John Herdman, but when Allan Massie came along that was great, because he was actually a fiction writer. I was moving into fiction, so I was taking him short stories, and would-be novels that would never come to fruition. He was the judge in the first ever short story competition I entered. He gave me second prize.

IM: Who got the first prize?

IR: Iain Crichton Smith. (L) So it's not bad. It was run by *The Scotsman*, so *The Scotsman* published the winning stories. So I was actually in print in *The Scotsman*. But that was postgrad.

IM: So your two Honours years are fun, it's all-American, basically?

IR: No, you didn't just do American; you did a course in Shakespeare. You came together with other students in the MA to do certain core subjects like Shakespeare – you did a whole term on him. I forget what the core subjects were. And you were still doing English Language.

IM: Even in Honours years?

IR: Yes, because it was an MA that was in English Language and Literature. So you were still having to do structural grammar and all the rest of it – Noam Chomsky and all that lot.

IM: So: did you have Finals, or was it a cumulative thing?

IR: You had Finals. Summer of '82, I had all my Finals. Lots and lots of three-hour papers.

IM: Did it appal you or inspire you?

IR: Mostly it was all right. I crammed like hell for it, and just missed getting a First. I think two folk got Firsts in my year, and there were about six of us that were champing at the bit, but they weren't going to give out eight Firsts. That would have cheapened it. So instead they gave out two, and the rest of us were borderline Two Ones. But I was very pleased with that, and then (L) headed off into the world of work, aged twenty-two.

IM: Were you at that stage interested in doing the postgraduate thing?

IR: I don't think so. I came to the end of that course and hadn't a clue what I was going to do with this. Miranda, who was a year above me at uni, doing English – American – she'd left the year before, she'd worked in bookshops in Edinburgh, and various bits and pieces. She'd headed off to France to work in a kind of co-operative vineyard. So the first thing I did when I'd finished my final exam was to head down to France to meet up with her. So I spent the first six months after graduation in France.

IM: That helps to explain how the pair of you later managed to disappear to France. I've always thought, my goodness, that was brave!

IR: We spent about six months down there, doing various things. We hitch-hiked around France and Italy, and we worked at Shakespeare & Company in Paris for a wee while, because when Miranda was a teenager she'd headed off to Paris on her own and worked there briefly, so she knew the guy that ran it. We got the kind of hippy, Kerouac-y thing out of our systems, came back to

Edinburgh in the winter of '82. What the hell do I do now? I got a room in a high-rise block in Oxgangs, and I had a series of bumming-around jobs, doing bits of research, like this alcohol study that was going on. But it was just dead end stuff.

IM: You weren't thinking in terms of career, because you still didn't know what?

IR: The thing was, I'd gone into English because I liked English, but I came out thinking, what do you do with this? I didn't want to be a high school teacher: I did fancy being a university teacher, but I knew you couldn't be a university teacher without a PhD. That must have been when I started thinking about applying for the PhD.

IM: (L) So what did you fancy about your idea at that time of being a university teacher?

IR: Well it seemed to me they had a pretty good job: they just sat there and talked about books all day, then went to the pub! (L) And talked about books a bit more. I did want to be a writer; I was doing my own writing. But I knew you couldn't do it full time. All the poets I met had other jobs, or were subsidised by the state, the Scottish Arts Council. Writers I met were librarians, they were teachers, they were university lecturers; they had other jobs. I thought, if I'm at uni, I can be a lecturer, but I can also have time to do my writing. So that was all part of this great idea of trying to get the money to do a PhD.

IM: Do you remember your title?

IR: Yes. It was 'The Novels of Muriel Spark: A Poststructuralist Critique' – God knows what it was. Something that was going to get me the money for three years. The man told me, there's precious few PhDs on Muriel Spark: he was right. So there was a big gap to fill. There was one skinny wee book by Allan Massie on Muriel Spark, and that was about all there was. One of the problems I had was that I never did pin it down. Having got the three years grant money, I said, right, what I'm going to do is write my own stuff for three years. This is a golden opportunity, just to sit in the library and write my own books and short stories. And do enough work on the thesis for them not to kick me out.

IM: But you did know sooner or later that you were not likely to finish the thesis?

IR: I think fairly early on. I knew a lot of people who never finished their theses (L), and I came to the conclusion that even with the PhD you didn't just walk into a job as a professor at a university. The guys I was meeting who were on one year contracts, part time work, these were people who had good PhDs, and they were just scratching along. I felt, I don't want that: I loved the idea of university as a safety-net, but that safety-net had just gone. I was much more interested in writing short stories and novels. The very first short story I wrote won that second prize in that *Scotsman* competition. That was about '83. The next year I won first prize in a Radio Forth competition, with the one about my uncle walking naked through the streets: it was called 'Walking Naked', a line from Yeats.

IM: Something that was bypassed somehow in my notes: you were ill when you were nineteen? Undiagnosed spinal meningitis?

IR: My Mum worked at this factory canteen, and she got me a holiday job working in the chicken hatchery. She died in February '79, and summer '79 I went back to the chicken factory to work, so it was the end of first year at uni. I ended up getting spinal meningitis.

IM: Sounds horrible.

IR: Yeah, it wasn't diagnosed for ages and ages, I just had this thumping headache that wouldn't go away. Doctors were giving me migraine tablets, and that wasn't doing any good. I was throwing up, and eventually got to the stage when I just couldn't get out of bed. My Dad, having just a few months before lost his wife, was up to high doh. God bless him, he was putting vinegar compresses on my forehead, because that's what his mum used to do. I was lying in bed reeking like a bloody fish and chip shop. We got the doctor in for another look, and he asked, can you sit up? I sat up, and said, oh, my back's really stiff. Oh, it sounds like meningitis. He said, has anybody at your work had meningitis? Yeah, there's a guy just had meningitis recently. I hadn't thought to say that to him: I didn't know what meningitis was. So he phoned the ambulance and I got taken straight to hospital, and I got a lumbar puncture. At the same time I picked up – what's that food-poisoning thing you get from chicken?

IM: Salmonella?

IR: Yeah: I got salmonella as well, so I was in a bad way. I just had to lie in hospital in isolation, in a ward on my own for a couple of weeks, in this belting hot summer, with all my pre-second year reading to do. So I was trying to read bloody Chaucer, having just had a spinal tap (L) Yeah: that was kind of grim.

IM: Back there, when you were finishing the PhD money, what next?

IR: Oh, God! The PhD money ran out in June,1986, by which time *The Flood*, the first novel, had been published. That was in February. And I'd finished *Knots & Crosses* [1987], the first Rebus novel. And that had been accepted by Bodley Head in London. And I had an agent, who was based in Glasgow. And I got married in July '86 to Miranda. She was working in London at that time as a Civil Servant, so I just packed my bags and headed down to London.

IM: Was she a civil servant because she really wanted to be, or. . . ?

IR: Mostly because it was the only job she could get. But she passed all these exams and got into the fast stream, so very quickly she was running a Minister's private office. But she was working all the hours God sends – like something out of *The West Wing*. (L)

I don't think we got anything out of London, really, because we weren't earning enough money. We had a one-bedroom maisonette in Tottenham. If you've got a lot of money, and you're living in the West End of London, I think it could be a very exciting experience: but if you're living in Tottenham, it's another London you're seeing. And when I first got there I wasn't working: Miranda was prepared to support me while I tried to be a fulltime writer. But I was making almost no money. *Knots and Crosses*, the first Rebus book I wrote – I got less than a thousand pounds for it.

In 1985 Willie McIlvanney was at the Book Festival. I went up to him and said, I've just finished a novel which is a bit like *Laidlaw*, but set in Edinburgh, and when he signed my copy of *Docherty*, he wrote, good luck with the Edinburgh Laidlaw.

IM: How important do you think Willie's books were to opening up the world of Rebus for you?

IR: They were very important, in that he was a self made, self taught man of pairts who was working-class, and was writing about issues of masculinity in post-industrial Scotland, which I was going to try to write about, having lived through it, with the coal-mines in Fife shutting down, and the sense of desperation that took hold of Cardenden in the sixties. I went through that whole period. When I was born, up to the age of six or seven, the local coal-mine was the biggest employer. You'd see guys going to the pit. You'd hear the klaxon going for the end of the shift. There were three shifts a day: they worked night shift, day shift, back shift, working all the hours God sends. And then suddenly it was over. The klaxon stopped going in the mid-sixties and that was the end of it There was a sense of hope went out of the village to a certain extent. Folk scrambling, trying to get jobs. The stuff Willie was writing about was stuff I could immediately latch on to: but of course he was just part of this huge exciting thing that happened.

Suddenly you had this whole Glasgow scene came along with James Kelman and Alasdair Gray – and Kelman's first two books were published by Polygon, a small press set up by Edinburgh University students, and run by Edinburgh University students, and because they'd had a success with Kelman's first book of short stories, and because they were publishing his first novel, they started looking for other young novelists. They published three new writers, and I was one of them. That was very exciting. It was great times. You had all these literary magazines that were springing up. It seemed like most of the writers were still Glasgow-based. It was always Alasdair Gray and Jim Kelman, and Liz Lochhead, and McIlvanney – they all seemed to be west coast writers. The east coast seemed to be Muriel Spark, Allan Massie – it was a different kind of book. (L)

IM: And your response to that was, I can write about much of the same subject matter, but I can be an Edinburgh novelist, and write from where I am?

IR: I just thought, Edinburgh's not been covered by Miss Jean Brodie: there's room for more books, and why haven't there been more books about Edinburgh? I just couldn't find novels about Edinburgh, from about 1961 when Jean Brodie was published. There were plenty poets, plenty playwrights, but there didn't seem to be a novel-writing scene at that moment. Edinburgh was a city I was fascinated by: all the stuff I'd done on Spark, all the reading I'd done around Spark, about Deacon Brodie, which took me to Edinburgh history, which took me to Robert Louis Stevenson, which took me to *Justified Sinner*, which took me to Calvinism, which took me to Scottish history – I thought, all of that is all contained in a small city. This is a fascinating city to write about: I should write about Edinburgh in contemporary terms. But the first book, *The Flood* [1986], was about Cardenden, really, where I grew up, but mythologizing it. It was an old-fashioned kind of Scottish book in a way; it was the sort of thing that Robin Jenkins or Neil Gunn would have done – trying to bring a magical realism, a mythology to this fairly desperate town. This town is going through industrial decay and blight.

IM: And the image of the burn –

IR: Aye, the hot burn. Which is something that happened to my aunty, according to my Dad. It was a story from our family history that as a young girl she'd fallen into the burn, and it was water coming down from the coal-washing plant, so it was actually hot. And she'd fallen into it, and somebody had grabbed her by the braid of hair at the back of her neck and pulled her out. And that was all it started with. It was going to be a short story about that incident, and somehow it just spiralled. I got to twenty pages, and thought, what am I going to do with this? It's too long – I canny give it to *Cencrastus*, canny give it to the BBC for their Morning Story slot that they used to have on the radio. I just wrote, Chapter One, and just kept going. (L)

IM: As I remember, I've only come across one case where you used material twice, when you wrote a short story about the disappearance of Damon Mee, and then you used it again in a novel. [*See the novella* Death Is Not The End *1998, and* A Question of Blood *2003*]

IR: Cannibalised it? There was a good reason for doing that. I wrote that novella specifically for an American bookseller, who wanted to get a new imprint going, of novellas, sold at a dollar a time. And he asked about a dozen crime writers to give him novellas, which we did, and then he couldn't get it off the ground. I thought, bugger me, that's never going to get published: I'd better use it. So that's why I did what Raymond Chandler would have done; he cannibalised a lot of short stories for his novels.

IM: Before I leave McIlvanney's example completely, my impression was that it was basically *Laidlaw* that struck you. [*Published in 1978,* Laidlaw *was an unexpected crime novel from a 'serious' writer.*]

IR: It was definitely the first one. I wasn't aware of any Scottish crime writing that I could read to become part of a tradition. There was no Scottish equivalent to Agatha Christie. There were plenty of thriller writers – John Buchan, people like that, if you wanted to look at a Scottish tradition of adventure; or Alistair MacLean. But I didn't think of myself as writing in the tradition of any of those guys.

IM: No. But I felt that *Laidlaw* by itself was the book that had affected you,

IR: Except I didn't believe in any cop who was thinking about Kierkegaard while he cleaned his teeth in the morning! (L)

IM: Absolutely, but on the other hand, what was it Gill Plain said somewhere about Rebus being a private investigator inside the polis? [*Gill Plain, Ian Rankin's "Black and Blue": A Reader's Guide 2002, p 38*] In that sense...

IR: But he's more a private investigator inside the police, because I'd no idea how the police worked! So he had to be a maverick: he couldn't be part of the system if I didn't know what the system was.

IM: Indeed. But Laidlaw was a maverick too, and so they had that in common.

IR: Very few crime writers, successful ones, have been cops or private eyes themselves. The reason that they make their cops either amateurs, in the British tradition, or private eyes in the American tradition, is because you don't need to know how the cops work. You don't have to do any research on how the police work.

IM: I had a vague feeling that John Rhodes, McIlvanney's hard man, might have just been something that went towards the creation –

IR: Of Cafferty? Naw. No, Cafferty was a *homage* to an American writer called Lawrence Block, who has a New York detective called

Matt Scudder, who's an alcoholic. He's left the force and become a private eye. [*Block on Scudder: 'In the early books, he's an angst-ridden hard-drinking ex-cop and unlicensed private eye. In later books he's sober. He's twenty-five years older than when I first started writing about him, and he's gone through changes, even as you and I.' The series, still going, began in 1976.*] I really got into the Matt Scudder novels in the late '80s, and he's got this villain whose name escapes me now, but he's nicknamed The Butcher Boy. He wears a butcher's apron, his dad's butcher's apron, whenever he beats people up to a pulp or kills them. And the relationship between Scudder and this villain is very much Rebus and Cafferty. Cafferty came into the series: he's a cameo in book three [_Tooth & Nail_ 1992] - he's only in it for about two lines – he's just another Glasgow gangster that Rebus is trying to put away. He's giving evidence against him; he's not a Glasgow gangster, but the trial's in Glasgow. And then he just got underneath my skin: I thought, there's a load I can do with this guy, especially sparking off Rebus. Because he has similar mentality, similar class, similar age; and both of them feel a bit like dinosaurs , coming to the end of their useful life, and younger and more ruthless and more careerist people are coming up after them. So to that extent I thought they're almost like Cain and Abel: you're never sure whether they're going to be like brothers or kill each other. Could go either way.

IM: If you finish the Rebus books, will you somehow finish Cafferty?

IR: I don't know how the Rebus books are going to end yet. I don't know if it's going to end with Rebus and Cafferty going over the Reichenbach Falls (L), or sitting having a drink in a pub and a good old singsong. Or Rebus getting happily married to somebody with Cafferty the best man. (L) There's all kinds of ways it could go.

IM: Oh well, we will see.
How much Ian Rankin is there in this book you've just finished, *Rebus's Scotland*? [2005] How did it start?

IR: It started with the photographers who do the jackets, Ross and Trish. They were the University's official photographers. I did a short story about Conan Doyle for the University a few years ago, called "The Acid Test", and when they sent me a copy of the magazine, there was this fantastic, moody, black-and-white photograph of Old College; and I immediately went wow, and sent it to my publishers in London: and they said wow, and they contacted Ross and Trish, and said, can we nick this for, I think it was *Dead Souls* [1999], the paperback. The publisher asked, have you any more nice moody photographs of Edinburgh? – and so they became my official photographers. Eventually they left the University and set up their own company called Broad Daylight, and are working very happily together. It was they who came up with the idea of a photographic book to go with the series, mostly for people who don't know Edinburgh that well. And so it's going to be lots of moody black-and-white photographs of Edinburgh. I was going to do a foreword or an introduction to it, so then we took the proposal to Orion, my publisher, who said, what about a nice big book about Rebus's Edinburgh? I said, it's not a big enough subject: what about Rebus's Scotland? Ross and Trish had some great photographs that weren't Edinburgh – they were Glasgow, the Borders, the Highlands: I said, it'd be great to use these. So it suddenly became Rebus's Scotland. At that point it was still mainly a photographic book, but when we did the deal, it turned out I was going to have to write 30,000 words of text. It's basically just my autobiography, because it's where Rebus comes from, and Rebus comes from me, which means telling you something about me, and about Cardenden, where he and I grew up. It's a series of mini-essays; there's Rebus in Edinburgh, there's Rebus and the rest of Scotland, religion, politics, booze, music – about eight essays.

IM: Anything about oil?

IR: Yes, there's a bit about oil.

IM: Did you do a lot of oil research for *Black and Blue*? [1997]

IR: I did tons. That was the first Rebus novel where I actually did lots and lots of research before I wrote the book. The early ones were mostly made up on the hoof, but this one. . . I went up to Aberdeen; - I was living in France at the time. A lot of what I did was to write to oil companies and get them to send me their literature. But I mooched around Aberdeen. I didn't go to Shetland. I wrote about Shetland without having gone there; I wrote about an oil rig without having gone to an oil rig.

IM: It's very convincing.

IR: I was kind of lucky. I spoke to a lot of oil workers on trains to and from Aberdeen. Drunken oil workers who were happy to talk to you about it. And also I knew a guy up there called Bill Kirton. And Bill Kirton is a crime writer, but also has worked in the oil industry; and he had videos, of helicopter flights and lots around the oil rigs, and that was great, sitting watching those. So in the end I didn't feel I needed to go out to the rig. And I didn't get permission anyway. You need to do all the safety stuff first, which means being dumped into a tank of water at Robert Gordon's. I didnae fancy being strapped into a fake helicopter and being ducked into a swimming pool upside down: that's not my idea of a good time. I think you're allowed to make stuff up in fiction.

IM: Absolutely! Does *Rebus's Scotland* purport to be non-fiction?

IR: The book is non-fiction, definitely. The first thing I say in the book is, look, this isn't Rebus's Scotland: he doesn't exist. However I exist, and I'll do my best to take you through the country. It started as a bit of a travel book. There's a hundred and twenty photographs in it, so the bulk of it is photographs. The rest is Rebus, me, and what the books say about modern Scotland. Which is why I've got chapters on religion and politics. They're inextricable. The main subject in many of the books is this mix of politics and religion. Which has made Scotland the country it is, and made Edinburgh the city that it is.

IM: Were either religion or politics important in your home?

IR: I went to church every Sunday until my Mum decided that I could stay at home if I wanted to. About the age of twelve or thirteen, she gave me the choice. Her and my sister Linda went to church every Sunday. My Dad never did; he stayed at home. When I was allowed to stay at home I would read the *Sunday Post* and drink tea. (L)

IM: Politics?

IR: My parents were not political at all. Well – one voted Labour, one voted Tory.

IM: Father Labour, mother Tory?

IR: But they never talked about politics in the house. I think they thought they were just so far away from the process, and unable to have any effect on the process. They voted at every election, but you've got to remember there weren't so many elections back then.

IM: But obviously we find both all over the place in your novels.

IR: I think my novels are political novels, to the extent that I will write about the effect that oil has had on Scotland; I will write about the Scottish Parliament, and the effect it is or is not having on the people it's supposed to represent; I do write about asylum-seekers; I do write about social policy. There's plenty of that stuff in the books. But they're not essays; they're not polemics. It's part of the story structure, so you either notice it or you don't. We put things in front of our readers, and make them question themselves. It wouldn't worry me if people read *Fleshmarket Close* [2004] and didn't fret about the asylum-seeker question, but I'd be thrilled if they did think about it.

IM: I'd be worried if they didn't worry at all, really. When it gets to the point that every sympathetic character in the book is accusing Rebus of something near racism. !

IR: Cops like every other branch of the armed services tend to be a wee bit racist. It's just part of your education. Cops always see the world in terms of us and them, good guys and bad guys. The danger is to marriages, because the job can become your partner, and the job becomes your life. And because you can't let off steam: if you've a bad day at the office as a lecturer, you can go home and scowl about it, or kick the dog. But if you've had a bad day in the police, you don't go home and sit around the table with your spouse and your kids and say, oh this horrible rape case I had today. . . or junkie overdose – or suicide or whatever. You just don't talk about it. So you never get to let off steam, except at other cops, or people in that line of work. So they become your family, they become your friends; you get shut off from your own family. It's a vicious circle. And there are a lot of busted marriages, there's a lot of drinking to forget, there's a lot of that stuff does go on. But there's also a lot more support than there used to be. If you want it, there's a lot of people on hand; if you've been a cop involved in Dumblane or Lockerbie, there'll be psychologists standing by to talk you through it afterwards, which never used to be the case. I've often thought about this: when my Dad came home from the war, he was working in a grocer's shop, and then suddenly when he was seventeen eighteen or nineteen, he was sent off to Malaya or Burma or wherever the hell he was, somewhere in the Far East. And he's supposed to go in and kill people, complete strangers, and then come back and be a grocer again, with no decompression in between. He doesn't talk it through with anybody. How the hell are you ever expected to let go of that?

IM: Yes; I'm very glad that Rebus had a nervous breakdown. There would have been something wrong with him if he hadn't.

IR: That Forces background – I lost both granddads in the Great War, so I never knew them. My own Dad served during the Second World War; my sister married into the Royal Air Force. I was very conscious growing up in Fife that the big jobs-provider was Rosyth, the Naval dockyard. Plus if you left Auchterderran High School at sixteen, you tended to get jobs either in Rosyth or in the police or in the army. I had friends who all did one of the three of those. When I started to write about Rebus he was always going to have an armed forces background, because I thought that was realistic. A cop who's come from Fife probably has had another life.

IM: There's an element of your life which I would sum up under the heading of performance. It's part of what made you want to be a university lecturer, it's what satisfies you when you go on stage with Jackie Leven; it helps you to be a public writer when some writers have to screw themselves up: might it lead you on to doing for example more stage shows? [*See – or rather hear! – the double CD: Jackie Leven Said Orion Audionbooks/Cooking Vinyl, 2005*]

IR: Not performing in them, no. I think I got that out of my system with the Jackie Leven project.

IM: Telly?

IR: I quite like telly. The thing about doing *Newsnight Review* [*BBC2*] is that it's live, which is always a bit nerve-wracking, but the reason I do it is that you get to go and see things that you wouldn't otherwise get to go and see. And the BBC pays you for the privilege. You get to go to first nights of theatrical things: you get to go to exhibitions before they open, when it's totally empty, just you and the exhibition. How fantastic is that! So all the stuff I can't do in Edinburgh with two kids. I go down to *Newsnight* for a kind of splurge of culture now and again, at the BBC's expense.

IM: And you thought you were going to be a rock star.

IR: Well, I was quickly disabused of that. The Dancing Pigs lasted six months, and only did about four concerts, one of them to some special needs children at the YW in Cowdenbeath. We had to turn the strobe off, because it was giving them all epileptic seizures, so we'd to play with the house lights up: that was our first ever gig! I think every teenage youth needs to get in a band; needs to get it out of his system. Then you find out you're never going to be a rock star. I did find performing fairly nerve-wracking; now I just find that it's almost like being a comedian – you've got to have new material every year. You are a performer, and I find that really frustrating, because that's not my job – I shouldn't have to stand up and give you new material –

IM: But you enjoy it!

IR: Sometimes I enjoy it, -

IM: You enjoyed that CD with Jackie Leven, and what's more you had the audience lapping it up. What I felt was that you really were enjoying it, you were reading it, making it mean more, they were laughing at the quips- you don't get that immediate effect when you're writing. And the lovely bit where the audience saw what was coming, and started laughing, and it didn't phase you for a second: you were enjoying the audience.

IR: Yeah, the audience like the idea of you interacting with them: actually saying you're ahead of me, breaking off the story just for that two seconds and then back in again: they quite like that. The communal sense that you get from that, from story-telling.

I had all sorts of fantasies going on when I was a kid: our house was a space ship, and a fireplace was the control centre, and there was a wee chip on one of the tiles, and I would pretend that was the button, and you could flip it open and press the button for take-off and go flying through space. And I'd have all my Corgi and Dinky cars lined up, and have wacky races with them, and different winners every day. I lived inside my head, almost totally. And about the age of ten or eleven I invented the Amoebas, my pop group, who lived only on paper inside my head. So I was a pop-star and I was travelling the world doing concerts.

IM: As a vocalist?

IR: As a singer, even! (L) Because not having to prove myself, I could call myself a singer. And I would write all the lyrics down, oh my God…Yeah, it was great: it was a whole universe, a parallel universe, where everything happened the way I wanted it to happen.

IM: I think you could have happily gone on to a whole lot of careers, such as university lecturing, where enjoying performance, or at least being able to seem to enjoy performance, is absolutely basic (L) because you have to spend all your time putting other folk at their ease.

IR: Several times I've been asked to give papers, or give lectures, and I always say no, because I don't like the idea of being – I don't mind making stuff up on the spot: I don't mind going in front of an audience who're there to buy my book, and just telling them stories, anecdotes, and I just go with the flow. But the idea of something prepared that you've got to read out – and its all structured, I still can't do that, so I'd have been useless as a lecturer. Tutor would have been ok. I'm not sure I would have made a good performer. The nice thing about doing the Jackie Leven set story was it was a very different kind of story from what I normally do. So it let me get to a different mindset. And also I was conscious that usually when people come to see me, they haven't paid. People come to a bookshop to see a writer flogging their book; they don't pay. And they might get a glass of wine and a bit of cheese. They're usually a fairly non-aggressive, non-threatening audience, because it's all free: they're getting something for nothing, so they're quite happy.

IM: And they buy the book!

IR: Yes, they might buy the book. But they don't have to. When you go in a situation where people are paying ten or fifteen quid a ticket to come and see you doing a show, they're expecting a show! They're expecting to be entertained and enthralled and all the rest of it. And I knew I couldn't just stand up there and read it off the page, the way I usually would a book, I would have to do gestures – you don't get this on the CD of course, but gestures and faces, and give each character a life of their own. So it was actually quite hard work; it was being an actor, more than reading a Rebus extract is, and so it was a very different skill skill set.

IM: You said you were re-reading the novels.

IR: I wasn't re-reading them. I'd never read them before. So it was a strange experience. I was up to about *Resurrection Men* [2001] before I remembered the ending. With *Black and Blue* [1997], *Hanging Garden* [1998] I had no idea how they were going to finish when I started reading them.

IM: But you did remember the early ones?

IR: No. I couldn't have told you anything about *Hide and Seek*. [1990]

IM: What about *Knots and Crosses*? [1987]

IR: I could have told you there was a tunnel scene at the end. (L) But I'd forgotten there was another guy in the tunnel scene who shot the bad guy. Once you write a book, that's it! You read sections of it when you do a signing tour, but being a crime novel you usually start at the beginning and read the first few pages. I was reading them as if they were the books of a stranger. And sometimes I was chuckling to myself and thinking, that's a good line.

IM: And didn't you ever think, oh I wish I hadn't written that?

IR: Yes! *Knots and Crosses* I thought was terrible. Rebus changes a lot between the early books and the books after *Black and Blue*. In the early books he likes jazz, because I thought that's what existential cops would listen to. And he's far too well read and always quoting from Walt Whitman or Dostoyevsky. He reads Dostoyevsky's *Crime and Punishment* every year. (L) And in one of the early books he listens to Radio Three, for God's sake!

All that got ditched eventually.   It was never intended to be a series. So I've found lots of mistakes; he went to school in Cowdenbeath in one of the books: in another he didnae: he went to school in Auchterdearn. That's just a mistake, because I had no idea of continuity. I gave Cafferty two lives. I gave Cafferty an early life in Edinburgh and an early life in Glasgow. You can't grow up in both. So there are glitches along the way, but no one's ever picked me up on those. The only time people pick me up is on wee, niggly things, like calling setts cobbles. Somebody wrote to me and said, they're not called cobbles in Edinburgh; they're called setts. (L) So I'd to correct that. And somebody else said, it's not a foot-rest along the front of the bar in the Oxford Bar. That I'd misremembered because I was living in France when I wrote that.

IM: You've always said that you try to write each book better than the last one. I would have thought you would wince occasionally at your early attempts at construction and things, because they're nothing like as smooth.

IR: Yeah. Though the early books are a lot simpler, less trying to connect various sub-plots; so there's not so much that can go wrong. There's much more that can go wrong with the later books, when you've got four or five plots and you're trying to connect them up at the end, without having any idea when you start the book about how or if they are going to connect.

IM: But the construction, I feel, just gets tighter and tighter as you go on, and these interpolated confessions, or journals, or diaries or letters of explanation are to a reader coming from the late Rebus sometimes a wee bit clumsy.

IR: Yeah, although things like the letter of confession in *The Black Book* – is it *The Black Book*? – no; the diaries in *The Black Book* were basically *The Confessions of a Justified Sinner*. I was just nicking from that book wholesale.(L) *The Black Book* [1993] was my attempt at a rewrite of *Justified Sinner*. You've got a kind of gangster figure who is convincing a young, naïve man to murder, basically. He's

208

got nothing to lose, and he can get away with it, because of who he is. So there's lots of consciously using stuff from my elders and betters. But that's because the early books were still influenced by the me who was an English literature postgraduate, which is why they're very studied, and very self-conscious, and there's lots of literary in-jokes. I'd spoil a scene just to put in a bad pun.(L) Rebus going back to Fife and looking at the chimneys where the smoke used to gush, and it's not there any more, because there's no mining any more, - it's the silence of the Lums. (L) At the time I loved that: this was the best joke I'd ever heard. (L)

IM: You're still doing it, because I remember in the story that's on the CD with Jackie Leven, it's 'one size hits all'.

IR: Yeah, but it's somebody saying that. I think it's OK if you've got a character saying that, because they might think that way. And also because it gets a musical reference in, because it's a reference from a Frank Zappa album, 'One All Size Fits All.' So the brother would know his other brother would get that reference. And it lightens the idea of abuse, spousal abuse and the abusive fathers. So there's all kinds of reasons for him to actually say that, but there's very few reasons for the narrator, or the author, to come out with 'Silence of the Lums.' And there's one book where it's got a joke running all the way through it – I think it's *Mortal Causes* [1994], but I don't remember: you never get the punchline of the joke - For hands that does dishes can be soft as your face with mild green hairy lipsquid – and it's so tortuous! When a mate first told me that joke I thought it was the best joke I'd ever heard. I got all that from an early love of books and stories, because I was just excited about using language. But also, doing all that Deconstructionist nonsense when I was a post-grad, the idea of a book being a game that you play with the reader, and signifiers, and all that. *Knots and Crosses* is just chock full of Semiotics, even to the extent of having a character called Eiser who is based on Wolfgang Iser the literary theorist. He's the person that gives Rebus the clue that finishes the book. He does Literary Theory at Edinburgh University. Well, I was a post-grad when I wrote it, and that was the only world I knew.

IM: Did you have to do a lot of that as a post-grad?

IR: You didn't have to, but I got really into it. Stupidly, I got completely obsessed with Derrida and Roland Barthes and all these guys. I wasted a lot of time trying to understand their books. Barthes was all right, but Derrida was impossible – grammatology ugh. No, I wasted a lot of time. And all I got was a couple of cheap jokes in my first novel. (L)

IM: And enough money to write it! But you never found any of that stuff useful for writing.

IR: No, quite the opposite in some ways. Studying Literature at university, you're picking books apart; you're concentrating on anything but the magic. You're concentrating on nuts and bolts; you're concentrating on the author's life; you're looking for themes and symbols and images; it's like picking a tapestry apart. And what you're left with at the end is lots of threads, but the tapestry is gone. And I almost had to unlearn all that stuff to become a writer. There are certain writers out there who write in a literary manner; they write with one eye on academe, but I made the decision early on that I wanted a wide general readership: I wanted people like my Dad reading the books. I thought my Dad would enjoy Kelman: a bus-conductor, it's about a working-class guy, but he found it really hard to read because it wasn't written in Standard English. I decided I would have everybody speaking fairly Standard English, with Scottish rhythms. And anybody Scots-speaking would use those rhythms to put the words back into Scots in their head. Also, Rebus left Fife a long time ago, so when he goes back to Fife in one of the books and meets an old friend of his from schooldays, and she says in the text, 'I used to know everybody around here', you then get the italicised version of what she actually said, which is, 'Ah used to ken a'body'. He's translating between the two. That's a nod to the fact that you're getting it filtered through a narrator's consciousness. But readers who want to read it in their own dialect are free to do it. And I did notice that towards the end of my time in London and moving to France, I put a lot more Scots words in the books, and I think it was almost a way of not leaving Scotland behind. And I noticed that a lot of the words I used were words that my Dad used to use, and of course he'd died just before I moved to France. I think he died in February 1990, and we moved to France in May 1990. So it was a way of hanging on to him as well. Rebus remembers things that his dad said, and they're exactly the same phrases that my Dad used to use.

IM: Can we talk then about how you approach the books? You seem almost every time to have had to decide, am I going to have short chapters here, or long chapters? There's a wide variety in the way you divide them up, and in the amount of focalisation from different characters.

IR: None of that's conscious. A chapter's as long as it is. I never sit down and think, right, I'm going to write a book with a hundred chapters; or, each chapter's going to be approximately three pages. I usually write it as one big block of text, then break it up later on, depending on whim, really. Obviously there's three sections to this book: or, there's obviously   ten days to this book.

IM: I liked that particularly: it gives a feeling of haste, and you can't stop reading it. [*A Question of Blood* 2003]

IR: There's a good reason for doing that, which is that in the early books, if you do try to work out the chronology you find that they're working Sundays, because I haven't worked out that they get a weekend off. I don't sit down at the start of each new day and say, it was Wednesday morning, so I forget where I am, and end up with them working weekends, then I have to go back into the book and have a weekend. (L) Wedge a weekend in there, which is usually about a page and a half: Rebus went to the pub and went to the pictures: right, that's it – back to the story again. (L) I don't do much pre-planning, before I start the books. [The one time I did try pre-planning a book in great detail, I satisfied myself that I knew what the book was about to such an extent that I didn't need to write it.] The whole point of writing a book for me's to find out what's going on. So the first draft of a book is like note-taking on a grand scale: there's lots of big gaps for adding stuff in later on.

Characters take on a life of their own: Cafferty's a case in point. Somebody who's meant to be a very minor character in one book, who just got beneath my skin, and I thought, I can do a lot more with you than I'm doing. [see eg titles] And sometimes characters who you think are going to be important to you, like the MSP in *Set in Darkness* [*Roddy Grieve, 2002*], you suddenly find thirty pages in you've got no place for him in the book, although you thought the book was going to be about him, so you bump him off. Then you've got another corpse on your hands: you've no idea who killed him or why, or how it connected with the other whodunnits that you've set up. In the first draft I set up a series of challenges for myself, which is that I've usually got three or four plots which have usually got a linked theme, but I've got no idea how they're going to link in the narrative. As I write the book I start to see the connections, and that's always my favourite bit of the book, when you start to see connections between one plot and another. That's never pre-planned.

And Rebus's various relationships are never pre-planned. What happens happens. I do depend a lot on the Muse, or inspiration, and some days I sit down and nothing happens, so I don't bother writing. Other days I can be writing all day, because it's going so well. It's quite scary, because there isn't this safety net underneath: it is kind of tightrope-walking. I never show it to anyone as I'm going. If I've got a narrative problem I'll sometimes talk it over with my wife, but she doesn't read the books while they are being written. And my editor never sees it until it's finished.

IM: And then does either of those attempt to make you change it?

IR: Oh yes, my editor does: I've had her for a long time. Caroline Oakley. Even though she's left the publishing world now, I've kept her on as a freelance, just to edit my books. The edit I've got upstairs for *Rebus's Scotland* is her notes from her little cottage in Wales, but it's only five or six pages. But that's five or six pages of notes for a seventy-page manuscript, so for a 350 page novel she would send me 35 pages of notes. And some of it's really small stuff, like, this guy's suddenly got a moustache – he had a full beard three pages ago (L) – and some of it is really big stuff, like, can you get inside Rebus's head a bit more here, or – a lot of it is getting inside Rebus's head, and why has he suddenly decided this? I've had a lot of editors. I used to just change anything they told me, because after all they are the reader. But now I don't change as much as I used to. I know the publishers will publish it anyway. That's just terrible laziness on my part. But I will fight my corner where I wouldn't have done before. And she's a good reader. Miranda my wife reads the finished manuscript, and she's usually got comments: my agent occasionally has comments, and then whoever ends up proof-reading it will have comments. So you're getting a lot of feedback. And sometimes your American publisher will say, this isn't going to make sense to the American market, so will you please change the word 'close' to 'alley' – Fleshmarket Alley. Or can we please add an extra chapter, which they got me to do – I think it was *Let it Bleed* [1995]. They asked me to tag an extra chapter on the end.

IM: I was going to ask you about that.

IR: It was a book where at the end he walks into the Senior Minister's office

IM: The fifteen minutes with Sir Ian?

IR: Yes. And that's the end of the book, Rebus walking into his office with all the evidence. But you never find out what happened afterwards. My publisher in America thought that American readers would want to know what happened afterwards: they don't like open endings. That's not why they go to crime fiction: they go to crime fiction for that sense of closure that they don't get in real life, loose ends being tied up, questions being answered. But of course that's one of the big sticks that the literary critics take against the crime novel, that it's too neat and tidy, and life aint like that. It makes it a puzzle to be solved, and at the end you've got nothing to be gained by going back and rereading the book. And I do love open endings. In *Dead Souls* [1999], even I wasn't sure what happened by the end of the book. (L) People still come up to me and say, is Damon Mee alive or dead at the end of the book?

IM: I think he's dead.

IR: But his mum thinks she saw him at the cash machine. So who knows? That's the whole point of Missing Persons, that we're never sure what happened to them, that huge gap in our lives.

IM: I like the fact that – I think it's in the last one – there's a couple of characters who're really quite important, who just kind of disappear off the edge, the Indian lawyer, and the woman who's been camping outside the place: they just do their bit and … [*Fleshmarket Close* 2004]

IR: The nice thing about a series is that there's always the possibility that someone comes back again. That's one of the great things about a serial novel. I do think that all the books put together basically makes one big book. I do feel that. I feel that there are enough shared themes between the books, and characters who come and go, a bit like *Dance to the Music of Time*, that you'll see a character in book 3, and you won't see him again till book 7. But life's like that. People come back into your life all the time from the past, and I don't see the point of having to invent a brand new character if a character used previously can fulfil exactly the same role. But reading the books recently, I thought, we never, ever meet Siobhan's parents: we hardly know anything about Siobhan's parents. Where are they? I suddenly thought, for the G8 book, that I'm going to start writing in September, perfect, because they're both lecturers; they probably would come back to Edinburgh for the march. So I can introduce them into the book. That's something that just would happen in life, and therefore why not have it happen in the book? I don't know what I'm going to do with them, but it seems natural to me that they would be there.

IM: Are they both English?

IR: They are both English. They pitched up in Edinburgh to teach, and she spent her early days in Edinburgh, and then went away, and then came back again.

IM: With her English accent.

IR: Yes, with her English accent. So I can talk about xenophobe Scots. (L)   There's a guy I went to uni with, and bless him, he's been a big help to me. His name's John Curt, and I made him Dr Curt in the books, because he never finished his doctorate either. (L) And John was a part-time barman as an undergraduate student in the Oxford Bar and he introduced me to the place – I'd never been there before he took me there. He's the pathologist. He was Dundonian, but he spent his early life south of the Border, so he'd an English accent. But he was fiercely Scots, very patriotic. There's a bit of him in Siobhan, I think. And maybe a bit of me as well, because my Mum was English; she never had a Scottish accent; she grew up in Bradford, and came up to Scotland during the war in her late teens, early twenties.

   We glided over punk yesterday, but I was thinking last night, punk was really important to working-class kids, because it told us you didn't have to have a skill set, and you didn't have to have money behind you, or influence, you just had to jump in and try something. You were talking about performance and how I performed early, and it might have been something to do with that, that I just got on with it. As soon as punk started, I was trying to do a fanzine, and I would type it up at home on a portable typewriter that I got from my sister's mail order catalogue, and I would take the sheets in and photocopy them in the Economics Department when nobody was looking and staple them together to make this punk fanzine. I think it's the same sort of gallusness that made me send my early poems off to places like *The Spectator* and *The Economist*. In retrospect I'd not a cat in hell's chance of them ever getting taken, but you thought, why not?

IM: Let's talk about Rebus himself: I'll start you, wickedly, to see what you think, a book you may not have seen yet, by a guy called Duncan Petrie, called *Contemporary Scottish Fiction: Film, Television and the Novel* [2004]. He describes Rebus as 'a maudlin obsessive, with an unhealthy lifestyle to match, seeking solace in alcohol, tobacco and the obscure annals of progressive rock.' [p149]

IR: I think that's a lazy description. I think he's more complex than that. In the early books, for example, he's very churchy, very religious.

IM: Yes; not churchy, but religious.

IR: He goes to lots of different churches, looking for one that suits him, and none of them do. He has a problem with organised religion. I think his religious quest mirrors the reason why he's a good detective, he's very interested in getting answers to big questions. . And religion is the biggest question of them all. Being a novelist, of course, what you are doing is playing God, so there's got to be a certain sense of the mystic about being a creative artist anyway, I think. So I channelled a lot of that down to Rebus, and he has these big questions, and eventually I introduce a priest, so they can sit and play devil's advocate with each other. Our Lady of Perpetual Help. . . (L) I'm not sure that he is maudlin: I think he's gone through maudlin stages in his life, but maudlin to me means self-pitying, and I don't think Rebus is self-pitying.

IM: I didn't agree with that description, but I do think he's more on the ball with the second quotation I have here, ' a contemporary study of Calvinist angst, with its curious and contradictory mix of fearless initiative and fearful, self-limiting doubt.' [*Petrie, p 153*]

IR: Yes, well, the Scots in general, I think, certainly male, working-class Scots in post-industrial society. The Rebus novels do straddle industrial and post-industrial working-class Scotland. Rebus grew up like me in a mining town, and then all the mines closed down, and he had to look for other channels to make a living. He had to look outside his home town for work. I do think that working-class male Scots have got problems anyway, with expressing their emotions, or expressing anything. Rebus is part of that. A lot of Scots have had to leave because they find the place stifling. The sense of community that you get in a place like Cardenden where I grew up can be stifling, because everybody knows everybody else, and sometimes you don't want that. You want to be a stranger: you want to have some privacy.

Why has he become a cop? Through investigating other people's lives he can put off investigating his own too much. And he's very voyeuristic, as are novelists. I don't want to too closely ally him to the McIlvanney camp, but he doesn't live where he grew up, and neither do I, so he never quite feels part of Edinburgh. He can't really comment on the community of Edinburgh because he doesn't know any community in Edinburgh. He lives in the student part of Edinburgh, where there's an ever shifting population every two or three or four years. His stairwell will change out of recognition that often because the students will move on and a new lot come in. That's the Edinburgh I knew as a student. The only reason he lives in Marchmont is that's where I lived when I started writing the books. So I can talk about the idea that it's very difficult to have a community in somewhere like Marchmont. But putting this cantankerous, middle-aged single man in there, next to these students, causes lots of little discourses on the nature of life in Edinburgh. While I lived here as a student, I never got to know my neighbours, but you thought what's the point of getting to know folk when six months from now I'll be in a different part of town?

IM: And you were so busy getting to know other folk, through your student life.

IR: Absolutely.

IM: Rebus is a funny paradox when it comes to family.

IR: Yeah. Here's a problem with writing a series when you never meant to write a series! In that first book, his dad's been a stage hypnotist; his brother's a hypnotist; he's had a nervous breakdown: he's been in the SAS; there's a lot of back story there, which you can't ignore in future books. As a one-off novel that would have been fine; I would never have had to think about it again; but having put all that in the first novel, I then had to take account of it all the way through the series, so that was a rod to beat my own back with. His memories of growing up owe an awful lot to my own background, but that's true of lots of other characters: there's bits of Siobhan where she's remembering things that I did, and Brian Holmes, when he goes to university, goes down to London, it's basically my memory of living in London and not liking it, and not getting on with it. And even bits of Cafferty's background – and various villains have got memories, like me being scared of crossing a pipe across a river – I've used that image a couple of times. But I think I gave that to the serial killer in *Dead Souls* [1999], so every incident and character in every book comes from inside your head.

IM: Sure. But I'm thinking about Rebus as if he were actually a real person - he has strangely hung up relationships with his brother in particular: it's almost a Jekyll and Hyde relationship that develops as Mickey goes into the drugs.

IR: It's pretty hard to be a cop when your brother has done time inside, so Rebus has got to distance himself from that anyway. But they were two boys quite close in age growing up with a dad and no mum, so there's going to be a power struggle between them in the early days anyway, and that filters down into the present.

IM: And when Mickey gets hung from the Forth Bridge in order to affect Rebus, [*The Black Book* 1993] his almost tribal reaction is quite strong, as it is when he's with Allen Renshaw in a later one and finds out what a beast he was to Allen Renshaw when he was a boy. [*A Question of Blood* 2003] He's got a real boiled up conflict with tribal things.

IR: The books are almost always about the past acting on the present, past crimes suddenly infecting the present, stuff being uncovered after centuries; it's a way of letting me write about Edinburgh past and present, and the interaction between the two, and the influence that history has on all of us without us necessarily realising it. There is a thematic element in there and a plot strand.

More than that, Rebus is – that horrible word! – conflicted. The army especially trains you not to see people as people, but to see them as objects that you've got to brush aside. Rebus was brought up in that sort of institutionalised way of looking at the world, and the police isn't much different. The institution becomes your family. The reason that I sometimes bring in characters who are ex-army or ex-armed forces is so that we can get a bit more of why he joined the army in the first place, how it affected him. So every few books you tend to get another character coming in who's got an army background, and you find out a bit more about either Rebus's training, which dehumanised him and dehumanised everybody who took part in it, or having to be in Ireland, in Belfast at the start of the Troubles and seeing how violence begets violence, and retaliation and recrimination come in early on. The reason he joined the army was because a mate of his got beaten up at school; he didn't want to, but in *Dead Souls* [1999] he felt guilt that he hadn't been able to save his friend, so he's got to join the army, which they were both planning to do anyway. And he was just on the cusp of saying to his friend that he wasn't going to do that. When he's in the army he only goes in for the SAS training to get away from the Parachute Regiment, because he's just witnessed some ugly scenes with them, and then the SAS thing breaks a friend of his, and so he leaves the SAS. So he's been running ever since: it's had a terrible effect on him.

IM: And then these horrible people from the SAS come back, in *Question of Blood*. [2003]

IR: The two army investigators come back armed with his past, basically, which he's been trying to shrug off and not talk to anybody about. His past impinges on him all the way through the series, and partly he can't get away from it because I gave him all that back story to start with, and it's obvious to me that it would keep resonating throughout his life.

IM: There is a feeling you get when reading a number of them in succession, that he has these strange conflicting feelings, say about his brother, and also about his former wife and in particular his daughter, that you're getting right inside his head. For long times he doesn't seem to think about Sammy, even when she's been disabled, and then something hits his nerves and he has very, very strong feelings.

IR: Yes: he spends a lot of his personal interior life shutting stuff out. And then something comes up that just jars it back into his consciousness again, and he's got to take account of that. He's surrounded by ghosts in various of the books, the ghost of every victim he's ever worked with, every colleague he's ever pushed away. He's haunted in the worst sense of the word, and it means that he's very tensed up about letting people get close to him, because his life is just full of fuck-ups, basically. This why he doesn't get into relationships, because he thinks, it's just going to go wrong so why should I bother to start with.

IM: Unless her name is Patience. (L)

IR: Well, if your name's Patience; but even Patience ended up just drifting away.

IM: Patience got on better with his daughter.

IR: I have tried throughout the series to give him happy relationships with the opposite sex; it just didn't work. Partly it doesn't work because my wife will say something like, oh she's boring. She thought Patience was boring.

IM: I think she's right.

IR: And partly it doesn't work because Rebus won't let it work.

IM: Yes; much more so, I would have thought. Gill Plain has some slightly critical things to say about the women. She identifies them as *femmes fatales* , and Siobhan is the plucky girl assistant, which seems horrible because she's more than that – but she is that so clearly, and she even has Gill Templer as damsel in distress, because Rebus has to go to her assistance in that book – don't expect me to remember the titles: I never do. What do you make of that? [*Plain, pp 48-51*]

IR: I've had this criticism for a long time. I did a gig once at the Book Festival with Helena Kennedy, and I thought my job was to interview her, but it ended up with her quizzing me on whores and madonnas in the Rebus novels. (L) I think it's a cliché of the male-written crime novel, and it goes away back to the beginnings of literature. If you go back to things like Circe, you can draw a line from Sirens luring sailors onto the rocks in Greek mythology, to women who come into a private eye's office, not giving him the whole story. The whole American private eye thing comes from the idea of the cowboy riding into town to bring order to the town. But that comes from the Grail myth. A lot of crime fiction comes from the Grail myth, the idea that there are dragons out there to be slain and damsels to be saved. It's archetypes: you can't get away from archetypes.

IM: Oh yes you can.

IR: No, I don't think you can; I think it's really tough to get away from archetypes, because they resonate on a subconscious level with all of us. These basic devices are very useful for saying things about the world around you. Earlier in the books there are few if any strong women characters, because I didn't feel comfortable writing from a woman's point of view, and I knew nothing about women cops, so how could I make that realistic? Then later on Siobhan came in.

   She was introduced as just another sidekick, like Brian

Holmes, she was just a female Brian Holmes, but there was so much more to her than that, I thought, there's stuff I could do with her that I could never do with Brian Holmes, the fact that she talks with an English accent, so I can discuss the relationship between Scotland and England, or racism and xenophobia in Scotland, or a woman in a man's world, because being a police officer is still seen as being a man's job, the glass ceiling that she's trying to break through; the fact that she is college-educated and Rebus isn't, so I can talk about that chip he's got on his shoulder –

IM: That's why I was disagreeing when you said you can't get away from archetypes: she outgrows the archetype.

IR: She does eventually, or I think she's starting to. Because she's such a multi-faceted character, because she's attracted to Rebus's way of policing, ie using instinct, but at the same time she can't afford to put a foot wrong, because she wants to climb that greasy pole, she wants to get up to Gill Templer's rank and above, and she's seen that Gill Templer has had to become less and less feminine to rise through the ranks. . .

IM: Can I interrupt to quote Plain again? 'Rebus and Templer compete like angel and devil for the soul of their apprentice Siohbhan.' [*Plain, p 24*]

IR: I don't think that's true. (L) You hardly see Gill Templer and Siobhan.

IM: It's more Siobhan's idea of Templer. She knows what she has to do to get on like Templer did. She often thinks that.

IR: I guess that's right. But she also knows that Gill's had to become less of a woman and more blokeish to succeed, and she doesn't want that. In the early books she started life as just a foil for Rebus. She's younger than him; she's got different musical tastes; there's just so many things I could do with her that could make sparks fly between them. Women cops and women crime writers started to say that they liked her, and thought she was realistic. So I started to think I could give her a bigger role in the books, to the extent that she's almost got parity now, I would say it's pretty much fifty-fifty in the books. She gets her own cases and goes off and does her own thing without Rebus having to come in and help her, or without her having to answer to him. If she keeps on the way she's going she's going to pass him in rank anyway in about two books time.

IM: What about the ending of *The Falls*? When he kisses her?

IR: No; that's the end of *Question of Blood* [2003]. He does: he picks her up and kisses her because he's so relieved that she's safe, because he's watched her die in a plane crash, basically. And then to get to the airfield and find she's alive - people read too much into that – that this was going to be it. A lot of fans want them to jump into bed together, which would be terrible on many counts. (L) Most because it would just ruin their working relationship.

IM: Well, if his working relationship is coming to an end anyway, you never know what might happen.

IR: Here's another thing, then. She's thirty and he's nearly sixty – that's never going to work. That's like all these Hollywood films, where they put Clint Eastwood in bed with some starlet (L): it's totally unrealistic. She would never jump into bed with him anyway, unless he plied her with plenty of alcohol.

IM: She does keep thinking about it , after the kiss she thinks about it in the next book, and says, we never talked that out.

IR: Because he wouldn't. Because he's a bloke and he just wouldn't talk it out.

IM: But he wouldn't have kissed Brian Holmes in the same situation.

IR: He'd have given him a nice big hug. Scottish men just don't kiss. Not even when they score goals at football. It's not a prelude to them heading off together to the motel by the Bridges. . .

IM: No, clearly not. But it still leaves the reader, and the lady, wondering.

IR: When I wrote *Fleshmarket Close* [2004] there was no reference to it, until my editor said, I think we need a reference to what happened at the end of *Question of Blood* [2003].

IM: She's a good editor; she was absolutely right.

IR: But I didn't want to make much of it.

IM: But it would have seemed odd if nothing had happened afterwards, no mention of it: it would have been very strange.
    I loved it – was it in *Resurrection Men*? [2001] – when Rebus was seeing a counsellor at the beginning and she was seeing one at the end. (L)

IR: Then she says let's get some chocolate. That's the answer to a lot of Siobhan's problems, is just get some chocolate. (L) How right she is! That's such a nice, simple and effective world view.

IM: It's also less dangerous than tobacco or alcohol.

IR: I'm a bit conscious that she doesn't have a life outside the police, that she's almost too much like a female Rebus, to the extent that she sits in her flat alone eating chocolate and listening to music while he's sitting in his flat alone drinking whisky and listening to music. I would like to give her an external life. Again, I introduce her to men, but she's got terrible taste in men.

IM: And terrible men have a taste for her!
    Can we move back to big Ger Cafferty? I get the feeling that there's more of him to come.

IR: End of the last book, yes. I think the last book's going to be Cafferty's book. Not the next book, but the one after. The relationship between him and Rebus is going to be coming to a head, I'm still not sure how. It's because they are two sides of the same coin. It's Jekyll and Hyde; it's Cain and Abel; it's yin and yang: it's all these things.

IM: But Jekyll and Hyde particularly, because Jekyll isn't all good, because Jekyll has a nasty side to him, and so does Rebus. He does things you wish he wouldn't do. And he's somehow complicit with Cafferty.

IR: Sometimes, but he doesn't like it.

IM: No, but that's not all.

IR: Cafferty saves his life in one of the early books [*Mortal Causes 1994*]. And I think that burden has been on Rebus ever since, the fact that Cafferty pulls him out of a fire in the discotheque.

IM: Yes, but elsewhere – there's the book where he gets Cafferty to dump some coke on somebody to make sure he gets caught? [*Resurrection Men 2001*] And somewhere he says, I've made a pact with the devil [*The Hanging Garden 1998*]. There's a complicity there that is disturbing.

IR: Yes. It's Rebus coming to terms with a failure of man-made justice to actually work. Sometimes you've got to cross that line. He's always crossing the line, but he never crosses it very far, and you do wonder, how far would he cross it, given the circumstances. Cafferty has offered up to him the guy who put his daughter in a wheelchair, and a Stanley knife. Here's the guy who did it, and a Stanley knife. [*The Hanging Garden 1998*]

IM: Wasn't that the Weasel?

IR: It was the Weasel, but it was through Cafferty. There's always that sort of temptation, that Rebus is going to go to the dark side.

IM: He does, in little ways. In that early one, the first one that goes to London [*Tooth & Nail* 1992], I really hated it when he beats up the gay guy for the greater good, as it were. (L) I found that unpleasant, and that leads me to a whole other thing, which is – how much is Rankin expecting the reader to go along with Rebus, and how much is he expecting the reader to criticise Rebus, and to maintain a critical stance? It's a very basic truism of fiction in general, that as a reader, if you're centred enough in one person you tend to sympathise with them.

IR: You empathise, certainly. I don't always like him: and he isn't me. I'm much more liberal than Rebus. I suppose he's sometimes the Hyde to my Dr Jekyll. A lot of the books are debates or dialogues between him and me, about how you look at the world. I'll plunk a paedophile on his doorstep, and say, right, what would you do in this circumstance? And what you do is out the guy. [*Dead Souls* 1999]

IM: It's horrible!

IR: As a result of which the guy ends up dead. And then Rebus has this incredible feeling of guilt, and has to go and find out who did it and why.

IM: It's not incredible: it's a justifiable feeling of guilt!

IR: He doesn't always make the right decisions, and often he makes very stupid decisions.

IM: But it's so easy, if you're following this central character, for the reader more or less to go along with it.

IR: No, I don't think so. You'd find it hard to read *Dead Souls* [1999] and come away from it thinking, right, I'm going to go and bump a paedophile.

IM: Oh no, because he learns in the course of the book, and he learns that paedophiles are very often themselves abused, and all that, and the whole plot tells you that. We're only talking about that wee bittie at the beginning, where he hasn't looked at it, any more than he's looked at a lot of other human conflicts, and he's just got this totally simplistic gut reaction – paedophiles – out them! I don't see how he got to be that age and that person without being a bit more understanding before the whole plot happened to him.

IR: If you talked to a few seasoned cops, you'd find that they've got blinkers for a few things, and one of them is nonces or paedophiles.

IM: And similarly with criminals in jail, I think.

IR: There's a code of honour that says, if you can grab a paedophile in jail, or a sex offender of any sort, you beat him to a pulp, because they're not proper honest criminals. (L) This darker side of us runs deep in human nature, I think it was P D James who said, we are all capable of doing terrible acts, and we've got to be self conscious. We all think we couldn't be nasties, but actually we could. Sometimes it just needs you not to do anything, or just to go along with the flow. I think the later books especially do have a dialogue going on about what you do about bad things, and who decides what's bad and what is good. You can't take the law into your own hands: that's basically what Rebus finds out. Even if the legal machinery isn't there to deal with something, you can't decide it for yourself.

IM: You can play God, but he cannae.

IR: That's an ongoing dialogue. What I'm doing is hopefully putting these questions in the readers' minds, and saying, what would you do in this situation? How racist do you feel? Do you know you're a racist? I think the most telling point in *Fleshmarket Close* [2004] is when the lawyer says, we're all racist, even me.

IM: I think that's a place where that particular question is very well posed, and forces the reader to think.

IR: I think the majority of people would say, no, I'm not racist. But what if an Asian family moved in next door? What if your daughter or son started dating an Asian? Things we never think about until they actually happen. And Rebus is casually racist as anybody else at the start of the book. Especially when you're living in a country like Scotland, which is a mongrel country anyway, and which has this reputation of having been quite welcoming to outsiders in the past, but suddenly seems to be pulling up the drawbridge, just at the time when we actually need an influx of skilled people to come in and work and pay tax. There were all kinds of questions I was trying to throw up in *Fleshmarket Close*, partly to try and answer them for myself.

IM: But also in both these cases, you're educating him. At the beginning of the one book he outs a paedophile: the whole book serves to teach him as well as us about its being more complicated than that, in the same way.

IR: Absolutely. The problem I've got is that a lot of casual readers just think that Rebus must be me, and therefore all Rebus's faults and feelings on the world must be mine. I'll get attacked for being pro-IRA, because in *Mortal Causes* [1994] the baddies were Protestant paramilitaries. I get letters from paedophiles, saying if you ever want to know about paedophilia, I'll be quite happy to help you, for future books.

IM: Often the individual paedophile has been, before you can ever start looking at it, himself a victim.

IR: Usually. Not all abused kids become paedophiles.

IM: And not all paedophiles have been abused, but there's a lot of it about.

IR: Another thing about *Dead Souls* [1999], of course, is that it was based on a true story. There was a paedophile up in the Raploch estate in Stirling who was outed by the media, and Big

Mags Haney got a vigilante group together to kick the paedophile off the estate, which they duly did. But then having empowered the community, they then kicked *her* off the estate, because her family were the neighbours from Hell. And she ended up going to jail for drug-dealing, I think. It wasn't that I was making this story up; it was already there, and all I was doing was saying, well, how would Rebus react? What if it happened in Edinburgh? Which is how a lot of the stories happen. A school shooting. What if that happened in Edinburgh? Protestant paramilitaries moving in; what if that happened in Edinburgh? – It *did* happen a few years afterwards, actually. (L) A racist killing on an estate: well that happened in Glasgow, on the Sighthill estate, the year before I wrote the book. The themes and stories are out there, and all I'm doing is adding a what if.

IM: Let's get back to Rebus and his daughter. Is it that he has deep feelings about her but he's always trying to hide from the depth of his feelings, and all his guilts and things?

IR:: Rebus and his wife split up when Sammy was ten or eleven, so he really hasn't watched her growing up properly, and the fact that she went with her mum means that again he saw it as an us versus them situation, that she'd chosen her side. He has emotional blocks, things he can't express, and he doesn't even want to think about them. So he doesn't think about his daughter, unless something traumatic happens, like she comes back to Edinburgh and gets involved in a hit and run, or she moves in with his ex-girlfriend.

IM : That was one of the interesting bits. Another is when she actually has complicity in a murder, because of her ideals. [*Let It Bleed* 1995]

IR: She passes a note across, yeah. She went into this job dealing with ex-prisoners and she was very naïve in her dealings with them And sometimes it just takes one tiny innocent action on your part. . . It was a traumatic knock-on effect for her, but stuff like this happens all the time: without us doing it consciously, we commit acts which lead to something happening that is not very nice. So she'd to learn her lesson. That was a hard lesson to learn.

IM: It's totally in character and right, and she's out-thinking her father, thinking that he doesn't understand, as one does. What about violence?

IR: I don't think my books are particularly violent. Violent things happen, but they usually happen off-screen. Usually the murder has happened before the novel opens, and what we're dealing with is the aftermath. I don't tend to linger on the brutalisation of innocence, like a lot of books that I cannae read, I have to flick through those bits, in those ugly, serial-killer books. I was lucky in my first editor at Bodley Head, the guy who actually took *Knots and Crosses*, after it was turned down by five other publishers. His name is Ewan Cameron, and I dedicated at least a couple of books to him. I gave him *Tooth & Nail* [1992], which was originally called *Wolf Man*, the one set in London about a serial killer, which was just me trying to do the Hannibal Lector book, to get some of that money, and there was one long sex scene in it, with Rebus, and there was quite a lot of violence in it, a lot of descriptive violence, and Ewan, God bless him, said, we don't need this. We don't need the sex scene and we don't need all this violence. And when I took it out the book was the same book.

IM: Probably a better book?

IR: Yeah. I get letters or meet people who say, that scene in the mortuary! I say, go back and look at it: it's four lines! All I'm talking about are the smells behind the doors. Your imagination puts in everything else. Things that are left unsaid can be much more chilling than things that are actually stated.

IM: But you don't even usually do that: you don't usually invite the reader to speculate about violence.

IR: I did it at the beginning of *Black and Blue* [1997]. The guy's tied into a chair and he watches them through a polythene bag as they open up the Adidas bag and bring out – I can't remember – it's a chisel and some nails. And that freaks him enough so he jumps through the window. That actually happened to a friend's brother: that's where I got that story. But they just left him tied up and went off. I don't know what he thought of his grisly end in the actual book. But really I don't think you need gratuitous violence. We're lucky in Britain, because I don't think people expect it as much as they do in the States. They've got gun culture for a start, so there are a lot more killings than there are in the British crime novel, but also this tough guy philosophy in their pulp fiction. You knock them down and they just get up again. When Rebus gets hurt in books he gets hurt. He can go through an entire book with his hands bandaged, because he's done that. He doesn't get back up again.

IM: B You can occasionally leave the reader wondering how, if his hands are so badly damaged and bandaged, and Siobhan runs a bath for him and then leaves him, how he's going to have that bath! [*A Question of Blood* 2003]

IR: And how can he go to the toilet? (L) I had to go back and put a couple of lines in, in which Siobhan says, how do you go to the toilet, and Rebus says, I manage. He's that stubborn and thrawn, he's not going to not manage. He will get in and out of that bath!

IM: Do you think so?

IR: He'll just use his elbows.

IM: I think he'll pretend –

IR: And he won't get in? Aye, something like that. (L)

IM: And occasionally you get an emotional scene. That scene where he fights with Jack Morton on the Meadows. And weeps. [*Black & Blue* 1997]

IR: Yeah; the King Lear scene. To me that was his King Lear moment on the heath. That's him reduced to the lowest possible human thing. He's gone from being a hero of crime fiction to being on his hands and knees with snot coming down his nose, having had a fight with his best friend, who's the only person in the world trying to stop him from killing himself. That's as low as he goes in the books. I did think of Lear when I was writing it, the 'poor forked animal' that Lear describes people as being. It was semi-conscious when I wrote it, and he comes out of it eventually.

IM: If one were going to read them consecutively and trace it, I think there would be a discernible drink problem.

IR: Yeah, which is now pretty much under control. Again, in *Black and Blue* I think it's about as bad as it gets. By the time you get to the end of it he's stopped drinking; in *Hanging Garden* [1998] he's stopped for the first bit of the book. When his daughter is hurt someone hands him a half bottle and he's off again, but always with a bit of control, always with the thought that he knows now what his limitations are, and so his drinking is never as bad as it was up to *Black and Blue*. Cops used to be famed imbibers: when I first started going to the Oxford Bar, it was full of cops at night, and at midnight a police van would turn up to act as a taxi service to get them home. But that institutionalised drinking is pretty much gone. Again, that makes Rebus a bit of a dinosaur; that he's the last of that breed that used to go out for a drink at lunchtime. More likely now, you'll find your cops in the gym at lunchtime. Or reading improving magazines.

IM: This sounds like a piece of unlikely PR. (L)

IR: But true. More and more are college educated; they're not the heavy-drinking working-class guys that used to be detectives. They need skills that you can't get by pounding the beat.

IM: *Black and Blue* [1997]. Is that named after Brian Holmes doffing up that guy, or what is the reason of the title?

IR: Oh no. *Black and Blue* is named after a Rolling Stones album.

IM: I know that, but –

IR: The previous Rebus novel *Let it Bleed* [1995] was a Rolling Stones album, and I thought let's keep this going. I looked at the various titles available to me, and I knew I was going to write about the oil industry, oil being black gold, so that was black, and the boys in blue was the police. Rebus gets beaten up in Aberdeen; Brian Holmes is beating up a suspect; it's black and blue everywhere in that book.

IM: I thought of black and blue as soon as I found Brian Holmes doing this unlikely thing: in a way, it's one of the most serious things that happens, because one has learned to read this man as dependable, and avoiding most of the Rebus traps, and having relationships with people, and here you go: he's following the stereotype: eventually can't keep upright, eventually is losing his woman, and eventually is beating it out of people. And it's very sad.

IR: Yeah. He's headed down the same road as Rebus, except there's room for one Rebus on the force: there's not room for two. And Brian Holmes doesn't have the same inner strength that Rebus has: he's going to have to leave the police, because it's going to destroy him. He was never going to survive as a cop. He's picked up all the worst bits of Rebus without picking up any of the good bits. The nice thing about Siobhan is you can't imagine Siobhan ever being driven to that sort of limit.

IM: Is that stereotype that he reinforces of the policeman's marriage doomed to fail, still true? Or are you telling me the new breed of policeman's got it licked?

IR: I've known a few CID guys for a long time who're happily married: I know other ones who aren't, or who were and aren't any longer. There's plenty professions that are like that, bad for your social life and bad for your family life. I just think the police is an extreme case, in that they can't talk to anyone about it, except other cops, and lawyers, and social workers, and people who have the same black sense of humour they have, like pathologists. I've heard a lot of stories from cops over the years that I couldn't put in the books because they would seem too outrageous, things that happened at Lockerbie and Dumblane that are funny, if you've got the right mind set, because you see that the humour is a defence mechanism against the horror that you're dealing with. But it would be too distasteful to put these real life incidents in a book. The problem with fiction is, you have to be realistic! The real world can be as fantastic and as outré as you like, and full of the most extreme coincidences, but start doing that in your fiction and you don't get away with it.

IM: A very early one, the London one has a few: you catch sight of your exwife in a museum. [_Tooth & Nail_ 1992]

IR: Yes, it's unlikely. But then it does happen. I lived in London, a city of ten million people, and I walk into Soho and bump into Allan Massie! (L) It's the sort of thing Anthony Powell does very well in _Dance to the Music of Time_. He makes it work in fiction. But coincidences happen to us all the time, extreme coincidences: like meeting a guy called Joe Rebus who lives in Rankin Drive in Edinburgh. Who would have given odds on that? But then when I met him in a pub in Edinburgh, and he said, the name's Polish. But to me a Rebus was a picture puzzle. So when I came to _Fleshmarket Close_ [2004] I thought, this is perfect, because Rebus is Polish! He too has come from immigrant stock, and his people came to Scotland at a time when lots of Poles and Eastern Europeans and Italians did come to Scotland. So I could talk about that.

IM: But you don't on the whole in the later books rely on coincidence very much. Also, my impression is you don't rely so much on the long inserted convention of a letter, or a suicide note, like Lawson Geddes left [_Black & Blue_ 1997], or Aengus's diary [_The Black Book_ 1997]: the device is just less and less necessary, because you've found different ways round it: you don't have to have these interpolations. One totally sees why they're there –

IR: I quite like using them though. You go back to nineteenth-century fiction, with all the letters and things, and revelations. I do love all that. I like the way *Jekyll and Hyde* is written, with different narratives and different people and diaries, I like that. And the Justified Sinner, with two different ways of looking at the same story. I think it's a great device. The thing about writing about Edinburgh, about a real city in real time, is that people recognise events or people, and you get that whole suspension of disbelief, that wonderful thing when it ceases to become a novel and becomes an experience.

Book by Ian Rankin mentioned in the interview:

The Flood 1986

Knots & Crosses 1987
Hide & Seek 1990
Tooth & Nail (formerly *Wolfman*) 1992
Strip Jack 1992
The Black Book 1993
Mortal Causes 1994
Let It Bleed 1995
Black & Blue 1997
The Hanging Garden 1998
Death Is Not The End (novella) 1998
Dead Souls 1999
Set in Darkness 2000
The Falls 2001
Resurrection Men 2001
A Question of Blood 2003
Fleshmarket Close 2004

Rebus's Scotland: A Personal Journey 2005 Photographed by Tricia Malley and Ross Gillespie

William Watson

William Watson [Bill] was born in Edinburgh in 1931, the son
of a very eminent lawyer and Writer to the Signet, and grandson of
a Professor of Celtic at Edinburgh University. Apart from being
evacuated for periods to the Borders and to Grantown-on-Spey, he was
raised in Edinburgh and went up to Oxford, where he was 'thoroughly,
thoroughly idle'. Sent down after two years, he passed briefly through
Law and English classes at Edinburgh University before joining
The Scotsman in 1954. He became Literary Editor in 1960, and
later Features Editor, and is credited with some part in a 'golden age'
of that journal. He wrote a number of successful plays, including A
Footstool for God (1972), acting as Literary Adviser to Joan Knight
at Perth Rep 1974-80. His serious fiction includes Better than One,
Beltran in Exile and The Knight on the Bridge. In 1981 he went to
Canada with the Scottish-Canadian Writers Fellowship, awarded
by the Scottish Arts Council. Meantime he began to publish a series
of thrillers featuring Colonel Harry Seddall, under the pen-name of J
K Mayo, in the hopes of subsidising the writing of more serious work.
He returned to journalism as a night sub-editor on The Herald in the
Nineties, for the same reason. He was permanently afflicted with the
aftermath of childhood osteomylitis; and he successfully coped with an
alcohol problem. He suffered a series of strokes, and died after a long
illness in an Edinburgh nursing home in December 2005.

Bob Tait joined me in interviewing Bill, an old and valued friend
to both of us. He came to Aberdeen for a weekend in 1987, and talked
largely, both on and off the tape. Where the indication (L) appears in
this interview, it usually means that Bill had us both giggling by his
insouciant delivery.

13th of February 1987, at Devanha Terrace, Aberdeen. Present:
Bill Watson, Bob Tait and Isobel Murray.

IM: We've known Bill for a long time, each of us separately. He
gave me my first reviewing job, on *The Scotsman* in 1962, and he was
enormously helpful to Bob in the difficult days of his editorship

of *Scottish International*. Given that his books don't reveal a great deal about himself or his background, I think the reader will be interested to hear what he thinks might be of interest in his youth, his background, early stuff.

BW: The second book I remember being given, I must have been about eleven, was *The Master of Ballantrae*. My sister Catriona gave it to me one birthday.

IM: Did you like *The Master of Ballantrae?*

BW: Oh yes, I seized *The Master of Ballantrae* right into my bowels. It was imprinted like a photograph. And the next books I remember reading were *The Three Musketeers*, and I had read *The Three Musketeers*, and I had been up to Morningside Public Library. I remember riding my bicycle down from the Public Library, because I'd got *Twenty Years After*, and there were shelves of Dumas to go.

IM: A wonderful feeling.

BW: And I didn't read them then because that's when I got a disease called osteomylitis, and I was ill for a long time.

IM: The kind of illness that meant you didn't want to read?

BW: The kind of illness that meant that for a start you couldn't read, and I guess the books were taken back to the Library by some conscientious person. Before the fines grew too big (L).

IM: How old were you?

BW: I was twelve.

IM: And you were ill for quite a long time?

BW: I was ill for quite a long time, and it was a dangerous illness, and I was one of the first people to get penicillin. It must have been 1943.

IM: What sort of age were you when you could be said to have recovered, and how recovered were you?

BW: Well, I was back at school in 4/4/44, because I remember writing an essay on that day in school.

IM: That was not so long.

BW: But I was back in hospital after that, because it was a disease that had a recurring effect.

IM: Do you think therefore it had a very big effect on your intellectual emotional and imaginative development?

BW: I think it had an effect on my imaginative development, because I was physically quiescent for a long time – for a long time I lay on my back – for a long time I was in plaster from one ankle up to my chest and then after that I was on crutches with a built up iron hoop on my right foot, and then I had a caliper from the hip to the foot and walked with walking sticks. So I was immobile for a long time, even though around and about.

IM: Do you remember how you felt about it, particularly when you were lying on your back?

BW   I remember going to an Infirmary in Edinburgh in an ambulance with the bell ringing … then I remember lights and doctors … and then I came to in this Ward 8 of the Edinburgh Royal Infirmary, and when it became real, you know, after about two or three days, I thought, God must have been very angry about something I had done, but I didn't manage to think what it was.

IM: Did you think you might die? Were you frightened?

BW: Yes I was … I wasn't frightened, but I knew I might have died. We were a Church of Scotland family. But my mother had a close friend who was a Roman Catholic, who apparently prayed with - there's a phrase in *Beltran in Exile*, 'a little cloud of moist nuns.' (L) (p. 215)

IM: Yes, that's wonderful.

BW: Well I had a cloud of dry nuns who were praying for me. I should not laugh at them. (L) I should not laugh at them. They prayed for me and they may indeed have helped the penicillin.
BT: What did your father do?
BW: He was a lawyer, a solicitor, a Writer to the Signet. He was very successful, a very good lawyer.

IM: And did he have any particular ideas of what you should be?

BW: That was quick, wasn't it? Yes, my father wanted me to be a lawyer. My grandfather was a distinguished Celtic scholar. He was the son of a blacksmith who came from the Black Isle and moved to Easter Ross near Tain, and my grandfather went to school at Tain, then he got a scholarship to Aberdeen Grammar School. Do you know this stuff?

IM: No: it's absolutely fascinating.

BW: He got a scholarship to Aberdeen Grammar School, and then he got a scholarship to Edinburgh University, and then he got a scholarship to Merton College, Oxford, and he got a double First and two half Blues. (L)

IM: What was his double First in?

BW: Greats.

IM: What was his name?

BW: W J Watson. William, I don't know whether it was James or John. Very likely James, as will become clearer. He became a school master, and he was Rector of Inverness Royal Academy. He was then Rector of the Royal High School.

IM: In Edinburgh?

BW: Yes. And then he became Professor of Celtic at Edinburgh University. He had quite a few sons. He had one who died of osteomylitis when he was a boy in Inverness. He had one who ran away to the war when he was sixteen, the First War, and got killed. I think he was undoubtedly an irascible man. I think that boy, his name may have been George, left the house in a rage or was kicked out of the house in a rage. My father was the oldest son. There was another son called Bill who became a soil chemist in Nigeria in the colonial service, and there was a son called Alastair. And when Alastair was being born his mother died, so my Grandfather wouldn't look at Alastair, and he was put out to be brought up by an uncle and aunt in the west of Scotland. So he was clearly a man of strong temperament and affections. In his second marriage he married the daughter of Alexander Carmichael of *Carmina Gadelica*. [*Carmina Gadelica* : *a series of prayers, charms and invocations, originally in Gaelic, collected by Carmichael in the Highlands and Islands, in the latter half of the nineteenth century.*] And they had a son called James Carmichael Watson. Which is why I suppose my grandfather's second name may have been James. And he was very fond of James, and James went to Bonn to study, and he succeeded his father in the chair. But he was killed: he went off to be a sailor and he was killed in the war.

BT: The Second?

BW: The Second World War, yes. Now there's one aspect of this I think which affects my upbringing, because my father very much wanted to be an advocate, to be called to the Bar in Edinburgh, and his father wouldn't do that, it cost something like five hundred quid in those days, and we're talking about 1920. So father wanted to be a lawyer.

IM: And I don't imagine a Professor of Celtic earned too much.

BW: I don't suppose he did. He must have put my father through university, and I suppose he paid something for Alastair's education, and he must have put Uncle Bill, the third surviving of the original marriage brothers, through his university. And my father also wanted to go to Merton College, Oxford, like his father had, and his father wouldn't send him there because of the cost.

Well, I heard of this from my mother, and how much she remembered, and how much she was closely informed at the time I don't know. But that was the story that came to me. Anyway, he would not send him to Merton. So Father went to Edinburgh instead. He was a very bright man: he did very well. He did his MA and LLB in Edinburgh, and he became a Writer to the Signet. And he wanted me to follow in his footsteps, but more than that, he wanted me to follow in footsteps he had not been allowed to tread, so he wanted me to go to Merton College, Oxford. (L)

In those days, in my day, about 1950, when you were setting out to get into Oxford or Cambridge or to get a scholarship to Oxford or Cambridge, whichever, you went and sat for a group of colleges. You'd go and stay in one college and you'd sit exams, and they would be for, like Merton, Corpus Christi and two or three other colleges all in the same group, same exams. A matter of convenience. And so I did two trial runs. I did Merton in Oxford, and whatever else was connected with Merton, and I did Queen's College, Cambridge, and whatever else was connected with Queen's College, Cambridge in these groupings. And at Queen's College, Cambridge, I didn't get a scholarship, I didn't get an exhibition, but I was next in line for an exhibition if somebody dropped out. (L) Which people did, because since you were all trying for different groups, people were doing trial runs. If somebody got a major scholarship, if somebody had got an exhibition at Queen's and then got a major scholarship at Christchurch, Oxford, that exhibition at Queen's became vacant. But I didn't get a scholarship to Merton (L), I got *in* to Merton.

IM: Lots of people didn't get in to Merton!

BW: Quite possibly having run out of steam. I know I'd run out of steam.

IM: Did you want to go?

BW: I wanted to go to Oxford or Cambridge. I wanted to go to Merton because my father wanted me to go to Merton. But I liked Queen's, Cambridge, because there were two spiffing guys there who interviewed me. One was called Armstrong and one was called Potts, and I liked their style a lot. I liked their manner: they were very open, breezy guys. I did not look upon their like in Merton, curiously enough, at least not among the dons, though I am sure there were some very useful citizens there. (L)

IM: (L) I am waiting with bated breath to find what you did find among the dons at Merton.

BW: Okay, what I was doing at Merton was, I was reading Law, not English. They hadn't got a place for me to read English, but they said I could go up if I read Law. And being a very slow developer, I didn't say, this is an occasion to duck out of Merton and go to Queen's, Cambridge.

IM: But you are half beginning to feel that you wish now you'd done that?

BW: No, I don't wish now that I had done that, I might not have – I mean life has been good, I mean life has *been* good, and I might not have become this person.

IM: Obviously you wouldn't have become exactly this person.

BW: I might have become a very, very different person, some other guy altogether. I might have known all about Chaucer. Like Potts did. (L)

IM: So you went to Merton to read Law.

BW: And my tutor was a man called John Jones, and I think it was at this time that some division of doubt entered my awareness, because when I went into John Jones's room for the first time, we were discussing some very simple elements of Justinian, like pages one to three of the *Institutes*. His bookshelves were lined with Wordsworth, Byron, Keats, Shelley, Aristotle (L). It later transpired that his main interest was the Romantic poets, and indeed he later became Professor of Poetry. [*This unlikely sounding account matches the facts: Henry John Franklin Jones lectured in Law at Merton, 1949-56, and then 1956-92 in English. He was also Professor of Poetry 1979-84. One would have expected such a man to understand the young Bill rather better!*]. This was really in a sense extremely ironic. Though the irony did not start to exist until much later for me. And I worked very well for a term.

IM: A term?

BW: Yes. And at the end of the term we had a thing called a Don Rag. All these jejune undergraduates (you can tell me what that word means later) went up and sat in front of the college dons. The Warden of Merton was a philosopher called Mure. [*Geoffrey Reginald Gilchrist Mure, 1947-63.*] John Jones actually said to him, and this is absolutely true, 'Watson is the most promising undergraduate I have had in this subject.'

IM: He was new in the job? (L)

BW: He was young. But one must at least hope he had done another year before we came along. (L) But I asked him whether there was any scope for the imagination in the study of law, and the Warden said, well, Watson – or possible Mr Watson, because everything was disguised with enormous courtesy at that establishment, there are good ways and bad ways of using the imagination. I should do without it, if I were you.

IM: (L) As if he were saying you should be celibate?

BW: Almost. Yes.

IM: And you didn't take this well?

BW: No. Apparently not. I'm very slow I think to recognise what I am feeling or what my reactions are, but I immediately stopped working. I *immediately* stopped working.

BT: Had you been enjoying your work up till then?

BW: Yes, actually, because it was in Latin.

BT: What prompted your question – what scope was there in Law for imagination?

BW: I don't remember, but something was obviously happening. It could well be the company I was surrounded by, the other guys doing Law. On my staircase as it happened was a Canadian Rhodes Scholar who was doing English, and won the Newdigate Prize for English Verse later. There was an American Rhodes – no, what do the Americans have?

IM: Fulbright?

BW: Something like that, who was the son of Professor Douglas Bush of Harvard: he was taking English. So my immediate buddies were studying English. So I stopped working and spent a lot of time going to movies, and spent a lot of time on the river, and fell in love with a girl with whom I spent a lot of time on the river and the movies, and some time in Merton, and I was sent down at the beginning of my third year.

IM: The beginning of your third year? So you had survived into the second year without working?

BW: Yes. I passed Law Mods, you see. Which come to think of it was quite an achievement – not having done any work.

IM: Not bad. So presumably this did not endear you to the father who never got there?

BW: Well, this must have been a great blow to him, and we were indeed from that time on - I've coined this euphemistic phrase before – a great nuisance to each other. (L) Father's prides, you see, were terrific, but they were not mine. Father could sit in St Andrew's Square in his office, with his legal fund and decimals, and he could look across to the East side of St Andrew's Square and he could look at what was then the Scottish Junior National Insurance Company, which was one block of it, and say, I am the Chairman of that. He could look at the next building in the middle of the Square which was the Royal Bank and say, I am their Law Agent; and he could look at the next building, which was then the British Linen Bank, and say, I am the Chairman of that bank. And it was obviously – I can see it now – inconceivable to him that I would not want to take up this place that he had made.

IM: You were the only son?

BW: I was the only son, yes.

IM: And one sister?

BW: Two sisters: Catriona, who was about three years older than me, and my sister Margaret, who is about fifteen months older than I am.

BT: When you just stopped working, what happened? You just stopped working, or something happened, and then you stopped working?

BW: It's very easy not to work at Oxford. For one thing, the terms are short, the town, as it was then is delightful, there are all sorts of things to do. Lots of people get Seconds or Firsts by just starting to work furiously half-way through the middle year.

BT: And so it didn't occur to you that you were being irresponsible?

BW: A very curious thing happened. When I was back home in vacations, it was clear to me that I was being irresponsible. When I was in Oxford, I was in a quite different place. Indeed, in Oxford, a kind of flowering took place, of me, among people, which was diminished when I returned home.

IM: Before this, had you got on well with your father, if only because you hadn't thought of wanting things he didn't want from you?

BW: Yes, in lots of ways. In fact my sister Margaret, who was very rebellious, thought I let him get away with murder. Indeed, we had this convention in which he called me Watson and I called him Sir, which was not entirely in the sense of the father in *The Four Feathers*, as you might say. [*In A E W Mason's novel, the timid son unironically addresses his intimidating father as 'sir'.*] (L) It was an affectation that grew up. But it was an affectation which came to represent in some measure the relationship between us.

IM: So there was an irony to start with which rather disappeared?

BW: Yes. Father had wonderful habits. He would sit at breakfast. He was a courteous man. He was a man of enormous integrity, which in the legal profession is a highly desirable aspect. He had that kind of integrity which derives from the study of Greek and Latin, particularly an admiration for the Roman virtues, which goes well, particularly with a Scottish lawyer. Because the law was based on Roman law. And he gave a lot of his time to all sorts of things for nothing. Anyway, Father's breakfast: Father would sit reading the paper, wearing his suit preparatory to going to the office, and he always had porridge and bacon and egg, and there came a time when he wanted the salt, which for some reason was never at his end of the table, and he put his hand round the paper and snapped his fingers. (L) Which would drive my sister mad, and which I thought was rather funny, and I would pass the salt. He never knew who had passed it, really.

BT: I'm interested in this conversion from a very filial sort of person who accepts his father's conventions and even adopts some of his mannerisms to some kind of dilettante.

BW: What do you mean dilettante?

BT: Well, you suddenly stopped working, and you experienced no feeling of irresponsibility whilst at Oxford.

BW: I don't think I actually did a dilettante at not working. That could sound purely defensive, but I don't think so – I mean I was ploughing the Elysian Fields. I was harvesting in the Elysian Fields. I had a wonderful sense of freedom when I got there. It was a wonderful new world to me – England was a wonderful new world to me. I wasn't a dilettante, I was thoroughly, thoroughly idle.

BT: What I'm driving at is that this was all remarkably guilt-free.

BW: Oh no: it wasn't guilt-free.

IM: He was a divided Scot, and while he was away from home he was happy and carefree, and when he was at home he was haunted, and son-of-Ballantrae-and-Weir-of-Hermiston and all that.

BW: Well I was son of Hugh Watson, and by God, was I son of Hugh Watson! Look here, I am 55. I live in a block of flats in Glasgow, and two weeks ago I was thunderstruck on my way to the psychiatrist when I was getting into the car, and a woman popped out of a door, and there are thirty flats in this block, and she said, 'You're not Hugh Watson's son, are you?' (L) When this kind of thing happens, unfortunately, I withdraw into myself a long way and I am extremely polite. I said, 'Yes, I am. How do you know that?' And she said that recently they'd had people up to dinner ('dinner!'), and one of them had been a secretary of my father's firm Dundas and Wilson, and she had said, 'That looks to me like Hugh Watson's son.' And first of all I was irritated, as one might almost be if one were in the Sahara and had gone for a long walk and found an oasis, and were just taking some necessary water when somebody said, 'Excuse me, are you Hugh Watson's son?' (L) I am in the middle of my life, and suddenly I was Hugh Watson's son.

But you're right, there were a lot of things about my father that I reproduced. I remember once going to a Walter Scott dinner, I was Literary Editor of *The Scotsman* then, and I went to the annual dinner of the Sir Walter Scott Club in Edinburgh, which was an occasion where I think mostly lawyers and their wives have dinner and somebody like the late Hesketh Pearson or Malcolm Muggeridge gets up and gives an address on Sir Walter Scott. Even Lord Longford has done it (L). And we walked into this event together, my father and I, because I had gone separately, but there he was and there was I. We were to an extent reconciled to each other's separate kinds of existences by then – to an extent. And there came up towards me, as I thought, a man who shall be nameless. He was a person who for some reason irritated me, annoyed me, vexed me beyond endurance. Then he said something polite like, 'Good evening,' (L), and I looked at him and walked on. And my father said to me, 'Do you cut him dead as well, Watson?' (L)

IM: That's wonderful.

BW: Which has only been beat as far as I am concerned by Brummell saying, 'Who is your fat friend?' [*Referring to the Prince of Wales*]

BT: It's hard to resist the impression you're very fond of your father.

BW: Very fond of my father, yes. And I also must have hated him at some point.

IM: Indeed. Can I –

BW: He might well have hated *me* at some point.

IM: Can I point out that the person that we have had an immense silence about is his wife and your mother?

BW: Yes. Mother had a brother called Charlie who was killed in the First War, and she certainly posthumously had the most enormous relationship with her brother Charlie, and during his life too. And I think to some extent I represent the possibilities of the kind of person Charlie was. He was a different kind of person from Father. I remember when I was about to get married my mother said to Catherine, 'Well, you know, Bill's just like his Uncle Charlie, he has the most awful temper.' When I think of Uncle Charlie whom I never knew because he died long before I was born, I think it's quite probable that Charlie did *not* have an awful temper at all, and I think the existence of dead Uncle Charlie being such a marvellous brother was a reproach to my father, certainly on occasions when he lost his temper, for example, or when he was not mild.(L) Or did things Uncle Charlie wouldn't have done. Oh, God knows what things Uncle Charlie would have done if he had lived to be older than eighteen. And there may have been a contest between my parents, invisible to me and possibly invisible to them, but certainly perceived by me.

IM: About who you were going to be, who you were going to be like.

BW: Who I was going to be like, yes. Whether I was going to recover Uncle Charlie to some extent. This is Mother again. After I was sent down from Oxford, as well as being Lord of one side of St Andrews Square (L), Father was also on the University Senate in Edinburgh. So in the middle of the term he got me into the Law Faculty in Edinburgh, and I was apprenticed to a legal firm in Rutland Square.

IM: In what kind of spirit did you go into this Rutland Square job? Did you still think you had any place in law?

BW: Aye, well, there was some exhaustion of spirit, because

whether you've been working or not, when you've been doing a subject for two years unsuccessfully, you're obviously not looking forward to another two years of suddenly tackling it successfully in a different university, (L) and I think after a year I clearly wasn't doing this with a lot of joy, so I said I wanted to quit. What I want to do is go and work in newspapers. So Father got me into the English Faculty at Edinburgh University, and I was clearly a very complaisant son. Though looking back one can see that all one had to do was not work, apart from the fact that I was now accustomed to this. (L)

IM: Doing it, I can imagine, with some grace by this time.

BW: Yes, I got very good at bridge at Edinburgh University.

IM: When were you there, incidentally?

BW: Well, I started in *The Scotsman*, April 12 1954. A date I don't easily recollect (L)… So we can assume that I was at Edinburgh University in the autumn of 1953; my year reading Law was the year before that, and the English Faculty was to me quite astounding, because it was nothing like English used to be in school; it was nothing like the glimpse I had had at Queen's College, Cambridge with the Messrs Potts and Armstrong, or even the sight of all the books on Keats, Wordsworth, Shelley, etc. in John Jones my law tutor's office at Merton College, Oxford. (L)

IM: Are we talking about Professor Renwick?

BW: We're talking about Professor Renwick, but more particularly we're talking about someone called Melville Clark.

IM: Oh yes, Arthur Melville Clark.

BW: Arthur Melville Clark.

BT: A historical note from Isobel.

IM: Arthur Melville Clark was in Edinburgh University for a very long time, and I am told by people who knew him early on that he was a man of great liveliness and promise. By the time I knew him, which was not that long after Bill did, he had become a kind of dictating machine. He used to come into lectures when I was there, and fill the blackboard beforehand with long words like London and Wordsworth that he thought we couldn't spell, and then he used to lecture to us at dictation speed, in the first year on Rhetoric, on 'style, unity, coherence and proper emphasis'. Bill is nodding; that's enough on that.

BW: I didn't stick the situation for long, and resumed the proposition that I wanted to go into newspapers

BT: What inspired that though? Why newspapers, as opposed to following in your Grandfather's footsteps – a distinguished career in school-teaching or something?

BW: Well obviously by this time I wasn't going to be a scholar. I must clearly have felt that I had exhausted the possibilities of becoming a scholar.

BT: Moreover, a career in newspapers would not normally be thought appropriate for the son of such a distinguished family.

IM: For the son of a quarter of St Andrew's Square.

BW: No, well mind you…

IM: Unless you were going to edit something?

BW: Quite clearly it was thought I wouldn't be capable of editing anything. Because I was being a scapegrace.

IM: A graceful scapegrace.

BW: Father was graceful as well.

BT: How did you manage your relationships during all this time? This is not a question about guilt in the same way that the earlier one was. It must have taken some managing to persuade your father that, well, something must be made of the chap, and he is being impossible, and he has this whim about newspapers, which is not the sort of thing I want my son to be involved in.

BW: Well, we had a stand-up row of course. We had several, but one particular stand-up row. Which he lost by actually slapping me in the face.

IM: Ah!

BW: He was obviously very, very angry about the whole thing.

IM: But presumably once he had slapped you in the face, he felt -

BW: He'd ended a chapter, so to speak.

IM: It can't have been something he ever expected to do.

BW: No, it can't have been something he ever expected to do. That's quite right.

IM: So did he help you get into newspapers?

BW: I got a job carrying tea. He actually tried to stop me getting into newspapers to start with. He had a good friend who was the editor of the *Evening News*, James Seagar, and he asked James to talk to me. I thought I was going for a job, but I was to learn that newspapers were a waste of time. Look at me, said James Seagar, wretchedly. (L)
    So then an extraordinary thing happened. Mother bought me a typewriter. Mother couldn't play or take part in these debates in public, but she went and bought me an Olivetti 22, as it then was, typewriter. Which is like buying a horse and a pistol for someone who wants to go West, and his father says, you're not going. (L)

BW: So I went to see Murray Watson, who was Editor of *The Scotsman*, and he asked me if I knew anything about art. He was looking for an art critic. And I said, no, I don't know anything about art.

BW (L) So then he said the only job he could offer me was as the Art Editor's tea-boy. The Art Editor being the Pictures Editor.

IM: All photographs and everything?

BW: Yes, that's right. So I thought that was just terrific – I mean it was a job. And then he said Roy Thompson wanted to see me, the next day. [*Canadian Roy Thomson (later Lord Thomson of Fleet) took over The Scotsman in* 1953] I went to see Roy Thompson, and he was probably the first robust businessman I had ever met in my whole life, as opposed to the Edinburgh kind of businessman. I thought he was absolutely terrific, and he said, wonderfully, as I was thanking him for giving me a job as Art Editor's tea-boy, 'That's all right, son,' he said, 'I wouldn't give you the job if I didn't think you could do it.' (L)

BT: (L) Why was Roy Thompson interested in interviewing the Art Editor's tea-boy?

IM: Because he was Hugh Watson's son!

BW: Because my father had phoned him up, and Roy bought *The Scotsman* by getting a lot of his money from those institutions in Edinburgh, some of which may or may not have been on the east side of St Andrews Square.

BT: (L) As a vote of confidence, this must have given you pause for reflection many a time.

BW: Right! Oh, it was great.

IM: Bill, had you ever made tea?

BW: Yeah, I could make tea. But I actually didn't have to make it, I just had to carry it. And you got to write picture captions. They mostly said things like, 'Vice Admiral so-and-so Flag Officer Scotland doing this or that at Rosyth.'.

IM: So, not trying to cut it short in any way, how did you move from being Art Editor's tea-boy to being the Literary Editor, which is what you were when I first met you in 1962?

BW: I became a sub-editor quite quickly, because any competent tea-boy could quickly become a sub-editor. That was how a lot of people went into journalism in those days. You got jobs as tea-boys, or copy-boys if they were in the news room, and then started sub-editing by making the appropriate marks for the printers on things like movements of ships. And then they graduated to doing things that needed headlines thought for them instead of just having headlines Movements of Ships. (L) I liked movements of ships. They said things like SS Francis Beam sailed Maracaibo for Leith with a cargo of pit props. And the phrases are evocative. 'Sailed Maracaibo', 'out of', all this stuff. So then I was a sub-editor for about six years and one day the Literary Editor, an upright six feet two called James Smellie, asked me if I would mind making some helpful arrangement about proofs which he was unable to do because he was off to some function or other. So I said, charmed to do this, and he said, 'Grazi.' I said 'Prego'. So at once he assumed to himself that he had here a person of some kind of culture. So the next day he brought me a book to review. (L)

IM: I hope it was an Italian book.

BW: I know what it was. It was a book about the Council of Florence in the fifteenth century, which was an attempt to resolve the schism between the East and West branches of the Church. And this is how I first learned – well actually it was just like going right back to school and swotting for an exam – you just read the book very hard, and then you could review it intelligently.

IM: In quite a small number of words.

BW: Quite a small number of words. And then I was given another book to review: it was the life of Madame de Genlis, who was the tutor to the children of Monsieur – the Duc d'Orleans. But I can't remember in the time of which Louis she was tutor – but I think it was Louis XVI.

BT: So you were suddenly a historical expert?

BW: In a way yes.

IM: And once you're typecast, it's quite hard. Anyway, on you go, about what you were doing.

BW: James Smellie decided to retire a little early, and when asked what should be done about his successor he nominated me. So they made me Literary Editor.

BT: That's a good story, but it's a bit brief. You had to ingratiate yourself with him by more than just reviewing the odd book. Did you demonstrate a general interest in literary matters?

IM: Or did you just set up the page for him a few times when he was busy?

BT: Where were you when Milne's Bar was busy?

BW: I wasn't in Milne's Bar, baby! I never looked at the literary pub hardly, except there was a time occasionally later on when I went to Milne's Bar with Sidney Goodsir Smith, I went to other places. I went to Betty Moss's bar in Leith.

BT: So in effect you didn't interest yourself particularly in where the Scottish writers happened to be congregating?

BW: No. You're on to something quite interesting, because when I was being a sub-editor I was being not a lawyer. Right?

IM: (L) More being not a lawyer than being anything else in particular.

BW: Yes. But when I became Literary Editor I knew I wasn't qualified in one sense – well indeed, in almost all senses except the journalistic sense. And there were plenty of people around to let you know that you weren't qualified too, because they thought they should have been Literary Editor! (L)

BT: Are we talking about the consciousness of intelligence or a kind of trade craft?

BW: Both. There are two things here. The consciousness of intelligence – this guy would be able to – it's a simple enough job to get books in from publishers and send them out to people who know how to review books, especially as you were bound to inherit a system from your predecessor, although there is something to qualify there. And the trade craft was there – the guy knows how to make up pages – how to deal with the printers, etc. But when I was given the job Alastair Dunnett said, I want you to bring the book page up to date. Which is *carte blanche.* [*Alastair Dunnett has been described as 'a key figure in Roy Thomson's effort to bring the paper out of its respectable but commercially disastrous torpor.' He was editor until 1972, and succeeded by Eric Mackay.*]

BT: And given your lack of knowledge of who'd been writing what in Scotland and who's been meeting for a beer or a dram, this was an interesting proposition?

BW: It was an interesting proposition. It also has this to be said about it, that I remember now that you asked me earlier when I first started thinking of writing. Well, I remember at school I must have been thinking of it, because I went to meetings of the Saltire Society, and there from a remote distance I saw Sidney Goodsir Smith and Hugh MacDiarmid sitting on the floor in a great mood, and Wendy Wood and people like that all buzzing their way about. I then realised that everything had to be written in Scots. And having been brought up *bourgeois* I'd gone to Edinburgh Academy with the sons of lawyers and other people, and having gone to Oxford any attempt by me to write in Scots would have felt quite unnatural. At school my love of English became big. It was an Eng Lit tradition; we did the English exams; we did School Cert and then we did Scottish Highers and then we did Higher Cert.

IM: It was called having the best of both worlds.

BW: Aye! And it was at school that I learned how to write the way I do write, because when I was doing School Cert and Higher Cert, you looked at the question and you started writing the answer. But in between when we came to do Scottish Highers we were told that for the Scottish Highers they liked you to have a beginning, an argument and an end. And I tried to do a beginning, an argument and an end for a bit, and I couldn't do it. So I began looking at the question and then starting to write the answer. So my books are not planned in that sense. I have an idea and then I chase it, but best I have an idea and then I have another idea and then I chase the two of them through the forest.

IM: I think that could well be something we'll come back to. For the time, it's just a useful trace laid.

BW: Aye!

BT: And you became Literary Editor at what date?

BW: About 1960. So that's curious, isn't it. There I was where I would have wanted to be if I'd had the wit to want to be it, if I'd got a degree at Cambridge. And I might not have got the job anyway. (L) You were talking about Scottish writing, I was taken out to lunch by a guy from Oliver & Boyd at the Café Royal, and Giles Gordon, who was in working for him. And he said, I presume now we'll be able to see more reviews of Scottish books on the new *Scotsman* book page.

IM: And was he right?

BW: Well, I immediately took this as a slur upon my predecessor, James Smellie, whom I had much admired, and anyway I liked him for nominating me for the job. And I said, 'Well, I don't expect to, no.' (L) And indeed I didn't.

What happened, though, was interesting, because there was a very conscientious system of handing book reviews. The book review was set in type and two proofs were taken. One for the Literary Editor and one for the reviewer, and it was then sent off to the reviewer, who could make any last minute emendations that he felt obliged to do, and corrections, and then the Literary Editor made his corrections and had his afterthoughts, and then the reviewer brought in his proof and the Literary Editor laid it beside his own proof, and a marriage was arranged. (L) So having come fresh from the newsroom at first I thought this was quite delightful, and then I thought it was a waste of time, and the pace it involved was rather sedate. When I stopped this process at least three of the book reviewers were cross, and expressed themselves in unfeeling language about it. So being kind of naïve I dropped them, and entered my bottom right hand drawer in which I'd got about thirty letters from people who on seeing that I had been appointed Literary Editor had written to ask if they could start reviewing for the *Scotsman*. Were you one? I can't remember.

IM: No.

BW: And among them was a letter from Robert Nye, who was then I think about twenty. And there was one from Martin Seymour-Smith.

IM: I would have guessed that.

BW: And so I wrote to Robert Nye and sent him some books, and I wrote to Martin Seymour-Smith and I sent him some books, and Isobel started reviewing, and quite soon we had in some respects a smashing book page. And almost in the first year I was Literary

Editor I started having the reviews signed, and I got the page set in Tempo, which is sans serif type, All these cheerful things I was able to do because Alastair Dunnett was my Editor and let one do it. He gave you a job and then gave you your head. And if he didn't like what you had done he didn't.

BT: Set the columns in sans serif type?

BW: No, set the headings in sans serif.

BT: Only a mad typographer would want to know the reason for me asking that question – it does seem strange.

BW: It would have been extremely striking. (L) However this was pretty striking because it was in *The Scotsman*, but the thing about Alastair Dunnett was, he didn't ask you on Friday what you were going to do on Saturday: he told you on Monday that you had screwed it up – if you had screwed it up. It's a perfect way to work. He let you get on with it.

      The first year I was Literary Editor, John Calder had his first Writers' Conference.

BT: Which is roughly where I come in, in autobiographical terms.

BW: That was stunningly exciting for me.

IM: Is this 1960?

BW: 1961.

IM: And John Calder himself was quite important for you, in all sorts of ways.

BW: Yes he was! He published a lot of what they called then avant garde writers, particularly French, and a lot of European writers. And of course he published Beckett's first novels. Indeed by knowing John one met some very interesting writers, who if you go back eighteen months before I became Literary Editor I didn't know existed. And suddenly I met lots of them at this conference talking in strange ways, and dammit, my first newspaper article, as opposed to a book review, was an article summing up the conference. And then I came to know John Calder well and indeed rented a cottage from him on his estate. At Ledlanet, which he had then.

IM: What about the other people at *The Scotsman*? Obviously you were being affected at this time by writers and reviewers, by John Calder and his particular set of writers. Were there any of the journalists in *The Scotsman* who were important to you? Or did you stay fairly separate from that?

BW: I became fairly separate from them. Indeed subsequently when I was running the Weekend Scotsman I was warned by one of my superiors (not Alastair) that I was becoming elitist. Perhaps I was: what does elitist mean?

IM: (L) What you want it to mean in any one sentence I suspect.

BW: It went like this. In the Weekend Scotsman we had Christopher MacLehose who is now my editor, and we had Ena Watt who was also the Travel Editor, and she later became Women's Editor of *The Scotsman* and she's now retired. We had a record-player in our office, we had a nice office, with an ongoing chess game and an electric kettle – all of which we provided ourselves. And it was a delightful environment, and not the kind of life people were living in the rest of *The Scotsman*. And one of my superiors, but not Alastair Dunnett, said well, why don't you sort of open it up a bit and let people come in for coffee in the morning? So I said, well, I don't want to do that – never get any work done, you know, for God's sake! (L)

IM: The non-Dunnett superior retires in confusion!

BW: I remember Magnus Magnusson came to start an investigative section of the paper called Closeup, and his team was David Kemp and Gus MacDonald, and at the same time I had become Literary Editor, and then I was given the Weekend Scotsman to do after three years of that to bring the Weekend Scotsman up to date and I brought in Christopher MacLehose.

BT: You brought him?

BW: Yes, at least they said, who do you want for an assistant?

BT: Where did he pop out of?

BW: He'd popped in the door some time in the preceding year quoting a mutual friend Archie Weir who had been and may still have been at that point Advertising Director of *The Scotsman*, and said, any chance of any reviewing? So we became friends.

BT: The sort of thing *The Scotsman* is famous for in that period, the early sixties, is for giving distinction to the idea of investigative journalism.

BW: No, I've never done that: it wasn't interesting to me.

IM: You were very happy to give the front page of the Weekend Scotsman over to the Closeup team when they had a good story.

BW: Yes, because they could only produce one every six weeks or so.

IM: So that suited you, it suited them and in between you had all these other things to do with it. So it wasn't a marriage of true minds all the way along. But that you and Christopher had more of a marriage of minds.

BW: Yes, that's true. And of temperaments. I wasn't an ambitious person: I didn't in fact know what ambition was, really. Christopher was ambitious, and has become very successful, and Magnusson was ambitious. Indeed I remember Magnusson saying something to me in what appeared to me then to be a deluded state, and subsequently I now see it as being correct. Magnusson said, 'One day one of us is going to be Editor of this paper, so I will make a pact with you that the other becomes Deputy Editor.' (L)

IM: I see. This tape could be worth something. Do you remember what, if any, ambition you had at that time? If you hadn't decided you wanted to write, you didn't feel ambitious about journalism, was it just a question of living what seemed a reasonable and civilised life and enjoying yourself?

BW: Yes, you see something happened when I became Literary Editor, which was that I reverted to attitudes that I had deserted when I went to Oxford, which was that you expect to be among the top three in the class. So I went back into working hard feeling like somewhere in the top three in the class and I worked very hard at it.

IM: And enjoyed it?

BW: Enjoyed it a lot.

BT: So you had no clear idea of ambition?

BW: That's right. I thought you went into a job and once I became Literary Editor and then became Weekend Scotsman Editor, I just assumed you went on working well and you ascended …

IM: From tea-boy to White House. (L)

BW: Well, you didn't actually ascend to the White House, you just ascended, vaguely.

IM: They went on clapping you on the shoulder and putting you up one.

BT: Did you in some way expect to be rewarded by being pushed into something even better?

BW: No, I didn't.

BT: And you had no ambition to go in any particular direction.

BW: No, just go on doing it and go up.

IM: Did you have a specific desire to stay where you were? Like stay in Edinburgh, for example?

BW: I think I didn't want to go to London anyway. I'd have had to be persuaded to go to London.

BT: Your account of it is difficult to believe, on the grounds that an intelligent person would figure it out otherwise.

BW: Well you've got to look at it that in the office I was having the time of my life. The same kind of time of my life that I had at Oxford, except that at Oxford I wasn't working.

IM: And in the office you were, and doing what you really wanted to do. You weren't sitting round feeling like an academic failure any more; you were feeling like a guy among his equals now.

BW: I was still out of my element. Something strange would happen: I would meet somebody because I knew John Calder. I would meet Samuel Beckett quite a lot. Either in John's house in London or John's house in Kinross-shire. And because Samuel Beckett was such a great man he was easy to talk with, and I met a lot of other writers. So I don't suppose I felt that being surrounded by Magnusson, Kemp and Christopher MacLehose was stunning. (L) Also there's another thing. One inherits a lot, and even though I was nowhere near being a lawyer, my father stayed at Dundas and Wilson until he became not the senior partner but the second senior partner, and he would have become senior partner except that he died. You said earlier that people living now wouldn't understand what we were saying about the fifties. I didn't think in terms of becoming, as it were headmaster. That's a very signal thing to say, I now notice.

BT: Yes, I think it is. I think it means that you're from a certain sort of background where that kind of absence of mind could occur.

BW: It's not competitive. I know Magnusson was competitive, and I recognised it even before I knew what competitiveness really was because the first time he came to see me with Roger Woods he sat in *my* chair behind *my* desk, and I said to myself, this is an intrusion that I don't like. (L) Then I realised that this was characteristic of Magnusson.

BT: It is quite important to pin down for people that there was a time when people from certain backgrounds, even from a whole variety of different backgrounds, didn't necessarily regard life as an enormous competition in which you struggle for a dominance.

BW: That is absolutely correct.

IM: Today off-tape we heard something about Bill's times as an evacuee during the war, which made us feel it would be quite nice to have that on tape as well. Perhaps you would tell us how it all came about, Bill.

BW: Yeah, when I was evacuated. I was evacuated first to Chirnside in Berwickshire, to a farm called Oldcastles, near Chirnside. I went with a family called Berry who lived across the street from us. At that time it was thought that the Germans might bomb Edinburgh, or even shell it, like Great Yarmouth in the First War (L). I was nine and I went to Oldcastles, and the household was Auntie May and Auntie Anne, who owned it and ran the farm. And Auntie Jean, who was in fact Mrs Jean Berry, but I called her Auntie Jean. And Joan and Ian and Jim, her children, in that order of age.

IM: Your sisters didn't go?

BW: No; they went to a school called Cranley, and Cranley was evacuated *en bloc* to Grantown-on-Spey. The next year we all went to Grantown-on-Spey. So this was winter time, and I have some very clear and fixed memories. One was of lots of snow, and a snow plough, having cleared out the side roads, and being taken along on a sort of small sleigh towed by one of the two donkeys, Day or Biddy. I remember we used to be allowed to roam the fields and play Cowboys and Indians, and hold up the train, which went past nonetheless. The school was an evacuees' school: in other words the kids were all wearing their uniforms from Gillespie's and the Marcia Blane School (L), Queen Street and Herriots, and Edinburgh Academy and you name it. But I don't actually, at this moment, remember anything at all of what it was like inside the school building.

IM: So what you remember is the freedom of the farm and the difference from city life.

BW: And a very strange thing – we went to a hotel for lunch everyday.

IM: Good heavens.

BW: Not the whole school, but just Joan and Ian and I. In fact I now begin to wonder if Joan was there at all, or if she'd gone up to – she was certainly there some of the time, it doesn't matter. The Misses Cowe; that's who Anne and May were. The name was Cowe, with an e on the end. Every Saturday we went into Berwick-on-Tweed to do the shopping. We went in two cars, a Jowett and a Humber. I had never seen a family with two cars in my life before, and they got petrol for the Humber, war-time rationing system, and used it in the Jowett, so it went further.

IM: A Jowett I take it was a smaller and more inexpensive car as opposed to the Humber.

BW: A very lovely and classic car, people think about them nowadays.

IM: I'm sure. So, did you go straight back from there to Edinburgh, or does Grantown-on-Spey come into this episode as well?

BW: Yes, then I went to Grantown-on-Spey. The Berry family moved *en bloc* leaving the father behind. So I went off with Ian and Jim and Joan, and Mrs Berry, who was known as Auntie Jean to me, and Granny Purvis, her mother. We went to live in a cottage called Birch View in Grantown-on-Spey, and I went to the Grammar School, and so did Ian, and Joan went to Cranley, which was now established in the Cairngorm Hotel.

IM: Do you remember whether you missed your own family?

BW: Well I know I missed my own family, yes.

IM: I wondered whether perhaps having a boy of your own age to play with more than made up for the absence of your sisters?

BW: I don't think it was my sisters I missed: I think it was my home. At one level obviously I felt very secure in that family, and at another level it was a serious disturbance for me. Becoming part of another family.

IM: Indeed, it's no small thing. And obviously if it hasn't left a terrible scar on you it's because of another super family who understood something about how to do it.

BW: Yes, I felt very warm towards Jean Berry, and she was a loving surrogate parent, yes. So then the girls stayed on at Cranley School, which was now completely a boarding-school in Grantown-on-Spey, and I went back to Edinburgh.

IM: And eventually to Edinburgh Academy and so on, and the unfortunate hospital times and everything we mentioned yesterday.

BW: We're leaving one thing out. When I went back to Edinburgh on the way to Edinburgh Academy I had four months summer holiday, because school like Grantown Grammar School had their holidays in June and July, and the Academy had their holidays in August and September. And that's when I experienced the merits of the interminable vacation. (L)

IM: Your first taste of what was to come to full fruit in Oxford.

BW: Very informative, yes. (L)

IM: I think we should now try to get to starting writing. Was *Better Than One* (1969) the first thing that you had seriously written, or did you write this play with Robert Nye first?

BW: No, I wrote *Better Than One* first, because Robert Nye didn't start writing until we noticed that we wrote in some ways similarly, then we thought it would be fun to collaborate on a play.

IM: So, as far as you remember, in what kind of spirit and with what kind of an idea did you approach writing *Better Than One*, and was it very important to you at the time? Was there a lot of Bill invested in it, and its success?

BW: No, there wasn't, oddly enough there wasn't a lot of Bill invested. It started with me writing in a very gloomy phase, and I remember I went to Glasgow for the paper to review *Armstrong's Last Goodnight*, and that was its world premiere, at the Citizens, and I wrote the review, and then I went back to Ledlanet, because John Calder had come to the premiere too, and I wouldn't be surprised if John had something to do with it, encouraging me that I could actually write something myself.

IM: You certainly spoke yesterday about John and his wide interest in European writers having had quite an effect on you. I would have said in a way that that is very clear in *Better Than One*. It's neither a Scottish nor an English novel, it seems to me. Very much more a European one. But if I was going to say 'like' anything, it might be Irish. A touch of the Flann O'Briens and a touch of the James Joyces, maybe.

BW: Well, when John first read it, he said 'James Joyce', and plucked his eyebrow, and that was for John a long sentence. (L) I said, well, I haven't read James Joyce, and he said, Beckett, then, Beckett: and that's possible, because I had read *Watt* and *Murphy* – indeed, I'd read the trilogy by that time.

IM: I wasn't at all suggesting that things were indebted, just that the nearest things that one knew in the language you're using tended to be these very European Irishmen.

BW: Yes, yes. I would have had difficulty writing as Scottish, and it shows everywhere. And what the problem is I don't know.

IM: Scottish writing in our time has been so self-conscious, so full of so many other things besides the ordinary ends of writing, I think it's not surprising at all that you found it foreign. You talked about going to the Saltire and hearing Hugh MacDiarmid and Sidney Goodsir Smith and Wendy Wood: these were people with whom you couldn't say 'Scottish' without a political act being involved.

BW: That's true, and their politics were nowhere near mine, because at that time mine were rather like the politics of Athos in *The Three Musketeers*, which is a curious kind of demanding loyalty to a monarch, not like the loyalty to the Stewarts, more like the oath that the nobles of Arragon swore to their king, that we who are as good as you will be true to you as long as you are true to us, and if not, not. (L) It was totally and utterly romantic, and I had no political sense at all.

IM: And a lot of Scottish writers, particularly in the time dominated by MacDiarmid, really did insist on making everything a political act in a quite unsettling way, I think.

BW: Yes. And the language is not mine, and I'd been brought up at a school that studied a lot of English literature as well as Scott and Stevenson. I liked Scott a helluva lot, I liked Stevenson a lot. But I liked T S Eliot, I like Gerard Manley Hopkins. I liked Bacon's essays: I didn't read Auden. Oh, I liked Thomas Hardy a lot, Dickens, Trollope, Jane Austen.

IM: So there was a sense in which you weren't self-consciously Scottish at all?

BW: No, not in the least: I just wasn't self-conscious at all. I was just going on being me.

IM: I mean in so far as you had a country, it was as much the UK or Britain, or something like that?

BW: No, it was Scottish. I had lived in the Highlands, we spent our holidays in the Highlands, or at Elie where we used to have holidays. Scottish guy living in Scotland. But there was always this invisible English influence which even affects the manners of the household you're brought up in. Even if you're Scottish. And indeed the Edinburgh Academy was set up as that kind of school. In its charter, which I read about somewhere quite recently, boys were to be taught the English language, and not to be encouraged to speak in Scotticisms – I mean, you did not sleep in: if you said you had slept in, you were told you had overslept, because that's a Scotticism, you were told.

IM: After all, Edinburgh Academy was the same kind of school as a whole number of Scottish schools, very much aping the English public school tradition, and finding socially for their products the sort of advantages that awaited the products of the English public schools.

BW: That's right. That's right.
    Better Than One was curiously very easy to write. I just wrote it quite happily and wrote it till it was finished. And it was a

lot of fun. It's a lot of word-play, and what it means I don't know. (L) But it means things get better.

IM: But also the play is fun in itself?

BW: Yes, the play is fun in itself: that's very right. That's good. That's Buddhist: that's not Christian. Yes, that's right.

IM: From my point of view it's a very serene book. No matter how awful the things that can happen to people are, if you're engaged on a level where word-play and these games are fun, even your characters, from time to time, both of them, enter into a conspiracy with you of enjoying games with language. That's OK. Did you have difficulty getting it published?

BW: Not really. (L)

IM: Why was that?

BW: Well, first of all I gave it to John Calder, who said he'd publish it. I mean, I took it along the road; about a hundred yards of farm track road to the house where he lived.

IM: You asked your nearest publisher. (L)

BW: Yes, and he said he'd publish it. But then he didn't (L), and then a year passed, and I looked at the contract and discovered that in that case he'd lost it. So it was published by Christopher MacLehose, who had by then gone from *The Scotsman* and was with Barrie and Jenkins.

IM: Or Barrie and Rockliff, I think.

BW: Barrie and Rockliff as it then was, under the imprint of the Cresset Press. It was published.

IM: So did you stay with Barrie and Rockliff?

BW: No, I didn't. Apart from everything else, I didn't write another novel for ten years, so such residence would have been vapid. (L) I wrote plays after that.

IM: For quite a long time as I recall it, it looked as if Bill Watson had been meant to be a dramatist rather than a novel writer, that *Better Than One* had been the odd one out, and really you were very much involved in –

BW: Being a dramatist? Yes, I was very involved in drama. I don't know at all what happened. I can't remember thinking, I'm not going to write another novel. I just started writing plays.

IM: And first of all you did this in collaboration, and this is part of the fun of it, isn't it?

BW: That's right, yes. Robert Nye published a novel called *Doubtfire* – it came out the same time as *Better Than One*. Robert was living in Edinburgh then, and we noticed that there were a lot of similarities of both joke and style, so we thought it would be fun to write something together, so we wrote a play. I've forgotten its name, and I've forgotten most of it, except that there was a beautiful lovesong in it, and the stage direction – 'Enter three tall grandfathers'. (L)

IM: And what happened to the play, Bill?

BW: We only had one copy, and Robert sent it to an agent, and it got lost at her hairdresser's. (L)

IM: At her hairdresser's. We could almost make a play about losing that one. But nothing daunted, you and Robert set to to write another one.

BW: It was a long one. We wrote a play called *Sawney Bean* on the Galloway coast cannibal and his tribe. (1970)

IM: Can you remember why you chose to write about such a bizarre and perhaps unpleasant subject?

BW: Well, once we'd thought of it it was probably irresistible. (L) Sawney Bean and his family lived on the beach, hid in the trees nearby, when people passed jumped down and killed some of them – well, caught as many as they could, and the others ran off shrieking. And they salted them and kept them in caves. The story is well known.

BT: I saw that play at the Traverse. That's where it was first put on, wasn't it? And enjoyed it very much.

BW: Did you?

BT: Yes, I did. I thought it was weird, and it was just the sort of crazy play you might expect someone to put on at the Traverse. Which is actually what I'm getting to. There was the Traverse, and you were living in an Edinburgh where all sorts of amazing things could be accepted: I was just wondering about the Traverse, and its perhaps influencing your idea of, all right, we can write plays, and here's a theatre which will happily put them on?

BW: That's quite possible! Because I spent a lot of time, at the Traverse, a lot of time in the Traverse bar, a lot of time in the Traverse restaurant. Finished work at *The Scotsman,* I'd go out and have dinner at the Traverse.

IM: And the bizarre licensing laws at that time as well – just about the only place you could get a drink after a particular time of night, wasn't it?

BW: Yes, well not me, because I was really drinking rather a lot, and I could get drink anywhere I wanted, just about – I mean places to get drink. I wasn't drinking rather a lot, I was drinking a great deal too much, but the great thing about the Traverse was it acquired a congenial company of people that went there..

BT: I remember that Mike Stafford Clark was Director of the Traverse for a period at the end of the sixties, beginning of the seventies.

BW: And he directed *Sawney Bean*, that's right.

BT: And he was a very clubbable man. It was pleasant to meet him and sit around and talk, quite apart from any performance you happened to be wanting to attend.

BW: It was good for the heart, soul and mind. It was a terrific place to be.

IM: So, having written *Sawney Bean*, was it great to see it on stage, or was it weird to see it on stage?

BW: It was weird to see it on stage. I went the first night, and it was the first time I had ever experienced this terrible first night feeling. I couldn't hear a line from the stage, because of the barking of the dogs and the traffic outside, and I thought, this is appalling, and I thought the same thing was happening to everybody else. But it wasn't. This never happened to me again at the Traverse. Never heard the dogs outside or the traffic in the street. It was just – it was a terror you get on the first night.

IM: And you went on getting that terror on other first nights in different places?

BW: Yes. Everybody gets it, the director, and the performers of course get it.

IM: But it didn't put you off writing plays for quite a long time?

BW: No. I'd started writing. Then I wrote a play called *A Footstool for God* [1972], which was about Rosslyn Chapel.

IM: About the apprentice pillar, as I recall. It was a sort of sampler pillar, with all sorts of amazing designs.

BW: And there's a fixed legend about Rosslyn Chapel, about why – which is that the mason building it designed three pillars that were marvellous, and he designed a fourth pillar and he couldn't carve it. So he went off to Rome to consult a chap who had been his master, and while he was away his apprentice did the fourth pillar, and it was better than the other three. So when he came back from Rome and saw this, says the legend, he stabbed him. But it is not historically established that he stabbed him, so I made him blind him instead.

IM: Apart from the moot case of *Sawney Bean*, this is the first of your historical things. Did you do a lot of research for it?

BW: I did a lot of unprofessional research, and I did it in a lot of really dirty books, dirty with soot, in the *Scotsman* library. Which are unreliable nineteenth-century books about Scottish history, and there's nothing better than an unreliable book for really giving you lots of grammatically possible hot news. (L)

IM: So it wouldn't have worried you if a historian had been to the first night and wrote you a gentle letter expostulating that you couldn't really have this or that?

BW: No, not one little tiny bit. The play was to find out why the guy who started building Rosslyn Chapel stopped building it. To hell with apprentices being stabbed. He'd started to build a collegiate sized church, and he ended up only with the chapel. He was stopped building it.

IM: Right. So although you had not been anxious to a fault about historical accuracy, a great deal of what you've written has been historical, one way or another, hasn't it?

BW: Yes. I think the reason I'm not nervous about historical accuracy is, I think the chances of me making a mistake from what I've read are very slim, because I go at it very close to the time I'm reading about it. So whatever the source is I'm very close to it.

When I wrote the book about the Templars, *Beltran in Exile* (1979), I actually knew an incredible number of things that happened in the particular year that the book was living in at that moment.

IM: 1291, as I recall. But I wasn't meaning just to ask about worrying about accuracy. Can you pin down at all what the attraction is of history? Why one would write in a different time from the time one is living in? You've done this both in plays and novels.

BW: Come at it this way. The reason that I started writing *Beltran in Exile* was that I went to live near a place called Temple, and so I wondered why, and so I became aware that it was the Knights of the Temple, and then I noticed that the Knights of the Temple had been twice overthrown. They were overthrown in the Holy Land when they were kicked out when they fought their last fight at Acre, and they were kicked out by the Moslems, and that was the end of the crusading kingdoms, and the Templars were the last out, like the French at Dien Bien Phu. And they were overthrown again back in Europe, when Philip the Fair destroyed the Order. And for me that was a picture of what happens in life: my hero Beltran was in it in Acre, he was brought up in the Holy Land, and he comes back to France, and holy smoke, the Order is turned over again. So twice the floor is taken out from underneath his life. And I think I'd actually be incapable of expressing that in a modern book. I would have no sympathy with the Beltran person in a modern book. I only understand him in the past.

IM: Because you've never yourself been a soldier, and you've never yourself been a religious? But you made the imaginative effort to combine both of these in Beltran, I think very successfully.

BW: Yes I did, but I could write about a schoolmaster who put a few schools up, so to speak. It would mean nothing to me at all. But I was very affected by Scott's historical novels; very affected by Dumas; very affected by other historical writers, and very embraced by the past. Yes, I have a strong sense of the past. And the value of the past. And I think I did feel at that time I was living in a world which had a strong sense of the present, which to me was swell to live in, but not significant with comprehensive symbols or messages.

BT: So it's the past, or historicised past that conveys meaning in the sense of symbols or messages?

BW: Yes.

BT: You know, I mean by historicised – I mean it already has to be turned into a story.

BW: I thought you meant I came across the historicised past and then imagined my way into it.

BT: Yes, that's actually rather what I mean – it's mediated by already being a story.

IM: There are ways in which it seems to me that you powerfully identify with Beltran. I was wondering if there was any sense in which you were conscious of any sense of code or belief that you could apply to your own life, whose basis is no longer sensible in any rational sort of way? In the way that Beltran's faith, particularly his Order, are just made obsolete, and he is left on living that?

BW: Well, Beltran's faith was in a sense a kind of challenge to God, it seems to me now. As if he said to God, OK, you laid this on me, and I have to go on serving the Order of the Temple even after it's been extinguished, and I will hold you to answer for it, and meanwhile I will endure. And if you're asking if I've survived that point of view, yes I have, because I don't think endurance is – I mean life is a lot better than that!

IM: Yes, I've even read a modern thriller in which the main character is described much in these terms, as somebody who, if he ever had beliefs and loyalties to live by, has outlived them, and he doesn't know where they come from, but he still tries to live by them.

BW: Really? Harry Seddall? Yes, that's right. But Harry Seddall's having a better time.

IM: We'll leave that for a footnote. [*IM had recently reviewed BW's second Mayo thriller, Wolf's Head, where Seddall is forced by his pretty sidekick Sorrel to admit to his outdated loyalties.*] *Beltran* then was about ten years after *Better Than One*?

BW: Yes, it was published exactly ten years after *Better Than One*. It was published in 1979.

IM: But before you came to *Beltran* you had written several plays; in fact you'd become a kind of playwright in residence, hadn't you?

BW: Oh yes: I was literary adviser to Perth Theatre for ten years.

IM: Tell us a wee bit about that. And the magic name of Joan Knight.

BW: Joan Knight moved Perth Theatre from having twenty to thirty per cent audiences into a highly successful theatre over a period of years. She was simply a very sensible, intuitive, experienced theatre woman from England.

IM: And did you write *Footstool* for her to do, or was it that she was interested in…?

BW: No, I wrote *Footstool* for a raking stage like the Old Vic when it was a National theatre.

IM: So you didn't have any particular company in mind at all? So, how did the play and the director find each other?

BW: The play and the director found each other because I had come to know her because my girl friend was working for her.

IM: Ah, that makes sense.

BW: And also Joan liked *Sawney Bean* a lot: she thought it was terrific, what plays ought to be. But before I gave *Footstool* to Joan, I'd tried London, because that's why I was writing plays – that's why I write, actually – is to be published in London and the world, as if it were an address, you know – London, England, The world.

IM: Would you then feel it was a kind of second-class publishing to be published in Scotland?

BW: No, I would feel it was more likely to be recondite.

IM: Or of particularly local interest. Your feeling if you wanted to be published in London for the world, is that the particular ways in which you were appealing to the reader or the spectator are ways in which you are appealing to things universal to everybody, rather than the person who wants to take the Scots, and particularly shake them about their own particular –

BW: Yes, I don't want to shake the Scots.

IM: Yet!

BW: Particularly. I noticed after a while when I'd been writing plays that I was trying to change the world. That I thought, for some reason, the act that was performed on stage would alter people's natures, and if a play was good enough it would do that, Oh, alter people's natures, to hell, alter people's perceptions and understanding. I noticed after I was doing it, this was what I was doing. It was quite an unconscious and quite nonsensical event going on in me.

IM: Perhaps dramatists have to have that? Hope, or confidence, and it was when you began to question it that you wrote less for the theatre? Perhaps you could tell us very briefly about plays after *Footstool for God* before you moved back into mainly fiction writing.

BW: Yes. I wrote two more plays, two modern ones which were staged at Perth, and one historical one which wasn't. *Footstool for God* was done at Pitlochry, directed by Joan Knight, who was the director of Perth theatre (1972). She commissioned two plays from me; one was called *The Larch* (1974): that was its working title. Actually it was going to be called *Mr Wintergreen*, but we ended up having to call it *The Larch*, because some advance publicity had gone out to Sydney, Australia, because it was done in the Perthshire, Scotland, Festival, but it had world wide publicity because of that.

IM: And what sort of a thing was that, then?

BW: That's a play about a man called Wintergreen whose car breaks down – or so he says – and he comes into this cottage where these two people, this young couple, are living. Great antagonism develops about his visit, and he's as far as I recollect allied first with one and then with the other, and goes off again into the night.

IM: Sounds positively Beckettian, as you describe it.

BW: Well, there's a lot of comedy in it.

IM: There's a lot of comedy in Beckett!

BW: I know: I hadn't thought of it as being Beckettian.

IM: Pinterian as well, in that things aren't explained, things just happen.

BW: Yes. Pinter was thrown at that play, and Pinter was thrown at the next play.

IM: And were you gratified or annoyed?

BW: I thought it was irrelevant.

IM: Did you, on the whole, tend to feel that comments on your work are relevant?

BW: When one gets good notices one thinks comments are marvellously relevant.(L) I find that comparisons with other writers seem to hold me up, bring me up short. This reminds me of the fact that we have been talking about writing historical stuff, and I think maybe the modern world makes me nervous, and I like to belong somewhere else. Or there was a time when I liked - my imagination – belonged somewhere else. Even when I was enjoying the world *I* was in. The noises that came from outside the bit I was in made me want to put my imagination not into that bit outside where I was in but into the past.

IM: So there was *The Larch*, otherwise known as *Mr Wintergreen*.

BW: Let's call it *Mr Wintergreen*.

IM: And then there was the next one.

BW: *Dodwell's Last Trump*. It's about a grocer.

IM: That's the other modern one?

BW: Yes. Dodwell's a grocer. Indeed there's a speech I love in it in which he recites a litany of things on his shelves. It consists of nothing else. This is because a supermarket has come up next door, and he's just sitting in his chair waiting for death, waiting for the end, waiting for the Gestapo to come, and they do come actually. The Gestapo do come, literally wearing Swastikas.

IM: Would you call it a comedy?

BW: Yes. Black comedy. It is a black comedy.

IM: And that one was also done at Perth?

BW: Yes.

IM: So then you wrote a historical one that wasn't done? Why was that?

BW: Yes. Because it was turned down by Perth and I didn't send it anywhere else. It's called *Mengart's Coast*. I'd like to write an original screenplay.

IM: You fancy doing that?

BW: Yes I do!

IM: And does your mind immediately fly to historical subjects for that, or - ?

W   No, I've got one modern one and one historical one.

IM: Are you going to tell us a little about them? Don't, if it's going to mean that you're getting tired of them before you ever do them!

BW: Well, the one about a man and woman playing tennis. He gets a telephone threat saying that he's going to be killed, so he hires a security outfit. And the security outfit gradually takes over the household. The servants have to go, the wife ends up cooking, people get shot. We never see the people from outside; there's a threat to the people from outside, and the people running the security outfit get more and more paranoid, and everything is bugged inside the household, and it's very comic as well, I guess, in my mind.

IM: At the risk of making you cross, it sounds so Pinterian to me. It has such apparent reminiscences of *The Birthday Party*, and the two who arrive and terrorise the chap whose having the birthday, and nobody knows who they are, or where from. The Pinter comparison does make you cross?

BW: Yes, I don't even see it now. I mean, I simply had this idea. Pinter didn't have it. (L)

IM: Do you think if somebody makes a comparison it's a vague kind of suggestion of plagiarism?

BW: No, I just don't seem to go in for comparisons, do I? (L)

IM: No, I'm interested. Are there none that you'd find complimentary?

BW: Yes. Stevenson I'd find complimentary, and Dumas I'd find complimentary.

IM: This is the Dumas things like *The Man in the Iron Mask*?

BW: And Maupassant, and Alice Munro, and Balzac I'd find complimentary.

IM: You named a woman there.

BW: Yes, Alice Munro.

IM: One!

BW: Yes, one! (L)

IM: Well, let us move on to what in some ways I find the most puzzling of the things you've written. I find it very enjoyable, but very puzzling, and this is the novel called *The Knight on the Bridge* (1982). It is about the time of the troubadours, Courtly Love and all that. But it involves a number of people who are, not to put too fine a point on it, either mad or missing at least one wit – they say it themselves. What kind of frame of mind should we read *The Knight on the Bridge* in?

BW: Quite a cheery one, because I'd written *Beltran in Exile*, which was much occupied with death, and my mother had died during the writing of that, and she was dying for the year up to which she died. And so I thought I'd do a book about love, and I set out quite clearly and definitely to write a book from the way we understand love now and relationships now, which would be me rewriting the start of Courtly Love in Europe. So I set it in exactly the time when it was starting. It was the twelfth century, and I set the joust in it just before the first joust was jousted in romantic Courtly Love terms, but I set it in a ramshackle household.

IM: There are two main male lovers, and one of them is Caesar, who has lost at least one wit, and who, in a fit of homicidal mania brought on by blood lust in a battle, killed not only most of the other side, but then most of his own side, and then cut his own little boy in two. Are we supposed to identify with Caesar?

BW: Well, it's quite easy to identify with Caesar -

IM: Indeed –

BW: It seems to me, because blood lust is a thing that happens in battle, which is not generally recorded in newsreels or news comments or political statements. Even movies rarely have a realistic blood lust. It's the thing that inevitably arises when people start killing each other, and they turn into something else.

IM: Can it actually in extremity do things like having somebody kill his own very beloved child? Slice him down the middle because he's in the middle of killing people?

BW: Well if he didn't see he was there. That is what this is based on, but, *but* the idea is also everything that is taken to its extremity, given what is already to the European civilised mind a nauseous proposition, that blood lust does arise, which is not because it's nauseous reached its extremity, so you take it to its extremity, which is then, in the point of view of the gods, colic.

IM: So you've got Caesar there and no wonder he's witless – he's having this *appalling* problem relating to the wife, who understandably is a bit bitter at what happened to her little boy (L): the knight comes along in favour of the daughter; he's just about your anti-knight, I suppose?

BW: Yes, Amanieu ?

IM: He is described as utterly revolting.

BW: Yes, he's utterly repulsive. To say something in passing that mothers and fathers cut their sons in two.

IM: Between them, yes. We touched on that yesterday.

BW: Yes. Amanieu, who now I come to remember it, is the seventh ...

IM: The seventh son of thirteen children and the first son of the third wife. Everybody can tell I reread this book for today.

BW: You sure have – wonderful of you. He's obviously numerologically engaged in his ancestry. He's very repulsive: he's amoral.

IM: He's physically repulsive, which is much more obvious than his being amoral. And yet he doesn't seem to put off the ladies, who communally lust after him, insofar as they are able.

BW: Yes, that's right, isn't it?

IM: Is that a very bitter comment on life universally? (L)

BW: No, no, not in the least. No, it may be the reverse. It may be a question. To some extent one feels repulsive, and can't understand. . .

IM: That each of us has ways of romanticising members of the opposite sex, but none of us can secretly imagine why the other person would find us individually attractive rather than repulsive?

BW: Yes. As far as I'm being subjective about the creation of Amanieu, yes.

IM: But the thing about him most of all. Flore, she's only twelve to thirteen and she'd just reaching womanhood when he rapes her, with her encouragement, and she's attractive, but he's described in a way that makes him like the foetuses that you see in Aubrey Beardsley or Edward Munch. His head's not properly formed, the first description of him; it's horrendous. I find it quite upsetting!

BW: Yes. Isn't that interesting, because here we are talking about a guy playing with words to create a repulsive character, and not thinking of painters, so the words to me don't represent that. I remember about him most that his lips seemed to have a life of their own, as if there was a snake . . . yes.

IM: Yes. That's not very pretty either.

BW: But I don't think of him gobbling, I just think of him . . .

IM: It's a sort of writhing motion that goes on down, ugh. . .

BW: But our Flore thinks he's cute. (L) I was thinking that she doesn't know anybody.

IM: Well, she knows the Captain of the Guard, and I suppose he's the standard against whom we are to judge Caesar and Amanieu.

BW: Yes. Vigorce is in love with Bonne, Flore's mother.

IM: Which is the appropriate Courtly Love thing to do, hopelessly in love with his superior.

BW   But he can't stop there because he hasn't yet learned that Courtly Love stops you there.

IM   And insofar as he stops he manages to carry on with the woman of the place.

BW   Yes, and this is quite modern – he thinks Caesar is quite the wrong person to be her husband.

IM   Actually the novel's being very very forgiving and humane about Caesar, and indeed Bonne, but given the blood lust thing, given this appalling fact, she has said a long time ago that it will always be a fact: there is no point in their separating: they might as well carry on together, and although he's freaking out through a strange phase when he feels that her soul must speak to his soul, and he behaves so intensely towards her that she's terrified or appalled or whatever, and she can't speak to him at all. Nonetheless, there's an astonishing amount of durability, or – what's the word I want?

BW   Will to love!

IM   Yes, and to make it new again between those two, and at the end you don't think it's all over the way you thought it was all over in the beginning and in the middle.

BW   Yes.

IM   So I suppose as far as that's concerned, given that that couple is still together at the end, and Flore and Amanieu are still together at the end, it's an optimistic novel (L).

BW   Yes, it is an optimistic novel. I remember my English master at school, Wilfred Hook, who was a brilliant English master, saying, just as well Romeo and Juliet popped their socks, because otherwise what kind of a home life would they have had?

IM   What kind of home life would their child have had?(L)

BW   How long would they have lasted? And so what I do with Bonne and Caesar is to make them as it were posthumous to plays like Romeo and Juliet where they have all ridden off into the sunset. And even at the expense of the extraordinary injuries they have imposed upon each other, there's a prospect of those two being healed, and they as two surviving.

IM   And healing each other as well as themselves.

BW   Yes. For me that is a very strong statement in that book.

IM   Indeed, indeed.

BW   And it contrasts also with Flore and Amanieu who go off not like Romeo and Juliet, but in the most practical fashion, counting where the money is coming from and how much they've got.

IM   And how they're going to play the circuses, as it were, and war and jousting and all that.

BW   And when Amanieu says they'll go to Spain by sea, and they're going to go to Barcelona, because they were the winning side in the recent wars, so you might as well be among the winners, says Amanieu. And they go by sea, and Flore says, well what if we're captured by pirates? And Amanieu says, more or less only in his language, 'Well, don't be a silly ass, then I become a pirate!'

IM   And he'd be good at that too!

BW   Scruple ain't in it!

IM   Now, right, pirates, scruples. An immediate thing that people might say about both The Knight on the Bridge and Beltran in Exile, is what a lot of violence. If they looked back again, they might qualify that and say there isn't really all that much of it, but Watson certainly has a way of making it effective and strong. Do you feel that the past is a country where things were much more violent that they are now, or -?

BW   No, but I do think the past is a territory where you can remind people how violent things are now, because they're just as violent now as they were then. But when I write about violence. . . Who's that film-maker – Sam Peckinpah? I mean the man at the start of whose movies you see the bits of the bodies fly out when they're shot, instead of people clapping their hands to their arms and saying dammit! (L) It was intentional with me to make the violence as realistic and terrifying. . .

IM   Sickening?

BW   Sickening? To me it's terrifying – it may be sickening to read – terrifying as possible. And I find in doing that that there's states of compelled imagination that you get into when you're writing which sometimes you seek and sometimes you don't: it takes three days to find them when you want them for a particular passage, or longer. Writing about, for example, violence, or describing a hillside, or writing an erotic passage, where you start writing in a very intense and to some extent transported way. You let that run – at least I let that run, and it will run for a certain curve of two or three days, or you have the energy for that amount of time, and then the passage naturally comes to an end. And to me that rhythm is an absolute gift, and I feel secure when I follow it; that it's in the right proportion for the book.

IM   The books are so different. The Knight on the Bridge is a more mixed book. Beltran excludes sex on the whole, and it has a sort of simplicity about a whole lot of the conflicts that isn't there in The Knight On the Bridge. When we first meet Amanieu, not only is he to me Beardsley and Munch-like, but also he is described – he describes himself – fairly happily, as having done a particularly manky murder on a harmless German prince. And we're not allowed to hold it against him, somehow. I would normally want to. I tend to have this wee prejudice against vicious murderers. Even if they haven't got a lot of money and the murderee has a lot! (L) It doesn't usually strike me as sufficient reason.

BW   Yes, I do in my daily self also have a prejudice against vicious murderers, but I have a great fondness for the callousness with which Amanieu does this, because he needs a silk shirt and some decent boots and a good horse. He gets a good horse out of it, yes.

IM   I suspect some of your readers are a bit nonplussed about that.

BW   Do you think so, because after all Amanieu has come up from what was the equivalent then in the war between Barcelona and Toulouse of the Thirty Years' War.

IM   He hasn't done anything, though. The only thing he's done is kill this chap. He pretends to have been three years at the wars, but he hasn't been.

BW   Oh, I think he has, actually.

IM   Has he? Oh, I misread it. Must go back.

BW   I think of the last War. Not to go beyond Europe, in 1939 we wouldn't have fire-bombed Dresden. And it's a long time since that war. If Amanieu's been in the wars, he would kill somebody without pause. It's true, what you say is true, in the sense that normally if somebody's going to bump somebody off like that, just because they happen to be riding by and they need what the guy's got, it's true that most often in a book you see him in these wars to start with, I accept that.

IM   One of the things that both these historical books are telling us is that blood lust and blood guilt are in everybody really, if the circumstances are right.

BW   Oh, yes. But I'm a Highlander, and I don't know about the English, but certainly the Albanians, the Italians, the Yugoslavs, the Germans from the forest, yes.

BT   Is this the same as searching for some kind of code in which a kind of release of blood lust is legitimated?

BW   You know, this is very interesting. I hadn't thought of anything like that, and I'm not really answering your question, but I do notice that we're talking about Courtly Love, and we're talking about a book that ends with a duel between two knights, one of whom is cheered on by his lady, wearing, physically or not, her favour in his helmet. And that this elegant encounter derives from people killing themselves in much less elegant ways. From having discovered that you can kill each other, and from the habit of blood lust.

IM   In the simple world of Beltran, it seems to me that the reader quite automatically prefers simple soldier knights who have their belief and who go on with it, to the perfumed and luxurious merchants of Sidon, who are convinced it's not going to happen, and that these terrible prophecies of doom are only ways to get money out of them. One is made to feel that these simple, stern knights are – you keep reminding us of Beltran, with whom we sympathise enormously. He's been killing for twenty-five years: his hands are calloused with killing. Although we don't see him very often killing, only in circumstances where it's sort of overpoweringly in his favour, like just when they're leaving Sidon and he and his friends have to kill five or six just to get to the harbour, but they're hopelessly outnumbered, and so they're noble and all the rest of it. Very strange! How much of it, do you think, comes from the movies? I wouldn't have dared say that if you hadn't spoken yesterday of a sense in which Western movies and all the rest of it from childhood form a lot of the basic things in this.

BW   By the way, I don't think they are outnumbered on the way to the harbour; just to let you know. Not hopelessly. [Defensively, IM points out that even several readings of the passage (pp 51-53) don't make that entirely clear to the uninitiated!]

IM   Well, there are just two of them, and there's five or six –

BW   Yes, but the five or six come at them in a slightly incompetent way.

IM   Yes, but they've got three foes each. Surely it's at least fair fight if you spit three men on the way to the boat, and save an infant blackamoor into the bargain.

BW   To me it wasn't supposed to be that number, because they were wearing armour and the other guys were not.

BT   Sort of the tanks to the infantry.

BW   Yes, yes.

IM   But we've already got this feeling because Sidon has been under siege and is falling, the only reason the Templars are going is it's falling, and everybody is waiting for the great rape and massacre to start, and we all know it's going to happen. So when Beltran and his buddy Geoffrey are actually able for a moment to strike the odd blow in return, there's some satisfaction in that.

BW   That's good. (pause) The reason they're leaving is that they're taking the Treasury. That's why they have to leave. The Treasury of the Order and the Grand Master with them. So the reason they are leaving is political. That's why the Templars are forbidden to defend the city.

IM   Yes, right. Are we going to see you writing anything more contemporary?

BW   Yes, I think I would like contemporary short stories.. I might write short stories about – I was thinking about my father, and therefore about the family, yes.

IM   Would you be thinking in the same way as before about your audience needing to be London and the world?

BW   No, I'll write these stories for me. Before, I meant to be published in London. I would like to make money from writing books, but I would very particularly like to make money from writing thrillers, which I do under a pseudonym, and I hope they will subsidise other writing. I don't see why any other writing shouldn't make money too.

IM   But with the Bill Watson books, you'd be happy to do something even if you knew it wasn't going to be as popular, was going to cut your audience, you would just do it. Whereas if you were writing a thriller you would go for the optimum possible audience.

BW   Yes, by writing a good thriller, of the kind I write. I wouldn't look and say, OK, Harold Robbins is notching up the dollars and therefore I will try to write a Harold Robbins book. There's a kind of thriller that it is natural for me to write. I think that's a Scottish thing too, I think a lot of Scots have been thriller writers – a lot of thriller writers have been Scots, rather.

IM   A lot of Scots writers have had two names. We could mention –

BW   The Author of Waverley?

IM   (L) There's Hugh MacDiarmid and C M Grieve. There's James Leslie Mitchell and Lewis Grassic Gibbon. There's William Sharp and Fiona MacLeod, there's Fionn MacColla and Tom MacDonald. There's quite a lot of them about. And then there's Bill Watson and this other chap (J K Mayo). Do you feel that there is a connection between the two writers that would make sense, if Bob were being allowed to ask you the questions he was thinking about asking, about cross-connections between the books that would be valid? Sooner or later posterity will have to know.

BW   I think it would be valid. But I think there would be imperfections in the validity because they are written in two such different states of mind – states of being, indeed. Because writing a straight novel you are in a state of being which can become quite extraordinary.

IM   That doesn't happen at all when you are writing a good thriller and you are really into it?

BW   No. Occasionally, occasionally it does, yes.

IM   I have got the impression when you were in the middle of writing the last one which shall be nameless [Wolf's Head (1987)] , that you had caught the bug of so much wanting it to be good and not just a thriller that you were in danger of getting quite as involved in that.

BW   Well, that would be great, yes.

IM   That makes you Graham Greene, and very rich. (L)

BW   Graham Greene, yes...

IM   His great thing has been to conflate these two things, and he writes thrillers all the time and he also writes novels all the time and they happen to be both.

BW   Well, I wrote plays in Scotland. And you write – either you write for God, or you write for some curiously virtuous purpose which is like living the life of Mother Teresa, or you write for reclame and you write for income. I write serious or straight fiction for reclame and I write thrillers for income, and if the one brings income as well and the other thing brings reclame as well, I think that would be just great.

IM   Do you ever entertain the quixotic thing that you have with the plays, that the novels, the serious novels, can change people?

BW   No, I don't think that at all now.

IM   You deliberately don't think like that?

BW   No, I only thought about it, I only noticed it, after I'd been doing it, and I think I wrote novels to be recognised. I write novels for the reader to recognise what I am doing, what I am saying.

BT   And also for reclame?

BW   And also for reclame. Why one writes books is for the reclame or the income, but when one is writing a book one is writing it for the reader to recognise what one is saying.

IM   And do you know when you have finished a book whether it's done what you wanted it to before you get the reviews, or is the review that important? Because it is a terrifying thought to me as a reviewer that the review is going to be that important to anyone, considering what an odd and kenspeckle lot they are. (L)

BW   No, you don't know whether you've done it – I don't know whether I've done it. But I remember when I finished The Knight on the Bridge, I sent one copy to Norah Smallwood, my publisher and another copy to Deborah Rogers who is my agent, by the same post. So they both read it over night and Norah phones me up and says it's marvellous – what does Deborah think of it?
I'd sent them a letter saying I'd sent it to the other by the same post, and I said, not having a clue, Deborah thinks it's wonderful. And I lay down the phone to pick it up again at once, and I phoned Deborah, and before I could speak she said I think it's marvellous, what does Norah think of it? And I assured her that Norah thinks it is totally terrific. So there they are – they are both in some state of doubt but now they think there is something quite strange and original here. (L)

IM: And reassured each by the opinion of the other. How clever. Can I ask a wee bit about Deborah, because particularly for a Scottish writer who's living a long way from the centre to have a good agent is terrible important these days.

BW: Well it is to me – and Deborah is a bloody good agent.

IM: What does that mean? Does she tell you what to do, ever, or does she do what you tell her?

BW: She's never suggested what to do with a book. You know, she's never proposed to edit the book with me, so to speak.

IM: Or even suggested what to write? I've heard of agents like that.

BW: Well, she has asked me to write a modern novel.

IM: Now why would she do that? (L)

BW: Well, she'd noticed that the sales of *Beltran in Exile* and *The Knight on the Bridge* were not large.

IM: Because in a way these days the historical novel audience is looking for lighter weight historical fiction than yours. The total simple escapist kind of thing – that's the ones that are very popular, aren't they?

BW: Yes, they are.

IM: So, the serious novel reader has a bit of a prejudice perhaps against historical novels.

BW: Yes.

IM: Expects them to be what Bob calls historicised, and too jolly, and intellectual slumming.

BW: Yes. There's no doubt at all the historical novel has been utterly debased at least since the first war.

IM: So you think when you go back to writing Bill Watson that it will be something else?

BW: Well, I want to write a comic novel about the Eglinton Tournament, or using the Eglinton Tournament. I can use all the people's names who were there because you can't libel the long dead. This is a tournament conducted in the same time as the retreat from Kabul. At Queen Victoria's coronation ceremony they left out for the first time the riding into Westminster Hall of the Queen's or King's Champion in full armour, who threw down his gauge and challenged anybody to impugn her title to the throne. They left this ceremony out. And this encouraged the demented nobility to think of men in armour. So the Earl of Eglinton actually had a tournament at Eglinton Castle in Ayrshire. Many people came and they got wonderful clothes made for the dances and stuff, and they got armour made, and there was a man in London who made a lot of money making armour. He was already making it for country houses anyway, to stand in people's halls. I just have a notion that the idea of this taking place, and that if with any luck historically that people roundabout were dying of cholera, or having a potato famine, that would make it more witty by point of contrast. (L)

IM: You were telling me about one or two possible characters.

BW: Yes, the book would start off with the Conde del Vesuvio setting off from Sicily and getting into a steam yacht lusting out for revenge against somebody who slighted him a hundred years ago. As it might be a German from the Forests who will be setting off down the Rhine, and it might even be a precocious Samurai leaving Hokkaido (L), and there will be Spaniards and there will be Frenchmen, and it will be quite giddy. And I see a sort of Britomart imitating Catherine Sforza and getting herself up in armour and possibly winning the tournament but forgetting or not realising you're not supposed to kill the other chap, and she was doing so. But I don't quite see a reason for it, except for the fun.

IM: One reason is surely that it takes your history and your modern thing and totally puts them together, and that's one of the magic things about it.

Published books mentioned in the interview:

By William Watson

Better than One, Barrie and Rockliff: the Cresset Press, 1969
Sawney Bean, With Robert Nye. Calder and Boyars, 1970
Beltran in Exile, Chatto & Windus, 1979. Later republished as
The Last of the Templars
The Knight on the Bridge, Chatto & Windus, 1982

By J K Mayo: the Harry Seddall series:

The Hunting Season, Collins Harvill,1985
Wolf's Head, Collins Harvill, 1987
Cry Havoc, Collins Harvill,1990
A Shred of Honour, Harvill,1993
The Masterless Men, Macmillan, 1995
The Interloper, Macmillan, 1996